GENDER AND GLOBALIZATION

A Comparative Perspective Between Europe and India

GENDER AND GLOBALIZATION

A Comparative Perspective Between Europe and India

Dr. B. Ratna Kumari
M.A. MWS. Ph.D. DIRPM.
Director
Dr. Durgabai Deshmukh Centre
for Women's Studies
Andhra University
Visakhapatnam, A.P.

KANISHKA PUBLISHERS, DISTRIBUTORS
NEW DELHI-110 002

KANISHKA PUBLISHERS, DISTRIBUTORS
4697/5-21 A, Ansari Road, Daryaganj
New Delhi-110 002
Phones : 2327 0497, 2328 8285
Fax : 011-2328 8285
E-mail: kanishka_publishing@yahoo.co.in

First Published 2010

ISBN 978-81-8457-113-1

PRINTED IN INDIA

Published by Madan Sachdeva for Kanishka Publishers, Distributors, 4697/5-21A, Ansari Road, Daryaganj, New Delhi-110 002, Typeset by Manas Enterprises, Delhi, and Printed at Rajdhani Printers, Delhi.

Preface

While gender is an ideological and cultural construct, it is also reproduced within the realm of social, economic, political and cultural practices. It is widely recognized that gender relations play a systematic role in the division of labor, work, income, wealth, education, productive inputs, publicly provided goods and the like. Its interdisciplinary relevance is rooted on the context of gender as the basis for the most pervasive study. The social, economic political and cultural dimensions of stakeholders are influenced by the gender.

Work has a gender based impact and it is important to know how this impact is embedded in the society. There is a theory of power, if it is equally distributed, it ceases to be power. Power is given by the society and this makes difference in gender. However studies in different parts of the developing or underdeveloped world, whether supportive or critical of the globalization, have all pointed to its effects of increasing women's vulnerabilities and insecurities. It is widely accepted that the advance of globalization has been marked by expanding forms of violence, insecurities and greater pressure in spheres of work, increased compulsion towards migration, trafficking, greater vulnerability to economic and social exploitation. There is an urgent need to see the consensus on the emergence of many new areas of concern consequent to the changes in women's lives being brought about by globalization across the globe.

The effects of liberalization and globalization processes on income distribution and poverty within and across different social groups and countries have been the subject of intense debate and critique. Just as they did across countries, the effects of globalization have also differed across groups within countries differentiated by gender (alongside class, race and ethnicity). This is because, as pointed out above, a discrepancy exists in almost all economies between women and men's access to resources, knowledge, ownership and control over assets, patterns of paid and unpaid work, the ability to generate income, educational patterns and political and economic power. Feminist researchers and activists have repeatedly pointed to a variety of gender biases of structural adjustment and macroeconomic stabilization policies since the mid–1980s. In fact, the critiques have to some degree found their place in policy-making and international mandates such as the Beijing Platform for Action.

The economic liberalization policies that have underpinned these processes are criticized as being "corporate-led", anti-poor, gender- and class-biased and destructive to the environment. Globalization and its discontents are being widely discussed over the past two decades but not with regard to work. Economic processes associated with globalization have deeply impacted the lives of men and women of all ages, nationalities, social classes and ethnicities. There have been differences across different segments of women. While some women have gained in terms of employment, who are less skilled or who have little control over assets, have lost their livelihoods as a result of import competition or open market systems, making them the weaker sections of society more vulnerable to economic losses. The origin of the research problem duly comes from the thought on how globalization has affected the equity on the gender relations and attaining social justice in view of economic development on women. One pervasive trait of gender relations across different cultures consists of the power asymmetries between men and women in the study of globalization. This globalization process may lead to social deprivation, environmental degradation and the destabilization of the basic rights of the women due to adverse impacts, especially on the livelihoods and empowerment of poor women.

When I attend a Summer Semester course on *'Globalization, Gender and Work'* in the International Women's University, Hannover, Germany, I have collected a number of research articles from well reputed researchers and feminists of Europe and India. I have also conducted empirical research on various topics like Globalization: Impact on Women's Work, Women's Education and Special Export Processing Zones. I have interviewed a number of Women Leaders across the globe during Women Leadership training by Haggai Institute in Hawaii, USA.

Considering the feminists and leaders who came from diverse disciplines were living in different countries and sometimes laid weight upon divergent standpoints and scientific approaches gives deep insights. It is a multi-disciplinary and international frame of reference, which is open for new ideas, new perspectives new concerns and new topics concerning the central theme *'Gender and Globalization: A Comparative Perspective between Europe and India'.*

Visakhapatnam **Dr. B. Ratna Kumari**

Acknowledgements

In the essay, "*Theorizing Gender Arrangements*," Regina Becker-Schmidt tries to develop a set of categories that is suitable to elucidate the connection between the organization of social systems and the structures of gender orders. Gender orders are constituted on two different levels. They entail a normative-cultural dimension in which practice is grounded on the one side, and factual constellation of living conditions on the other side. Both levels are intertwined. If we wish to grasp the disadvantages against women, we have not only to find out the criteria that lead to discrimination. We also have to search for their socio-historical formation. "Relationality" the yardstick for comparative evaluation and the adviser of its points of reference, has to be understood as a medium that links the female and the male gender in institutionalized contexts. As a consequence, the alignment of relationality modulates the assessment of what is called "female" of "male" work. The term "Geschlechterverhaltnis," which is not identical with the notion "gender relations," stands for the societal nexus of such links, which combine comparative evaluation with the interlacement of gender positions. Relatedness can be based on parity or imparity. In the cases in which relationality stipulates asymmetries between the genders, relatedness is a mode that shapes hierarchies and constitutes social inequality.

We asked *Brigitte Young,* who did not belong to the CAG "Work," but is one of our key-professors, to leave us a text dedicated to "globalization," a process which changes labor markets, political systems, and ways of life on a world wide scale. We thank her very much for her willingness to do so.

Brigitte Young discusses "globalization" in an European horizon. She points out that this complex of transitions has to be seen as an open and contradictory process. She argues that not everything which comes in contact with globalization can be subsumed under the logic of capitalism. "Globalization is thus not only a process of expansion and breakthrough of political, economical, social, and ecological barriers. It always also involves the development of counter-tendencies, those that set barriers to globalization."(Young, p. 2)

Her analysis follows up two central questions. First, how can a broderless global market and the territorially bounded concept of democracy be reconstituted? Second, how are gender regimes and gender orders reconfigured in the new "network societies?" She shows ways in which the increasing internationalization of capitalism, marked by the change from industrial to "informational capitalism," undermines the existing Fordist regimes of accumulation and modes of regulation. Simultaneously, the economical and political influence of the national state is weakened in the face of global markets and the lack of institutionalized structures of control.

As Fordism promotes a male breadwinner model, the decline of this period touches the entire gender order. Therefore, the author anticipates new flexible gender arrangements. This outlook supports the conviction that women are not necessarily losers of globalization processes, but also winners of changing constellations within the employment system and the private sphere where patriarchal power fades.

It will be interesting to discuss whether this concept of globalization is transferable to countries of the "Third World."

Three of the contributions of this reader lead directly into the regional center of our project area: Western, Central and Eastern Europe.

Christiane Lemke explores the crisis of all European welfare states caused by the dissolving of traditional gender orders. The comparative orientation of her essay refers to "*New Family Patterns: Germany after Unification.*" As she argues, modern welfare states were based on the assumption of a male worker, who provides the family with his income. This ideology of a male bread-winner, which ignores the paid and unpaid work of women, loses credit in times where labor markets are characterized by high unemployment, increasing job insecurity, and wages insufficient to support a family, especially solo-mother households and female single existences.

A short detour through modern history makes clear that the three possible criteria for making claims on the welfare state-work, need and citizenship—were associated with men.

Relying on recent feminist discussions which the importance of family care work has become a focus of systematic and comparative welfare state analysis, the author intends to present a conceptualization of a welfare state model that includes relevant issues of gender equity. Lemke writes: "Embracing the variety of paid and unpaid services, such as care within family units, this more sophisticated approach identifies a complexity of services and opens the field for variety of potential policy changes in European state." (Lemke, p. 4)

Her comparative study of the two different "west/east" bread-winner models starts with a suggestions: the story of German unification can be read as the story of the clash between two contrasting ideas of welfare state provisions. While the West German welfare state was based on the dependency of women on men's income, the East German bread-winner model considered women as part of the labor force, who have welfare rights as benefits for their own work. After the unification, these differences were leveled, and the conservative Western German model was re-established.

We add to this paper of *Christiane Lemke* a second text, published together with *Katrin Tons*. We thought that it would be useful for the students to know in what theoretical contexts conceptions of welfare state are embedded. The contribution of Lemke and Tons deals with the rise of postmodern discussions, which are dedicated to "*Feminist Theory of Democracy and the Dispute of Difference.*" The text reconstructs a piece of the history of American political theory influenced by postmodern discourses. The examination of Lemke and Tons is focused on feminist critiques of liberal democracy models, which refer to concepts of group identities grounded in gender, class or ethnic differences-foundations to represent their special issues.

Katalin Koncz analyses–as the title of her text indicates – "*Gender-Specific Division of Labor in Hungary after the Regime Change.*" A short foreword introduces the problems of transition all East and Central European countries are confronted with. Then she outlines the developments which are specific for Hungary. Combining a political perspective with an economical approach, she claims that the position of women in political decision-making processes must be strengthened in order to get more influence in women's issue–*e.g.* their status in the labor market and their exclusive responsibility for family tasks such as domestic work and child rising. Koncz also pays attention to the socio-historical dimensions that are constitutive for the connection of politics, labor market and family. The difficulties in the present transitional period result from two divergent time-structures. On the one hand, changes in the political and economic system are taking place simultaneously: the transformation of society implies the reconstruction from a communist dictatorship to a democratic society as well as the rearrangement of the state-centralized economy to a market oriented economy. On the other hand, obsolete social structures characteristic for the time before the regime change are still effective. That can be said for the recruiting of politicians as well as for the accesses to the labor market–both phenomena are marked by androcentrism. Traditional gender stereotypes have survived in the family, too.

Taking this into consideration, Koncz proves by documentary evidence the limited participation of women in political institutions as well as in the different fields of the employment system. Her research is well founded in empirical material–statistics exemplify significant advantages and new disadvantages (*e.g.* unemployment) which touch women's entire life conditions.

Elena Y. Meshcherkina presents a differentiated survey on *"Women at the Labor Market in Russia"* As a general trend she lines out the gender-based asymmetry on the labor market. But looking at rural districts on the one side, and urban areas on the other side, considerable differences of employment and unemployment of women become visible. Even in the urban labor markets the economy in transition does not follow a one-dimensional logic that always discriminates the female gender. Objective agents such as the decline of certain industries or regional barriers against economical progress, but also personal factors like age, family situation, and reproductive behaviour have influence on the position of women in the labor market. Furthermore, we have to acknowledge that women profit from the emergence of new working places and new vocational programmes. Meshcherkina refers to an–in former times unknown-phenomenon that she interprets as open of the key problems of the present employment system: the switching of employees from old jobs to new jobs. These changes are combined with the cutting of wages. Because women are concentrated in low-remunerated industries (non-manufacturing sectors), for them the search for new working places is often followed by loss of money as for men. Therefore, the restructuring of the employment system widens the gender-related gaps of payment. Meshcherkina points at another discrimination against women: their higher level of education in comparison with men in not accompanied with an equally high social status.

In her conception of the future of women's work she interfaces socio-economic and psychological perspectives: the future depends not only on objective tendencies, but also on the adaptation of new skills required for the labor market, on flexible reproduction behaviour, and on the destabilization of traditional gender stereotypes.

In her paper, "*Professionalization and Gender Hierarchy,*" *Ulrike Teubner* discusses the employment situation of women in industrial societies. Referring to gender-based professional segregation, she suggests that the discrepancy between changes on various social levels and the maintenance of gender related inequality in the labor market requires complex research strategies that are theoretically and methodologically suitable for the investigation of this phenomenon.

Teubner points out that there is a need of socio-historical and intercultural approaches. The construction of gender differences – related to assessment as well as to social status–which are responsible for forms of gender segregation in the occupational system, are historically constituted. This fact becomes visible when we take into consideration those occupations that altered the gender designation. The awareness of historical shifts must include the recognition of deviating cultural traditions. In one society a certain profession may be connoted with "maleness," in another one with "femaleness." But in despite of these variations we can see that an important impact of different forms of gender segregation remained constant over space and time: that is the dualistic conception of "femaleness" and "maleness" that goes along with separation and herarchization.

That leads to the question "to what extent the dualistic differentiation the sex provides the basic mechanism controlling the creation and reproduction of gender hierarchies in employment." (Teubner, p. 7) Following the arguments of the author, this question can only be answered when the gender-coding of work is understood as a complex and flexible process. The principles which link gender to work are to be found on two different levels: on the one hand, the higher rank of men and men's jobs is related to women and women's work, on the other hand, the procedures that establish division depend on the definitions of differences between the genders for each specific occupation.

Teubner claims research strategies that consider intrinsic aspects as well as structural constellation, which are not reducible to the context of market-mediated work. The association of women's work with domestic tasks and child care influences the images of women's professional potentials.

The world-wide process of globalization includes two contradictory tendencies. On the one hand, globalization takes command under the neo-liberal rules of those stakeholders who have uncontrollable power for decision-making. Global inequality, gaps between rich and poor countries, is the risks of these unmanaged developments. On the other side, we can recognize shifts in global policy due to the alliances of democratic governments, non- governmental organizations which strengthen local empowerment, and agencies of marginalized groups.

Whether globalization will have a human face in the future or not depends on the emergence of new coalitions "across geographical borders and traditional political lines to move public policy in ways that meet the aspiration of a global citizenry" (Mark Malloch Brown, Foreword for "Human Development Report, 1999", P.V). A global civil society entails equality of its members, democracy in all institutions, and transparent structures of global governance.

Gisela Notz essay, "*Shaping the Future of Work*" is written in the spirit of a world-wide civil society. She scrutinizes the reform concepts discussed in Europe, especially in Germany, which propose alternatives to the present distribution of gainful work and benefits of the welfare state. Notz points out similar contradictions on a regional level as we find them in a global context. Established interest groups are the barriers that confine ideas how a citizenry could guarantee a "good life" for all people. The point of reference of her critical remarks is in the first place the social situation of women. Notz asks: "What kinds of work do scientists have in mind, when they react to the running out of labor in western societies?" Her answer is that the reform concepts are focused on market-mediated labor and male life pattern.

Women's work is not considered an ensemble of social activities (subsistence work, domestic work, care work, work in the formal and informal segments of the labor market). Regarding unemployment, women are supposed to have an "alternative role" in the family, so that this misfortune for them seems to be less dramatic than for men. The scientists ignore the desire of women to have—like men—both a family and a career.

The ensemble of women's activities, which are all necessary for the maintenance of social life and societal reproduction, shows that work in its variety forms a whole. That is the background of the authors conclusions: Simply extending the notion of work to include domestic work and care work will not be enough (...). And the concepts of action will not only have to be directed towards employment creation measures and working hours, but also towards the humanization and democratization of work, its structuring with regard to content and organization, and towards the usefulness of products and services. For the future the issue is socially necessary and meaningful work in all areas of production, services and private reproduction. (Notz, p. 13)

I am particularly grateful to *Regina Becker-Schmidt,* Coordinator of Gender and Work, IFU, Hannover, *Margot Poppenhusen,* who generously helped to realize the reader, and to *Rebecca van Dyck, Julia Grrundlack, and Ellen Leinwohl Jennifer Menzel,* who translated and corrected the papers.

Contents

Preface *v*
Acknowledgements *ix*

1. Theorizing Gender Arrangements 1
REGINA BECKER-SCHMIDT, HANNOVER

2. Globalization and Gender: A European Perspective 31
BRIGITTE YOUNG, MUNSTER

3. New Family Patterns: Germany after Unification 60
CHRISTIANE LEMKE, HANNOVER

4. Feminist Theory of Democracy and the Dispute of Difference 71
CHRISTIANE LEMKE AND KATRIN TONS, HANNOVER

5. Gender-Specific Division of Labour in Hungary Since the Regime Change 95
KATALIN KONCZ, BUDAPEST

6. Women at the Labour Market in Russia 137
ELENA Y. MESHCHERKINA, MOSCOW

7. Professionalization and Gender Hierarchy 152
ULRIKE TEUBNER, DARMSTADT

8. Shaping the Future of Work 173
GISELA NOTZ, BONN

9. Work and Gender: A European Perspective 186
DR. B. RATNA KUMARI, INDIA

10. Globalization and Its Impact on Women Workers in Visakha Special Economic Zones 194
DR. B. RATNA KUMARI, INDIA

11. Globalization and Its Impact on Women Students in Higher Education 225
DR. B. RATNA KUMARI, INDIA

12. Financial Inclusion for Women Empowerment in South Asia Context 258
DR. B. RATNA KUMARI, INDIA

Index 282

1
Theorizing Gender Arrangements

REGINA BECKER-SCHMIDT, HANNOVER

From Women's and Gender Studies to Research into Geschlechterverhaltnissen[1]

It is often argued that globalization possesses the potential of bringing economic and social benefits to societies all over the world. But there are also critical voices pointing put the negative, disruptive and marginalizing impact of globalization. The ideology of neoliberalism which asserts the strength of worldwide market processes regulated by free competition conceals the fact that globalization "has the capacity to do extraordinary harm as well as good."[2] Poor people and poor countries risk being excluded from the increasing concentration of income, resources and wealth, as well as from the global exchange of knowledge.[3]

Not only are those regions located on the periphery of the rich and powerful possessors of international economic and political influence becoming increasingly marginalized in the worldwide market, where the flow of money, trade, technological know-how and information freely permeates national boundaries; the gap between men and women in also widening. However, we cannot claim that the female gender does not profit at all from globalization processes.

During the period between 1990 and 1997, the net secondary enrolment of girls augmented from 36 per cent to 61 per cent. Over the same time period, the rate of women's involvement in economic activity rose from 34 per cent to nearly 40 per cent. Women have found new opportunities for jobs in the labour market, especially within the formal and informal service sectors, although wages here are often extremely low. Nevertheless, in comparison with men women are subject to discrepancies in education, economic activity, distribution of paid and unpaid work, social security benefits, political participation, and to higher proportions of suffering due to physical and sexual abuse.

Confronted with data such as these, feminists have reacted with a shift of concepts with regard to empowerment strategies. Activists within the international women's movement have reflected on whether measures aimed at benefiting women or anti-discrimination laws to protect they are effective enough to bridge the gender gaps. These discussions have led to a more radical claim: social changes to the advantage of women will only occur if feminist policy can sufficiently alter gender orders and gender regimes. The social organization processes. "Development and gender" — so the feminist understanding — is the connection requiring investigation.[4] However, to be able to do so it is first necessary to clarify the different dimensions implied in the term "gender relation" and/or "gender relationships." The definition of "gender" selected determines the frame of reference and thus the scope within which scientific investigation takes place. This epistemological problem requires that the theoretical approach used in gender studies be more precisely clarified in this respect. There is an apparent lack of transparency with regard to this issue in feminist theory.

The following reflections will attempt to provide some orientation in this direction by asking in which ways the social organization of gender relationships structures society and *vice versa,* how gender relationships are mediated by society.

At the beginning of the nineties, Ursula Beer called "gender" a "structural category."[5] This formulation comes out against oversimplified or one-sided approaches in the field of women's studies. It compels feminist scientists to go beyond those ideas which seek to define "gender" in terms of role theory: a separate behavioural report corresponding with the gendered division of work and belonging to being a man or being a woman. It is not sufficient to view the gender as social construction of "femininity" or "masculinity" inscribed into the symbolic order. "Gender" is not merely the point of reference for classifications through which human beings are sexualized in a one-dimension way and are forced into polarized gender groups. U. Beer emphasizes another dimension: the structuring effects of gendering processes, which are based on social inequality – the participants in the discrimination produced between women and men sediment differences in their societal status. Along this line of separation, discrepancies in socio-economic opportunities and those for political participation emerge between them that conform with the structures of dominance inherent in the prevailing social framework. In her investigation "Geschlecht, Struktur, Geschichte" (Gender, Structure, History), U. Beer asserts that "all of our known cultural formations are based on gender inequality.[6] "With example of the transition from the 19th to the 20th centuries in Prussia, she verifies to what extent the newly forming society continues to be characterized by traditional gender hierarchies – despite the social change from agrarian and trades-based feudalism to industrial capitalism: the ranking of the genders belongs to the social structure along with its organization according to class; the subordination of women through birth control remains a distinguishing feature of patriarchal population policy; the gendered division of work is an essential pre-condition of social reproduction; economic, cultural and political relations of power are organized around male bonds. This can be seen from the androcentrism of the legal system, ownership structures, authority in the family, processes of professionalization, the educational systems, the sphere of employment, and the welfare state. Feudal a feminist angle, the liberal emphasis on freedom and equality is an ideology insofar as women remained excluded for a long time and to this day, real equal status has not been attained.

The phrase "gender as structural category" suggests a general theoretical and methodological shift. The social interrelatedness of the genders becomes relevant within the context of societies situated in social history. Alongside women's studies, gender studies come to the fore and – in a widening of perspective – so does the discussion concerning the societal organization of gender relationships. The notion of "Geschlechterverhaltnis" stands for this institutionalized interlacing between women and men as social groups.

Women's studies focus on the members of the female gender group. On the one hand, its intention is to bring out the significance of their experience and their knowledge in the establishment of social spheres and to retrieve their role in cultural history as well as in the development of the science. On the other hand, women's studies reveal the discrimination women are exposed to while taking account of the difference in women's living situations, which can be traced back to differences in class, ethnic origin or skin colour.

In contrast, gender studies takes up a different comparative angle when discrimination against woman is the issue: The male gender group is logically the point of reference for assertions concerning situations of gender inequality. Is attention diverted—either politically or scientifically—from women's problems because now men also appear on the scene? Are explosive social disparities between women and men neutralized by a comparative point of view? I think the contrary is the case. We only gain precise insight into society's unequal treatment of women due to their social gender groups merely out of methodological considerations: the fact as well that both gender groups are made up of heterogeneously cannot be disregarded. When investigating gender discrimination, female and male gender groups must be comparable with regard to other criteria of social status and esteem. For this reason is it necessary to take into account social differences within and between the gender groups that cannot be traced back to gender membership.

Gender studies are not an alternative to women's studies: the kind of approach I select is dependent on the problem dealt with by research projects. There are critical objections to both approaches. Women's studies can run the risk of getting stuck in "hyphenated sociologies" such as "Women and Work", "Women and Education", "Women and Culture", "Women and Power." What is then omitted from the sociological analysis is how the unequal treatment of the genders that we find in one social sphere is linked to hierarchical constellations in another social sphere. Furthermore, the points of reference for the diagnosis of social inequality—namely men's privileges—do not become transparent.

Criticism can also be raised with respect to the gender studies' approach. Gender studies unquestionably lose their connection to feminist positions and to the women's movement when research interests become purely academic and the sting of criticism that comes out against social injustice is lost. Furthermore, it cannot be ruled out that gender studies are conducted by scholars in the service of men.

In their introduction to "Frauengeschichte-Geschlechtergeschichte" (Women's History-Gender History), Karin Hausen and

Heide Wunder, the editors of this anthology, concisely formulate what the differentiation contained in the title of the book amounts to. They write: "Insofar as women's history reflects its methodologies, insofar as it is grounded in academic research and seeks to be more than just a reprint of the popular cultural history of 'the women' in the 19th and 20th centuries, women's history cannot avoid conceptualizing itself as gender history Even if the focus of the investigation is directed towards a certain group of women, these women must still also be thought of and regarded as human beings of the female gender and thus in relation to the male gender. Because women's and men's lives are bound in the respective prevailing cultural orders of gender relations which up to now are still hierarchically constructed and which permeate all social spheres. Correspondingly, from the onset the interest of women's history has been accompanied by the intent to research the history of cultural gender order." [7]

The identification of "relationality" as a mode that interlaces the genders is a central precondition for the investigation of the societal phenomenon we call Geschlechterverhaltnis. But what does "relationality" mean/what implications are concealed in this term? How much it be developed so that the concert configuration of gender interrelatedness can manifest itself according to historical and socio-cultural conditions? Within society, the genders collide as "social magnitudes" in different spheres (family, educational system, labour market, employment system, welfare state). Does the way they are placed in relation to one another arrange itself according to the same pattern of assessment in all of these social spheres? If so: Are modes of interrelatedness combined to form a nexus that we can decipher as a complex societal arrangement?

Determining Factors in Geschlechterverhaltnissen: Relation, Connection, Nexus[8]

Let us first of all more precisely clarify what is implied by the term "relationality."

Firstly, relations indicate the elements—the relation into a relationship with one another similar to quantities in an equation. In our case, these are men and women, who are taken as gender groups. I will discuss below the mechanisms through which such group formation is achieved although neither of the two social genders is homogenous with regard to class or ethnic membership.

Secondly, it is a matter of the contexts within the gender groups—if they are not treated as equal—get caught in an interrelation of upgrading and downgrading. Interrelations between the gender groups have manifold nodal points, *e.g.* relationships of kinship, love and cooperation; economic cultural and political conditions that determine women's and men's opportunities for material security and receiving recognition.

Such constellations are by no means based on the same principles of order in all societies. In a comparison of cultures we encounter relations of similarity and difference, symmetry and asymmetry, equal treatment and hierarchies, inclusion and exclusion. Within a context of cultural tradition, historical investigations can unearth changes from epoch to epcoh. That means: The way in which the interrelatedness between the genders takes shape is dependent on history and society. In view of these premises, can we even speak of one Geschlechterverhaltnis or is the use of the plural appropriate? I will attempt to answer this question further below.

By referring to the necessity of considering "relationality" within a historical and sociological context, we arrive at a further layer of the meaning of this term. It not only indicates what enters into relationship, but rather how the relationship between the interconnected elements, and what are the standards for these assessments, what modalities or conditions do they adhere to? We find answers to these kinds of question if we look for the socio-historical determinations that regulate the interdependency, if we look for the *verhaltnisbestimmungen*[9] characteristic of a relation. Whether gender groups have equal value or whether one of the genders is furnished with superior value to the extent that the interrelation amount to an assignment of inferior and superior positions is dependent on the measures that rule a relationship we can identify the set of measures that mark societal interlacing as symmetrical or asymmetrical, equal or unequal "connections."

The term "connection" equally refers to both structure and agency. It contains "nexus", which means as much as joining together, becoming entwined, as well as "nectere", the verb for "to link" and "to combine." Connections therefore refer to the modalities brought about by thinking and doing as well as to the societal arrangements in which agency is embedded.

Thus, on the one hand, the investigation of connections supplies information on the alignment and the social framework of the rapport existing between the gender groups. On the other hand, their analysis throws light on the conflicts in which women and men struggle for the esteem and social status they believe the deserve. If connections that establish ranks prevail in the social relation between the gender groups, then the controversy over equal social treatment implies social conflicts that can lead to crises of legitimization and to the orgnization of resistance. In contrast, an association of solidarity between the two can express itself in a balanced reciprocity or in a complementariness that allows for difference—for instance in terms of the practices assigned to women or men—without, however, positioning these within a hierarchy.[10]

An extract from U. Beer's complex analysis "Geschlecht, Struktur, Geshcichte" puts into concrete terms how one institutional context–a nexus–develops from the joining together of concurrent connections across the boundaries of private and public realms. It concerns the meaning of legal systems for the social regulation of gender relationships.

The point of departure of U. Beer's investigation is the adoption to a large extent of the General Prussian District Law of 1794 – the foundation for gender orders within the agrarian-corporative social formation—into the German Civil Code of 1900, which canonizes the competencies of men and women in the family, in the labour market, and in the formation of property under the new conditions of the industrial age. Despite the fundamental restructuring of German Society around the turn of the 20th century, few changes were made to the German Civil Code to correct the unequal legal status of women and men. The patriarchalism that had developed within feudal contexts and in which it was legally safeguard lived on in the modern age with only slight modifications. In both time periods and well into the 20th century, laws legitimized that heads of families and/or husbands could rule on the employment of female labour, that they alone were competent to contract, that they represented private matters in public. Men were reconfirmed in their role as the legal guardians of women, as was a woman's commitment to the family based on her material dependency within marital relations. This included obligating woman to perform housework, childcare and child-rearing.[11]

U. Beer brings out the objectives pursued by civil legislation at the turn of the century. First of all, it aimed at maintaining the availability of women for the regeneration of the commodity of labour and for the generative reproduction of the population, thereby minimizing the costs for house-keeping and the social factor of procreation. This interest, which is immanent to capitalism—which does not make reference to private reproduction as a necessity for industrial production–corresponded with a male interest: If Women's work was defined as unpaid housework, in the reverse conclusion one could maintain: Men's work was gainful employment. In the consequence of this logic, the securing of the family budget primarily through the man's wages granted him the role of main breadwinner of the family and thus strengthened his authority as head of household.

Secondly, the exclusion of women from employment that secured their livelihood was meant to guarantee male superiority in the labour market.

In this case, we are therefore dealing with a male-bonded interlinking of interests which also appeared to be socially functional: The civil constitution was intended to connect the supremacy of the male gender group in the family with its supremacy in the labour market. U. Beer's investigation enables us to study under what social conditions and based on what interest the Geschlechterverhaltnis assumes that impartiable form which is characteristic for the modern age.

The separation of the private sphere and the sphere of employment carried through in the course of industrialization through the spatial disassociation of lifeworlds and workplaces outside the home for the majority of the population had fatal consequences for women: they were forced to take on the domestic responsibilities, their professional possibilities were restricted. In contrast, the representatives of the other gender, who held the reins in legislature, succeeded in doubly securing the supremacy of men by combining what was socially distinct–family/employment system—by way of a uniform, legally homogenized principle. The subordination of the female gender under the guardianship of a head of the family and/or husband guaranteed that in all of their dimensions, women's lives were subject to the control of the pater families. It was emphasized in all three codices—the laws concerning ownership, family and labour—that a husband could dispose of the labour of his wife. With this, a dual objective was achieved: binding the security of a woman's livelihood to her husband and granting him the power to be in-charge of her on all matters. Sexuality, housekeeping, market-mediated work—everything was placed at his discretion. Middle-class as well as proletarian husbands profited from the patriarchal family law: the German Civil Code allowed the patriarchalization of the family to spread to all classes.[12]

Placed within the context of the investigation as a whole, U. Beers's analyses based on one aspect of a sociology of law make plausible that it is not possible to attempt to determine the social status of the female gender solely in relation to the family, as constitutive this institution may be for the unequal positions of the gender groups.[13] Neither can change in the Geschlechterverhaltnis be exclusively derived from the development related to the expansion of the capitalist mode production.[14] The multi-dimensionality of the phenomenon of "the oppression of women" becomes clear in the nexus "legal system": an andocentric claim to oppression of women becomes clear in the nexus, legal system: an andocentric claim to power converges with capitalist interests in dominance. Across the boundaries of class, this fusion causes the synchronization of connection we find in the various gender arrangements of our culture and that work to the disadvantage of women. Under the key work "gender as master status", below, we will consider the fact that gender membership more strongly influences the social status of women and men—although in a diametrically opposed way–than does their class position.

Let us now look at the other side–based in the theory of action—of the term "connection." Verhaltnisbestimmungen did not only evolve and as such are socially constituted, they are also made, negotiated, changed. Let us linger on the problem of "gender hierarchy and the history of law" and this time looks at it from the actor's perspective.

It was above all Ute Gerhard who opened up this approach in that she not only investigated legal material with regard to gender bias, rather she also addressed the conflict-ridden processes of negotiation surrounding the equality of the genders under the law. From this viewpoint, which focuses on the opponents in the struggle for justice, she brings up the history of the women's movement.

Women are not only victims of the legal systems, which U. Beer exposed in its feudal-patriarchal and capitalist-androcentric forms of violence. Women also force revision.

U. Gerhard refers to the contradictory character of the civil code, which gave the women's movements the impetus to vehemently strive for the equal treatment of genders.

On the one hand, in its liberal turn against the "ancient regime" the civil code legally stipulated claims for protection against public as well as personal infringement on individual lives, for the equal treatment of individuals, and for the observance of human dignity. On the other hand, it was a controlling device that could be used for the purpose of defending positions of power. This ambiguity was revealed in the revolutionary demand for "liberty, equality, fraternity", above all by its completely ignoring the other half of humanity — the sisterly one. The women's movement responded to this. Anja Wolde comments: "U. Gerhard sees the initial decades of the 19th century. This cannot only be traced back to the structural changes accompanying the change in modes of production, but rather also to the fact that the ideas that arose from the Enlightenment—equality, liberty and justice—had developed their own dynamics as social and political demands and provided women with the starting point for petitioning for a right to equality. The legitimization based on custom of the unequal treatment and subordination of women could no longer be sustained and had to be replaced by new patterns of legitimization."[15] U. Gerhard does not conceal the fact that in the history of law, women did not merely act a agents of modernization. They also accepted the gender orders and contributed clichés laid down by the norm.[16]

And yet it cannot be overlooked that in the social conflict surrounding the early women's movements, important steps were taken for the dismantling of patriarchal positions of power: In the 20th century, women were finally forced to be granted the status of legal subjects.[17] Contradictions between normativity and factuality, between progression in certain gender arrangements and backwardness in others, have remained the targets of women's policy.

Let us sum things up and record how the analysis of two important positions in feminist research has brought us much closer to understanding the term "Geschlechterverhaltnis."

We can say with certainty: The social status of women and men cannot be deduced from their status in one social sector. Rather, their positioning within one sphere qua gender membership affects their status in other spheres. This true in its positive as well as negative effects" where the ideas of gender quality is reached by societal consensus, there will surely not be any socially relevant areas where the violation for rules of equality does not provoke anti-discriminatory measures. In contrast, where the discrimination of women concerns the key issues of social participation and securing livelihood–for instance in a legal system that legitimizes disproportions in the gender-based division of work and authority—it is unlikely that the logic in the organization of gender arrangements changes from institution to institution. Thus there is not only a need to clarify under what circumstances gender distortions come about in individual social spheres—for instance in the educational system; rather, above and beyond this there is a need to clarify the modalities through which structures of discrimination against women link themselves together across individual social spheres such as the family, the labour market and the welfare state.

One could also indicate the point of departure for comprehensive disparate connections: the interaction between the cultural construction of difference, which is based on the unequal valuation of "femininity" and "masculinity", and the hierarchical positioning of women's and men's work.[18] The combination of the diverse institutionalized gender arrangements on both levels—the ideal as well as the material level—is surely essential for the consolidation of what we call "Geschlechterverhaltnissen." However, an important factor is still missing in the determination of this social inter-relationality. For this reason, let us go step further and ask how the respective living conditions of the two gender groups are socio-structurally intertwined.

If we consider the entanglement of genderized realities, the term "relationality" leads us to what we want to determine from societal perspective: the relational structure between the gender groups in the sense of a social interlacement. "Relationality" then not only provides the standard according to which the positions and areas of responsibility are marked out for the social genders. Within this context, "relationality" is a medium of dominance that establishes constellation of social dependency. We can also say that "relationality" has the function of building up societal structures by regulating social interdependencies. Interdependencies can involve reciprocity, but it is also possible that they are undermined by assumptions of power.

Three components work together in gender relationships. Firstly, human beings are subsumed via gender classification under social totalities ("Women or men"). Gender difference paves the way for gender hierarchies. Secondly, women and men are characterized by the label "female"/"male", women and men are channeled into engendered fields of practice that are not assigned the same amount of prestige. Lastly, the engendered fields of practice that are not assigned the same amount of prestige. Lastly, the engendered fields of practice are embedded in social spheres that are part of the societal reproduction process, which only functions through the division of work. Although all spheres are dependent on one another, there are differences in the level of societal influence. We will see later on that the hierarchies in social spheres correspond with hierarchies in gender orders.

In any case we are confronted with dialectical connection: none of the elements in the different constellation has identity of its own; it is always also the non-identical element of the other, which it needs for its own self-definition. None of the elements is independent; they do not acquire their status until they have been placed in reference/contrast to the other elements. If we leave the order of the societal sectors aside for the moment, we can discern a "soziales-verhaltnis" into which distinct classes or groups have been integrated in such a way that they have referential connection. Although they are separate from one another, they are bound together; although they are bound by reciprocity, they are separated by antagonism.

A social relationship may be symmetrical or asymmetrical, balanced or antagonistic: it is always characterized by an ensemble of connections that forms and organizes society. In our culture, the gender groups are subject to an entanglement that equally encompasses opposition and dependency. They are power and status differences despite reciprocity. For this reason, we can say that "gender" is a central point of reference for social stratification. The position of one gender not only provides the standard for the positioning of the other one; above and beyond this, "gender" implies the reciprocal inclusion of social positions. This will be shown in more concrete terms below in my implanation of the structural significance relationships between couples.

If we accept the mutuality development and the genesis of gender systems, then we can see the influence the framework or form existing in any given society has on gender policy. If a gender relationship is marked by superiority and inferiority, then we are dealing with a phenomenon of social dominance and compulsion. Oppression on the one side and dominance on the other can only then be cancelled if the entire nexus of hierarchical relationships is broken up. This does not mean that a gender relationship that assumes the form of dominance is static. On the contrary: gender inequality contradicts gender democracy, a clam formulated in our society's constitution. Conflicts are unavoidable: Social developments in favor of women which follow this calm affect male claims to hegemony. In the alternation between attack and defense, fissures develop in this structure of authority that cannot be permanently covered up. Furthermore, in view of social dynamics, traditional gender relationships can be become socially dysfunctional and discrepancies can develop between individual gender arrangements. Karin Gottschall has pointed out that problems have emerged in the educational system and in the labour market that question the legitimation and functionality of the unequal treatment of the genders: "First of all, the structural discrimination of women's work in the employment system can no longer be primarily traced back to women's educational deficits or their orientation towards the family. Secondly, at the level of individual firms and industrial sector—within the context of rationalization and reorganization, new social demands on the quality of service, and new forms of job consciousness—it by no means proves to entirely functional: in particular the traditional deprofessioalization in the typical fields of women's employment (sales, health care, social and educational sectors) is approaching its limitations."[19] Thus genderized segmentation in industry is in motion.

In this instance, too, fissures develop that more precisely illuminates the phenomenon of the entanglement of genderized positions in society as a constituent of a hierarchical Geschlechterverhaltnis; I would like to come back to two controversial problems in gender studies.

(a) Disagreement prevails over whether it is even possible to talk about one Geschlechterverhaltnis in socially differentiated societies

where different living styles coexists or undermulticultural conditions where we encounter different ethnic milieus. In other words, are we rather not forced to assume a plurality of Geschlechterverhaltnissen? The following can be said in this regard: if we want to express the reciprocal social interrelatedness of the gender groups, if the phenomenon of relationality is to be brought up then only the term "Geschlechterverhaltnis" makes sense from an apistmological perspective. Empirically, if we come across conditions of disparity on all social levels of a society, if in a clearly determined context all gender order turn out to be based on similar Verhaltnisbestimmungen, then the singular is necessary as well. We are then dealing with **one** social network in which the gender groups are unequally involved. It is possible that we find different gender orders in a society in which different culture coexist. However, in this case it still needs to be clarified whether one of them is dominant, as majority societies influences the gender-based power relations in minority groups through claims to hegemony and the pressure to conform.[20]

The plural is called for if we leave the boundaries of a social structure situated in space and time and contemplate international variability. In this case, in view of ethnographic variety we must talk about "Geschlechterverhaltnisse."

(b) In view of the variety amongst women and men with regard to social origin, ethnic membership or skin colour, cam we even talk about gender groups? The answer to this question is important: If despite social differences on both sides we cannot identify important correspondences in the social situation of all women, all men in a society, if they are not subject to connections which more or less apply to them all qua gender membership, then the term "Geschlechterverhaltnis" does not make sense: The criteria are missing for generalizations which result in the two totalities that make up the elements of this relationality.

There are two possible ways of identifying "gender" as principle of social group formation without suppressing the heterogeneity of either gender group. On the one hand, we investigate whether women and men from similar socio-cultural and economic strata are treated equally or not. Their status quo gender in relevant social spheres is then the tertium comparation is that enables us to compare their living conditions. On the other hand, we systematically track where women across different milieus are discriminated against as opposed to men. Such investigations cover sexual violence in all strata of our society and of other societies, the global dissemination of job discrimination, and exclusion from the control mechanisms of power relatively independent of ethnic contexts. There will always be exceptions. But it is questionable what weight they have as opposed to the rule. In any case, however, they can release fantasies about relationships between the social genders that deviate from existing ones.

The processes by which women and men are assigned to a gender group—whether by choice or whether they are aware of it or not—can also be indicated. Their "Versamtlichung" (Hedwing Dohm)—the assembly of all women in to unit and all men into an opposing unit-comes about on the hand through social psychological mechanisms.[21] As different they may be as individuals, all of them are confronted with stereotypes of femininity and masculinity—whether in contexts that vary historically, culturally or class-specifically. All of them are subject to such patterns of generalization, which does not mean that people do not resist and change them. But first of all, individuals are subsumed under gender classification as a general grid.

On the other hand, the forms of socialization are gender-dependent. Some people can step off the prescribed social path of female or male biographies; however, even they are reminded of the factuality of the Geschlechterverhaltnis by the cost of their deviation from the path, by the resistance they are compelled to overcome. Because it is a part of the whole of society, the Geschlechterverhaltnis affects all those who are dependent on its conditions of reproduction. We can also say: The Geschlechterverhaltnis cannot be considered in isolation; rather it is built into comprehensive structural and functional constellations within society. We will see this in the next section: Our life courses are institutionalized in such a way that we can hardly avoid processes of genderization.

The structuring of the Geschlechterverhaltnis—Organization of Society as a Whole. The Paedox of the Connection of Separation and Linking

In our discussion of U. Beer's analyses of gender order we became acquainted with a strategem that consolidates dominance and at the same time obscures power relations: the connection of separation and linking in the juridical structuring of social relations. On the one side legal matters are broken down into independent codices (family and labour laws, property right); on the other side they are networked to form a coherent system by means of a unidirectional logic oriented towards andocentric interests.

We again encounter the construction of "separation and linking" in the everyday lives of working women; however, it is without the involvement on their part of interests in dominance. Rather it is due to the calm women have to not allow themselves to be narrowed down to one sphere of activity – namely the family – but to participate in the labour market as well. The functionalization of this dual orientation is a matter of society's agencies and their male actors.

Women circumvent the boundaries between domestic and market-mediated work by commuting between both fields of activity. In doing so they swim against the current although their individual recombination of what has been socially disassociated is more beneficial than detrimental to society. Firstly, female employment earmarked for female personnel, women are needed on the labour market. Women nevertheless experience little support in their effort to bring together what has been torn apart by society. They alone are responsible for ensuring the compatibility of family and career. The public is hardly aware of the psycho-social pressures associated with this.

It is so difficult to accommodate family and career because the organizational structure of society is not geared towards this. The private sphere is cut off from the employment system. In turn, market-mediated work is considered separate from the private sphere. Because different functions are to be fulfilled in both places, each place must be seen to display a relative measure of independent logic. The production of commodities and market-mediated services call for different maximize of action and organizational forms than do the care of family members and child-rearing. For working women this also means being forced to equalize their behavioural orientations when changing fields of activity. At the same time, the contrasting spheres are not completely isolated from one another. For reasons of reciprocal dependency they must be permeable.

In the family, the maintenance and regeneration of the labour expended in working life must be ensured through psycho-social care and material housework. And *vice versa*: in their own interests, factories and firms cannot conduct the destructive exploitation of human resources – they must show consideration for needs for rest, time with the family and recreation. These facts affect women differently than men: First and foremost, women perform the regenerative work at home; this is not taken into account in the structuring of their working hours in the labour force. For this reason, working women have less free time than working men. Furthermore, while we can observe that the requirements of the working sphere strongly encroach on women's private lives, *e.g.* in determining the rhythm of their life spans, the disciplining of their senses, and the distribution of energy, the same cannot be stated for the reverse case, *i.e.* for consideration of family matters in the employment sphere. Within this context as well, women are exposed to other provocations than men are: Women mediate between both unequal and separate worlds by providing services in the home that create the prerequisites for their family members to tackle duties outside the home. In the process they cannot count on receiving the same support for their own regeneration that they render others.

Housework and gainful employment – coordinated in the ensemble "women's work" – are two conditions of social reproduction but they are not treated by society as equal in value or as belonging together. However, the fact that this dilemma is dealt with at the expense of women is already the result of another insertion based as well on the double-edged principle of "separation and linking."

In an empirical investigation, Claudia Born, Helga Kruger and Dagmar Lorenz-Meyer (1996) trace how the disassociated areas of "family" and "profession" become connected in relationships between couples.[22] Something that remains undiscovered occurs in private which has obvious consequences for the social organization of the Geschlechterverhaltnis. Women and men first of all through career biographies that take place in separate institutional channels. However, their differently arranged life courses then interests in marriage or in permanent non-marital relationships. This is of central importance for the emergence of forms of the gender-based division of work because contributions to work within the family and to gainful employment are negotiated amongst couples in personal contracts according to objective prerequisites, upon examination of normative prescriptives, and lastly also in consideration of individual needs.

This social construction is analyzed more closely in the essay *"Dominanzen* im *Geschlechterverhaltnis: Zur Institutionalisierung von Lebenslaufen"* (Dominances in the Gender Relationship: on the Institutionalization of Life courses) by Helga Kruger.[23] She does this under three aspects. Firstly, she inquires into the way the courses of biographies are moulded by a general institutionalized framework and what role "gender" plays in the context. Secondly, she investigates how discrimination against the female gender group accumulates in their passage through the institutions of the educational system and the job market. Thirdly, she looks at the institution of "family", where the genderized biographies become entangled in relationships between couples. H. Kruger can show that – and why – men are the winners in this entanglement.

In her opinion, genderized socialization and engendering processes[24] in all of the institutions relevant to career biographies are responsible for the discriminatory structures that women encounter in all phases of their life courses. The idea that women should primarily identify themselves with family duties and only on second thought plan a career continues to live on in concepts of female education despite the growing status that women – even mothers – have attached to education and gainful employment for several generations. In all of their status passage, women are confronted with clichés of feminity that make deviation from this normative setting of priorities more difficult. In all stages of their career orientation, women experience that they are treated unequal in comparison with men. Women are more likely to be denied long-term career motivation than their male colleagues; that society assigns them domestic matters earns them the verdict of being unreliable for, or only sporadically available to, the labour market. Under such auspices, investments in training schemes appear as worthless as the opening up of opportunities for advancement.

In contrast, the construction of male socialization allows for a more consistent life plan: in this case, the desire for a family can be combined with career ambitions because his contribution to securing livelihood is not seen in his work performance, but in the money his gainful employment makes available to the household budget.

Such a premise, which overlooks the existence of female career interests, is consistent with the social practices that provide men with the space for self-assertion, competitive behaviour, ambition, and for demanding preferential treatment. The gate-keepers of institutions that must be passed through in the course of career socialization open their gates more widely for the male than for the female gender.

H. Kruger considers this gender bias, which crosses through the institutions that structure people's life courses—to be the leitmotif to which all of the advantages for the male and all of the disadvantages for the female gender can be related. She is able to show convincingly in what way "gender" assigns status in all institutions and thus can be considered a consistent principle of organization in society. In her opinion, as opposed to other characteristics of social situating (age, education, social origin), "gender" has a "master status" (Hughes).[25] However, this affects the two gender groups differently. H. Kruger sums up: "In male life courses, which are in fact mediated by the market and sustained by the family, 'gender', 'labour market' and 'family' add up to produce a positive result; in female lives, which are split by the market and by the family, gender stands for the accumulation of discriminating factors in the employment of resources for the individual securing of livelihood. Internal positions on the labour market and with the family, which from the very beginning can be considered status differences, become consolidated with a status hierarch between the gender in which the gaps continuously widen."[26]

H. Kruger's analysis of life courses is positioned on a meso-level of social theory: on the level of gendered institutional structures. However, to a certain extent she goes beyond this. She emphasizes that the institutional structures. However, to a certain extent she goes beyond this. She emphasizes that the institutionalization of male biographies enables giving precedence to labour market demands and ranking family matters low without the emergence of conflicts. Within the context of female life courses, however, such an unproblematic, society-condoned ranking of fields of activity cannot be taken up. According to Kruger, women's striving for a rearrangement of the priorities laid down for them in accordance with social norms falters "on the weakness of the family to assert itself."[27] This means: there is no social lobby for the demands by women to be relieved of housework and the care of small children and/or their interest in a just distribution of these tasks amongst the genders. The issue of housework does not carry political weight.

With this H. Kruger points out that the institutions in our society are themselves subject to a hierarchy: The labour market and the educational system have a greater influence on social objectives than does the private sphere. This opens up a macro-sociological perspective which I would like to pursue further by asking: How are gender rends mediated by hegemony of the social spheres or by comprehensive social principles of organization?

I see a possibility for finding an answer to this question by relating the connection in the Geschlechterverhaltnis to those between social sectors. In doing so, I take up Adorno.

In his "Einleitung in die Soziologie" (Introduction to Sociology), Adorno formulates "society as relational phenomenon, that is a notion in which the Verhaltnisbestimmungen between the individual social elements are of prime importance.[28] By "elements" Adorno means members of society.

Individual human beings—who are united in a population, do not merely form an agglomeration of monads. Depending on how they are socialized, they belong to social groups, strata and classes that are connected to each other. However, as social gender is not given central status is Adorno's sociological thinking, I must fall back on my own considerations.

His comprehension of society as relational constellation requires further elabouration: the social sectors also belong to the elements which are placed in relation to one another within the scope of the social division of work. It is not until this extension is made that it is possible to search for the homologies already mentioned—relations between gender positions/relations between the spheres of the societal reproduction process.

Let us begin with the members of society, whose social gender we have to take into account—as the elements of relations.

If we take the term "socialization" (Vergesellschaftung) seriously in Adorno's sense, then the position of the gender groups in the Geschlechterverhaltnis does not represent the end of their social situating, rather it is more like a vehicle to bind them—each in a special way—into the comprehensive social system.

This can be demonstrated particularly clearly with respect to the female gender group. The human capital women make available to society is subject to two different modes of integration: Housework is not market-mediated and consequently unpaid; gainful employment is market-mediated and is rewarded. This discrepancy in the assessment of practices equally necessary for society leads to contradictions and disproportions in the context of women's lives. There is a further reason for the imbalanced socialization of women, who are more strongly integrated into the private sphere than into the employment system. As long as the majority of children are nor produced in test tube, the generative maintenance of the population is based on the child-bearing ability of women. But because the birth of a child is considered a private matter, the procreative significance of women reinforces their normative situating within the family. Thus when emphasize the imbalances women are marginalized in the employment system in areas with high training levels; where they perform work equal in value to that of men they are paid less. Despite all of this, members of the female gender group represent a broader spectrum of social competencies than do their male counterparts. Because of such implications in women's living situations, the term "two-dimensional socialization" should not simply be extended in an undifferentiated way to male biographies – as is the case, for instance, with Kreckel.[29]

"Socialization" is a construct that remains empty of content without recourse to historical developments and social dynamics. For this reason, reference to the "two-dimensional and ambiguous socialization of the female gender" needs to be contextualized appropriately.

Let us again start with the separation of family life and work outside the home in the course of capitalist industrialization. We can use this to illustrate both things: how disparate relations occur in the Geschlechterverhaltnis, and how this goes together with a new ranking of the social spheres.

In the course of the replacement of the home economy by the national economy, which accompanied the expansion of the industrial-capitalist mode of production, housework was removed from the context of market exchange laws. Secluded in the private sphere, it not only lost public recognition. As housework did not share in the development that led from the simple exchange of goods to the money-mediated exchange of commodities, household management furthermore developed into a commodity difficult to assess. In comparison with work and utility goods, money became the historically further developed intermediary on the market and thus the more crucial medium of social exchange processes as well. It was no longer—as it had been in agrarian feudalism–the possession of land but the possession of money that was associated with power and standing. This change, which received it specifically industrial form in the interrelation of wage labour and capital, did in no way spare the family despite its being excluded from events on the job market. Here, too, money began to prevail over work: the monetary contributions by the head of the household to the household budget, which were intended to function as the equivalent of housework, had more prestige because they stemmed from the sphere of social exchange and not from private interrelations, which could not keep pace with modernity. Until this very day, the exchange between housework and income—the one inassessable in time expenditure and effort, the other fixed by earning–is based on disparate initial conditions: As women do not have the same opportunities as men in the labour market and are therefore in general unable to contribute comparably high earning to the family's income, in the distribution of housework and employment male partners are granted more scope for their careers.

The fact as a medium of exchange money has more value than work not mediated by the market can serve as a further indication that there is ranking between the social spheres—in our case: family/employment. We have already discussed that the employment system can have more influence on private life worlds that the other way around. This can be generalized. Despite the interdependencies between sectors that in a division of work contribute to social cohesion, our society is not a balanced system in which all subsystem carry their due weight. The fact that spheres of state policy, military facilities and economy have a more powerful impact on social decision-making than do the education system or non-public agencies of socialization points to hegemonies. This is where we should search for the structural homology to hierarchies in the Geschlechterverhaltnis.

The relations between the spheres of society are also characterized by modes of connectedness such as the establishment of difference, disproportionality and power hierarchies. Here, too, disassociations are bridged by interlacings. But these forged links have the character of "false linkings." The separation between "free" scientific research and the economy are undermined by research centers financed by large corporate groups. The order of the overall social structure is heteronomous, as is the order of the Geschlechterverhaltnis. And there is a correlation between the two heteronomies.

The prestige of and the influence of social sectors does not only follow a politico-economic logic, but an androcentrist logic as well.

Male fields of action (the military, the higher echelons of politics, business management, and applied research) are primarily granted social relevance in historical continuity In contrast, viewed from this perspective female practices have been degraded. The male gender has been able to assert its own standards in the devaluation of housework as an unpaid, non-professionalized activity not mediated by the market in comparison to paid, public and professionalized work. This hierarchical ranking affects women in a two-fold way: The low assessment of housework, which is considered a female sphere of activity, also rubs off onto women's employment, which likewise is not "men's work."

If the establishment of a hierarchy within the sectors corresponds with the esteem granted to male spheres of power, so do the different forms of work correspond with this ranking. The position of the genders is a result of such upgrading and downgrading, and the gender-based division of work is linked into this.

The discrepancy in society's assessment of the production of devices of power means of information and subsistence goods in comparison with its assessment of the procreation and reproduction of life along with its cultural requirements is astounding. This cannot be explained solely by the indifference of the logic of capital, technology and the exploitable sciences towards human beings. Rather it is related to a male-bonded structuring of the social world as well. The dichotomy between individual and society corresponds with the downgrading of the feminine to represent only the particular on the one hand, and the stylization of the masculine to represent the general on the other.

My reflection on the term "Geschlechterverhaltnis" have no claim to universal validity. They refer primarily to modern Europe, in particular Germany. Which question would have to be asked in order to be able to bring out differences in the development of gender arrangements in other cultures and regions? A few suggestions in this regard:

- In order to understand the connection between societal reproduction processes and the genderization of society, before analyzing international interdependencies we have to scrutinize the constellations that characterize historically constituted, country-specific gender relationships.
- 'Work' is an important mediator of societal reproduction. However, in the mainstream social sciences we can observe a narrowing of how it is understood: 'work' has been reduced to mean market-mediated labour. Of we look at the composition of women's work we can see the variety of social activities upon which the permanent revitalization of society is dependent: domestic work, care work, works within the labour market. This wealth of social activities is characteristic for women's work—the horizon of men's work is less multifaceted.
- What are the components of women's work in different cultures? How does this composition differ from country to country?
- From a socio-historical perspective we are compelled to ask: How did the development of a given society influence the assignment of women's and men's work in different social spheres? And *vice versa*: How did these assignments structure our society as a whole (*e.g.* the stratification system, the patriarchal legal system)?
- What does the gendered division of work have do to with gender orders? How is it connected with stereotyping femaleness and maleness, the normative impact of engendering processes? What are the social sources of the efficiency of these genderized clichés?
- In which ways do given social arrangements of the gendered division of work support the functioning of social systems? Under which circumstances do they sustain hierarchies, power structures, inequalities and asymmetries? What are the preconditions for equal rights, redistribution and recognition?
- What are the mechanisms within globalization processes that affect societal gender arrangements? Are women the sinners or the losers in worldwide transformations? In which

social realms can we observe changes occurring, both negative and positive/ what strategies have been formulated by the international women's movement to establish a feminist concept of empowerment suitable to correct the detrimental effects of globalization to the female gender?

LITERATURE

- Adorno, Theodor W. (1993), Einleitung in die Soziologie, Frankfurt a.M.
- Adorno, Theodor W., Familie (1956), in Adorno, Thedor W./ Dirks, Walter, (Eds.).
- Soziologische Exkurse, Frankfurter Beitrage Zur Soziologie, Vol. 4, Frankfurt a.M., pp. 116-132.
- Becker-Schmidt, Regina (1998), Relationalitat Zwischen den Geschlechtern, Konnedionen im Geschlechterverhaltnis, in: Zeitschrift fur Frauenforschung, 16 (3/98), pp. 5-21.
- Beer, Ursula (1984), Theorigen geschlechtern, Konnexionen im Geschlecterverhaltnis, in: Zeitschrift fur Fraeunforschung, 16 (3/98), pp. 5-21.
- Beer, Ursula (1984), Theorien geschlechtliehtlicher Arbeitsteilung, Frankfurt a.M./ New York lechterverhaltnisses, Frankfurt a.M./ New York.
- Beer, Ursula (1990), Geschlecht, Struktur, Geschicte, Soziale Konstituierung des Geschlechterver-haltinesses, Frankfurt a.M./ New York.
- Born, Caludia, Kruger, Helga and Lorenz-Meyer, Dagmar, (1996), Der unentdeckte Wandel. Annahe-rung nad das Verhaltnis von Struktur and Norm im weiblichen Lebenslauf, Berlin.
- Butler, Josephine (1869), Education and the Employment of women, London.
- Connell, Robert W. (1987), Gender and Power, Cambridge/ Oxford.
- Gerhard, Ute *et al.* (1983), Herrschaft and Widerstand: Entwurf ZU einer historichen und theoretic-schen Kritik des Patriarchats in der burgerlichen Gesellschaft; in: Heckmann, Friedrich Winter, Peter (eds.), 21. Deutscher Soziologentag,

Bamberg 1982. Beirtage der Diskussions-und Ad-hoc-Gruppen, Opladen.

- Gerhard, Ute (1990), Gleichheit ohne Angleichung. Frauen im Recht, Munchen.
- Gildemeister, Regine and Wetterer, Angelika (1992), Wie Geschlechter gemacht werden. Die soziale knostruktion der Zweigeshlechtlichkeit und the ihre Reifizierung in der Frauenforschung in: Knapp, Gudrun Axeli and Wetterer, Angelika (eds.), Traditionen Bruche. Entwicklungen feministischer Theorie, Frankfurt a.M./New York, pp. 151-200.
- Gottschall, Karin (1995), Geschlechterverhaltnis and Arbeitsmarktsegregation, in: Becker—Schmidt, Regina and Knapp. Gurdun axeli, (eds.), Das Geschlechterverhaltnis als Gegenstand der Sozilalwissenschaften, Frankfurt a.M./ New York, pp. 125-162.
- Haug, Frigga (1990), Erinnerungsarbeit, Hamburg.
- Haug, Frigga (1990), "Okonomie der Zeit, darin lost sich schlieblich alle Okonomie auf", in: Das Argument, Vol. 32. No. 184, pp. 879-895.
- Hausen, Karin and Wunder, Heide (eds.), (1992), Frauengeschichte-Geschlechtergeschichte, Frankfurt a.M./ New York.
- Heise, Hildegard (1989), Gleichstellung and Ungleichstellung von Frauen und Mannern (im entwik-kelten Kapitalismus): Vor-und Ruckesite "Desselben", in: Muller, Ursula and Schmidt-Waldherr, Waltraud (eds.), FruenSozialKunde. Wandel und differenzierung von Lebensformen und BewuBtsein, Bielefeld, pp. 261-297.
- Knapp, Gudrun Axeli (1990), Zur widerspruchilchen Vergesellschaftung von Frauen, in: Hoff, Ernst-H. (ed.), Die doppelte Sozialisation Ersachsener, Mucnchen, pp. 17-52.
- Knapp, Gudrun Axeli (1993), Der "weibliche sozialcharakter"–Mythos order Realitat? Soziologische und sozialpsychologische Aspekte des Sozialacharakter-Konstrukts, in: Kruger, Marlis (ed.), Was Beibt eigentlich feminsitisch? Zur theoretischen Diskussion in den Geistes- und Sozialwisseschaften, Bermen, pp. 93-120.

- Knapp, Gudrun Axeli (1993), Segregation in Bewegung. Einige Uberlegungen Zum "Gendering" von Arbeit und Arbitsvermongen in: Hausen, Karin and Krell, Getraude (eds.), Frauenerwerstatigkeit. Forschungen zur Geschichte und Gegenwart, Munchen/Mering, pp. 25-46.
- Kreckel, Reinhard (1992), Politische soziologie der sozialen Ungleichheit, Frankfurt a.M./ New York.
- Kruger, Helga (1995), dominanazen im Geschlechter-verhaltnis: Zur Institutionalisierung von Lebens- laufen, In: Becker-Schmidt, Regina and Knapp, Gudrun Axeli (eds.), Das Geschlechterverhaltnis als Gegenstand der Sozialwissen-schaften, Frankfurt a.M./New York, pp. 195-219.
- Lachenmann, Gudrun (1999), Entwicklungssoziologie. Geschlechterforschung in der Entwicklungs-politik, in: Dausien, Bettina *et al.* (eds.), Erkenntnisprojekt Geschlecht, Feministische Perspekitven Verwanddeln Wissenschaft, Opladen pp. 72-94.
- Lenz, Ilse (1995) Geschlecht, Herrschaft und internationale Ungleicheeit, in: BeckerSchmidt, Regina and Knapp, Gudrun Axeli (eds.), Das Geschlechterverhaltnis als Gegensatnd der Sozialwissenischaften, Frankfurt a.M./New York, pp. 19-46.
- Marx-Ferree, Myra (1991), Gender Kritik der Politischen Okonomie, Berlin.
- Marix-Ferree, Myra (1991), Gender Conflicts and change: Family Roles in Biographical Perspecitves, in: Heinz, Walter R. (ed.), Theoretical advances in Life course Research, Weinheim, pp. 144-162.
- Morschhauser, Martina (1993), Frauen in Mannerdomanen, Koln.
- Nietzsche, Friedrich (1910), werke, Vol. VII, Leipzig.
- Ott, Cornelia (1998), Die Spur der Luste. Sexualitat, Geschlecht und Macht, Opladen.
- Patzig, Gunther (1973), Relation, in: Hamdbuch philosphischer Grundbegriffe, 4, Munchen.
- Weib, Florence (1991), Die dreisten Frauen. Ethnop-sychoanalytische Gesprache in Papua-Neuguinea, Frankfurt a.M.

- West, Candan and Zimmerman, Don (1991), Doing Gender, in: Lorber, Judith and Farell, Susan A. (eds.), The Social Construction of Gender, Newbury Park/London/New Delhi.
- Wolde, Anja (1995), Geschlechterverhaltnisse und gesellschaftliche Transformationsprozesse, in: Becker-Schmidt, Regina and Knapp, Gudrun Axeli (eds.), Das Geschlechterverhaltnis als Gegenstand der Sozialwisseneschaften, Frankfurt a.M./New York, pp. 279-308.

REFERENCES

1. In German, the term Geschlechterverhaltnis refers to the societal organization of gender orders. A social "Verhaltnis" implies not only the arrangements of gender relations, but also the independence of genderized positions.
2. Mark Manoch Brown, Foreword, Human Development Report 1999 (New York, Oxford, 1999), P.V.
3. *Ibid.*, p. 6.
4. Gudrun Lachenmann, "Entwicklungssoziologie: Geschlechterforschung in der Entwicklungspolitik," in Erk-ennttnisprojekt Geschlecht. Feministische perspektiven verwandeln Wissenschaft, eds. Bettina Dansien *et al.* (Opladen, 1999), pp. 76 ff.
5. Ursula Beer, Theorien geschlechtlicher Persoektiven Verwandeln Wissenschaft, eds. Bettina Danise *et al.* (Opladen, 1999), 76 ff.
6. Beer, Geschlecht, Struktur, Geschichte. Soziale Konstituierung des Geschlechterverhaltnisses (Frankfurt a.M., New York, 1990), p. 9.
7. Karin Hausen and Heide Wunder, eds., Frauengeshcichte-Geschlechtergeschichte (Frankfurt A.M., New York, 1992), p. 9.
8. This chapter is a continuation of the following article: Regina Becker-schmidt, "Relationalitat zwi-schen den Geschlechtern, Konnexionen im Geschlechterverhaltnis," Zesitschrift fur Frauenforschung, 16(3/98), 5-21.
9. Verhaltnisbestimmungen are the criteria and factors which constitute the social construction of femininity and masculinity and the social positions of the genders.
10. Florence Weib studied such a constellation in the Iatmul community in Papua New Guinea and investigated the social conditions of a balance of power between the genders within this ethni group. cf. Florence Weibm Die deristen Frauen. Ethnopsychoanalytische Gesprache in Papua-Neuguinea (Frankfurt a.M., 1991).
11. It was not until 1977 that the direct, juridically legitimized dominance of husbands over their wives was rescinded by the German Marriage Law Reform.

12. Cf. Regina Becker-schmidt, "Geschlechterverhaltnis als Herrschaftsgefuge. Frauenpolitische Stra-tegien," in: Wider das schlichte Vergessen. Der Deutsch-Deutsche Einigungsprozes. Frauen im Dialog, eds. Chistine Kulke, Heide Kopp-Degethoff and Ulrike Ramming (Berlin, 1991), pp. 234 f. Refer also to Anja Wolde, "Geschlechterverhaltnisse und gesellschaftliche Transformationsprozess, "in Das Geschlechterverhaltnis als Gegenstand der Sozialwissenschaften, eds. Regina Becker-Schmidt ad Axeli Knapp (Frankfurt a.M., New York, 1995), pp. 279-308.
13. This is sometimes the tenor in essays by Frigga Haug, even though she takes up a perspective that includes society as a whole. She makes the domestic division of work the starting point of the social inferiority of women. However, the private sphere is not the only place characterized by the division of work according to gender hierarchies. This structures the employment system as well and manifests itself in mechanisms of closure, marginalization and segmentation. Cf. Frigga Haug, Erinnerungsarbeit (Hamburg, 1990); Haug, "Okonomie der Zeit, darin lost sich schlieblich alle Okonomie auf," Das Argument, 32 (1990), No. 184.
14. Hildegard Heise makes attempts in this direction. However, in patriarchal dominance she sees only personal dependencies and not social structures. Cf. Hidlegard Heise, "Gleichstellung und Ungleichstellung Von Frauen und Mannern sind (im entwickelten Kapitalismus) Vor-und Ruckseite 'Desselben," in frauenSozialkunde. Wandel und Differenzierung von Lebensformen and Bewubtesin, eds. Ursula Muller and Hiltraut Schmidt-Waldherr (Bielefeld, 1989), pp. 261-297.
15. Wolde, p. 294.
16. Ute Gerhard *et al.*, Herrschaft und Widerstand: Entwurf zu einer historischen und theroretischen Kritik des Patriarchats in der burgerlichen Gesellschaft," in 21. Deutscher Soziologentag, Bamberg 1982. Beitrage der Diskussions-und Ad-hoc-Gruppen, eds. Friedrich Heckmann and Peter Winter (Opladean, 1983), pp. 60-74. Gerhard, Gleichheit ohne Angleichung. Frauen im Recht (Munich, 1990).
17. It must, however, be taken into consideration that the enactment of laws governing Geschlechterverhaltnisse, in which patriarchal traditions play such a major role, is a development peculiar to Germany and cannot be generally applied to all of Europe.
18. Within this context, U. Beer makes emphatically clear that authority qua masculinity is not limited to the possibility of degrading women's work and controlling how women are utilized. Women's bodies are also made available to men. Birth control and sexuality belong to the patriarchal realm of dominance.

19. Karin Gottschall, "Geschlechterverhaltnis und Arbeitsmarkt-segregation", in Das Geschlechterverhaltnis als Gegenstand der Sozialwissenschaften, eds. Regina Becker-Schmidt and Axeli Knapp (Frandkfurt a.M., New York, 1995), p. 134.
20. Cf. Ilse Lenz, "Geschlecht, Herrschaft und internationale Ungleichheit" in Das Geschlechterverhaltnis als Gegestand der Sozialwissenschaften, eds. Regina Becker-Schmidt and Axeli Knapp (Frankfurt a.M., New York, 1995), p. 40.
21. Cf. Gudrun Axeli Knapp, "Zur widersprichlichen Vergesellschaftung von Frauen, " in Die doppelte Vergesellschaftung Erwaschsener. Zum Verhaltnis von berufichem und privatem Lebnesstrang, ed. Ernst H. Hoff (weinheim, Munich, 1980), pp. 17-52.
22. Claudin Born, Helga Kruger and Dagmet Lorenz-Meyer, Der unentdeckte Wnadel: Annaherung an das Verhaltnis von Struktur und Norm im weiblichen Lebenslauf (Berlin, 1996).
23. Claudia Born, Helga Kruger, "Dominamzen im Geschlechterverhaltnis: Zur Institutionalisierung von Lebenslaufen, "in Das Geschlechterverhatnis als Gegenstand der Sozialwissenschaften, eds. Regina Becker-Schmidt and Axeli Knapp (Frankfurt a.M., New York, 1995), pp. 195-219.
24. What is meant by this are processes in which social construction of gender difference function as guidelines for social behaviour and maxmis for action. "doing gender" and "making the difference" are strategies that are at work in all institutions - as Robert W. Connel shows in his book Gender and Power.
25. I will not go into more detail about the methodological problem involving the lack of a distinct differentiation here between ascriptive and socio-cultural criteria for the assignment of status.
26. Kruger, p. 206.
27. *Ibid.*
28. Theodor W. Adorno, Einletiung in die Soziologie (Frandkfurt a.M., 1993), p. 63.
29. Rheinhard Krckel, Politische der sozialen Ungleichheit (Frankfurt a.M., New York, 1992).

2
Globalization and Gender: A European Perspective

BRIGITTE YOUNG, MUNSTER

Globalization

Globalization has to be understood as an open and contradictory process that entails resturcturing the nationally bounded economic system and its Keynesian institutional regulatory structures. More specifically, we are facing a process of de-nationalization of the political and economic spaces that symbolized the proceeding period of capitalism, generally referred to as the Fordist regime of accumulation (Aglietta, 1979; Jessop, 1988). After 1945, Fordism came to mean the highly successful synchronization between mass production and mass consumption. The novelty of the post-Second World War Fordist regime was based on the way liberal democratic societies were able to assert themselves against the destructive forces of the market. At the center of the unique historic Fordist compromise was the synchronization of real (male) wages with productivity growth, and the national anti-cyclical monetary and fiscal policies that led to one of the longest growth, and the national anti-cyclical monetary and fiscal policies that led to one of the longest growth periods in history. The Keynesian welfare state was key in stabilizing consumer demand and expanding social rights to average citizens who. For the first time, were given access to mass consumer goods. Since 1973, the "virtuous circle" between mass production and mass consumption has come under increasing stress. The neo-liberal answer to the crisis has been the deregulation and flexibilization of the Fordist model of nationally bounded economic and social system.

Therefore, globalization cannot be reduced to quantitative comparison of international trade and financial statistics as many critics of globalization assert. Hirst and Thompson (1996) cite export quotas and data for direct investment between 1870 and 1973 to show that the process of globalization is nothing new. These scholars maintain the present global trade and investment data does to significantly differ from the imperialist time. But globalization is not about quantitative indicators. In contrast to globalization, internationalization prior to World War I was based on an exchange between nation-states. It starts with the nation-state as the central actor in this exchange (Strange, 1996). The major difference between internationalization and globalization is that now national economic and political actors are exposed to the logic and conditions of global competition. The nation-state continues to be important, but is forced to adjust to the economic logic of the global economy. The state logic no longer is that of Keynesian demand management. Hirsch refers to the new state as a "competition state" (Hirsch 1995). The state acts primarily as geo-economic actor and its traditional role as geo-political actor becomes secondary (Altvater and Mahnkopf, 1996)

For the first time in history, the global economy has the capacity "to work as a unit in real time on a planetary scale" (Castells, 1996: 92). Whereas the space-time relations in modernity were shaped by the separation between time and space–time was the invention of mechanical clock that first made possible a precise classification in space and time zone–globalization means an expansion of such processes. In other words, a network architecture is emerging as a form of connection between different social contexts and regions across the entire global surface (Giddens, 1995). The many "time" across different continents shrink to one world time. This process of creating "a timeless time" despite events that happen at different times has produced an artificial "world rhythm," making it difficult to discern between the "real" and the "virtual." In this virtual reality, which Jean Baudrillard calls "hyper-reality", citizens of the first world live in the "time." These inhabitants, linked via telecommunication and computer technology, experience the globe as a village. They are no longer restricted by their spatial environment. Inhabitants of developing world experience the space-time dimension in reverse to the people of the first world. They live in the "space which is heavy, indestructible, and untouchable, ties down the time, and is beyond the control of its inhabitants" (Bauman, 1996: 661).

In this "hyper-reality", in which the spatial and temporal distances between local and global events are "stretched," a complex relation develops between "local involvement" (a situation of simultaneous presence) and the "interaction across distances" (connection between presence and presence) (Giddens, 1995: 85). With globalization an intensification of global social relations spanning local and distant social events starts to take effect. One gets the impression that with economic globalization all other social relations also become globalized, even those aspects which cannot be subsumed under capitalist forms of utilization (Alvater and Mahnkopf, 1996: 13). As a result, globalization always also encounters barriers. Not everything that comes in contact with globalization can be subsumed to the logic of capitalism. Globalization is thus not only a process of expansion and breakthrough of political, economic, social, and ecological barriers. It always also involves the development of counter-tendencies, those that set barriers to globalization.

This chapter is guided by the central question of how a borderless global market and the territorially bounded concept of democracy can be reconstituted, and how gender regimes and order are reconfigured in the new "network societies." The theoretical insights of the French Regulation School provide the basic building materials to explain the complex connection between transformation of the Fordist regime of accumulation and the reconfiguration of new post-fordist gender regimes and order. To explore this argument I focus first on the decline of industrial capitalism and the present rise of "information capitalism" with its new network structures (Castells, 1996). I proceed with an analysis of why and how globalization has undermined the fordist gender regimes and discuss the merging new "fledible" gender orders. Finally, I explore the significance of these changes for feminist state theory and practice.

"Information Capitalism"[2] and the Development of Networks Structures

The globalization literature defines the new mode of production as a transformation from industrial production to service economy. The existing data surely does provide some evidence for this assumption. Not only in the USA has the share of the service sector risen to 70 per cent as part of the gross domestic product. In other industrial countries as well the share of the service sector has increased while the share of industrial production has declined (Thurow, 1997). From this, a linear sequence of historic regimes of accumulation is extrapolated: agrarian capitalism until the 19th century, followed by industrial capitalism, and now the rise of the tertiary economy. These different accumulation regimes vary fundamentally in how profits are extracted. In agrarian capitalism, profits were appropriated through the extensive use of land of labour power in the production process. Industrialism relied on the intensification of technology and labour power, made possible by the fossil fuel revolution. Not only was it feasible to abstract high energy efficiency with low amounts of energy input, the profits form this production process were used to advance social, political, cultural and economic living standards of the population (Alvater and Mahnkopf, 1996). Energy efficiency is no longer the basis for profit accumulation in the merging informational capitalism. At the center of the present value generation is the quantitative and qualitative intensification of electronic information and communication processes (Castells, 1996).

The source of productivity lies, as Castells points out, in the technology of knowledge generation, information processing, and symbol communication. "... What is specific to the informational mode of development is the action of knowledge upon knowledge itself as the main source of productivity" (1996: 17). Information processing is focused on a "virtuous circle" of "interaction between the knowledge sources of technology and the application of technology of improve knowledge generation and information processing" (1996: 17). While industrial capital pursued the goal of maximizing output, information capitalism is oriented towards technological development: the accumulation of knowledge toward higher levels of complexity in information processing. This information production does not take place in an abstract space. It is embedded immaterial production processes. As a result, neither industrial nor agrarian production lose their economic importance in the global economy despite the continuing decline in overall numbers. On the contrary, as a result of the new information technology, for example in genetic engineering, new horizons open up for the agricultural and the medical and pharmaceutical sectors, which were inaccessible until now. The tapping, manipulation, and decodification of human, animal and plant life and the future reprogramming for genetic codes of living material open up new doors, however critically this is viewed form an ethical standpoint. We are not even able to fathom the effects on human beings and the nature at the moment (Haraway, 1997; Wichterich, 1998). To quote

Castells once again, "... what characterizes the current technological revolution is not the centrality of knowledge generation and information processing and communication devices, in a cumulative feedback loop between innovation" (1996: 32). The present interpretation of the sequential development from agrarian to industrial, and now to a service economy, is a simplification of the very complex interconnection of different production developments.

The change in the technology paradigm has also led to fundamental transformations in the type of economic organizations and control mechanisms. The new types of organizational structures are based on a combination of features inherent in the market and the state. On the market side, the characteristic plurality of autonomous actors is combined with the typical capacity of the state to coordinate strategies for the purpose of achieving specific goals (Messner, 1997: 57). Manuel Castells defines the emerging plurality of the inter-organizational weblike-connections as a network society. Networks are the new instruments for a goal economy based on innovation, globalization and decentralized concentration, "for work, workers, and firms based on flexibility, and adaptability; for a culture of endless deconstruction and reconstruction; for a polity geared towards the instant processing of new values and public moods; and for a social organization aiming at the supersession of space and the annihilation of time" (1996: 471). The new economy no longer relies on the vertical organizations of the multinational era, but is organized around global enterprise networks of capital, management and information, whose access to technological innovation is the driving force for competition. The new logic of this network society not only pervades the economy, it substantially alters the entire social structure and dramatically reorganizes existing power relations. According to Castells, "switches" connecting the networks are the new instruments of power. Financial flows taking control of media empires influence political processes furnishing the interoperating codes and switches that shape social processes and the social structure. This type of capitalism differs from the previous industrialization in that it is global. Second, it is structured largely around a network of financial flows located in a few strategic "global cities" (Sassen, 1996). Profits are mainly accumulated in the sphere of circulation and no longer in production. Whatever is extracted as profit "is reverted to the meta-network of financial flows, where all capital is equalized in the commodified democracy of profit-making" (Castells, 1996: 472).

The transformation from vertical structures of industrial organization to the new interconnected global networks has fundamentally changed the gender-specific Fordist division of labour between the highly paid male industrial workers and the female part-time earners. I now turn to examining how and why this has occurred and to explore the reconfiguration of gender regimes in the context of the emerging global "flexible regime of accumulation" (Harvey, 1989). In the new decentralized "flexible accumulation" processes (Harvey, 1989), the organization of work is based on the spatial dispersal of informal sub-contracting and outsourcing activities to a wide net of contractors, sub-contractors, and sub-sub-contractors. The preferred workers in the "global factories" specializing in cheap electronic, textile, clothing and shoe products are young, uneducated, poor rural women who are strangers to labour organizing. Women no longer earn money only as an additional source of income to the male breadwinner. They increasingly subsidize the seasonal work of their husbands through their permanent integration in the labour force, or their wage labour functions as the sole income to feed the family (Ward and Pyle, 1995).

Associated with this spatial dispersion of economic activities, we witness a new a new division of labour between an international, hypermobile, professional class of "information carriers"—mostly white and male—and the low-skilled, place-bound workers of all colours. In her studies on "global cities", Saskia Sassen criticizes the mainstream accounts on globalization for operating like a "narrative of eviction." They concentrate on the global culture, the hypermobility of capital, and the power of transnational. By neglecting the material production sites for running the advanced information and global communications technologies, we miss the place-bound capital that is at least still partly embedded in national territories. Focusing on the practices that provide the infrastructure for the production and reproduction of global capital, we recover a multiplicity of work cultures ranging from immigrant to female cultures where the work of globalization gets done. These include secretaries, pizza delivery persons, cleaning crews, truck drivers, industrial service workers, maids and a host of other low-skilled, blue-collar workers that have become "invisible" in this narrative of hypermobile capital. The invisibility of the material work culture has produced a change in the valuation of labour inputs. Increasingly, many of the unskilled jobs are regarded as irrelevant and no longer needed in the global economy. Saskia Sassen warns that the corporate culture with its emphasis on specialized information services is overvalued while other kinds of work cultures are devalued. In simple terms, it is the work of women and immigrants that has become revalorized. Thus we need to proceed from the bottom up in studying how the global economy works. "Power is not a silence at the bottom; it absence is present and has consequences" (Sassen, 1996: 21). If we include the precarious activities of women and immigrants as part of the capital-bound globalization process, then women and ethnic economy are important components of the global information economy.

The informal sector of the global economy employs many more women than the formal sector.[3] The major "carriers" of the informal economy are the subcontractors that produce for the transnational corporations. Particularly in the Free Export Zones, found anywhere from Central America to parts of Africa and East Asia, the new type of "global factory" has emerged. On the border between the United States and Mexico these global factories work on a contract basis for American transnational corporations, such as J.C. Penney, Sears & Roebuck, Walmart, and Montgomery Ward. The "maquila businesses" profit from the high unemployment rates in these regions, and from the desperate need of women and men to earn a living.[4] These Export Zones benefit from the extraterritorial status they enjoy. Import and export activities are handled in these zones and are cut off from the national territory; companies in the zones do not provide living space for the their work force; building and factories are exempt from taxes; the enterprises do not pay local taxes, nor land, corporate, or income tax; imports and exports are exempt from tariffs; the host countries provide infrastructure, build streets and harbours, and offer telephone, water and energy services at low prices (Lemoine, 1998). The new cheap-wage "El dorado" countries in Asia are Vietnam, Cambodia, Laos, and China at the moment. These countries are replacing the former cheap-labour countries that included South Korea, Taiwan, and Hong Kong in the 70s, followed in the 80s by the Philippines, Thailand, and Indonesia (Wichterich, 1998).

Transnational production is increasingly associated with local informal activities that range from sweatshops, home-based work, to street alleys and back yard conditions. Increasingly, the rural countryside is opened up for even cheaper sources of labour. Transnational corporations take advantage of the still existing household economies by paying below the subsistence minimum. As a result, the subsistence work of the women in the household economy relieves the companies from paying even the minimum wage. The search for ever cheaper production sites means that the firms are constantly on the move either to locate their business to cheaper areas, take advantage of further outsourcing into back-alleys and sweat shops, or rationalize the production process and thus get rid of most of the labour force (Ward and Pyle, 1995).

In contrast to the Fordist production techniques, the new flexible accumulation can be housed in small and the mobile "global assembly lines." The new precarious unregulated, and very exploitative activities of the informal economy have also appeared in western industrial countries. In Eastern Europe and in the periphery of Europe, the interaction among globalization, in formalization, and transnationalization has promoted the flexibilization of the work force and strengthened the gender-specific division of cheap labour (Wichterich, 1998; Mahnkopf, 1997). Transnational labour-intensive corporations are found from Greece, Spain, and Ireland to the United States, the country in which the centralized Fordist production techniques originated at the turn of the century. Many of the European textile and clothing industries, the Italian producer Benetton for example, are marketing enterprises that coordinate globally their cheap-labour sub-contracting firms dispersed among networks of world-wide sweatshops (Harvey, 1989). In the US, labour-intensive transnational corporations are found in the same industries (for example, electronics and the clothing industries) as in cheap-wage countries of the developing world. In contrast to the widely held belief that the low-skilled and work intensive industries have migrated to Third World countries, the, United States shows exactly the reverse. The clothing and textile industries are not shrinking sectors. The number of workers in the clothing industry alone is greater than the combined work force in the auto, steel, and electronic industries (Fernandez Kelly, 1989).

Despite important differences there are commonalities between the Eastern European transitional societies, parts of the "Third World," and the industrial countries: everywhere we find "cheap-wage zones" (Mahnkopf, 1997). These enclaves of the informal economy have become a permanent feature of the formal economy.

The informalization of the economy is thus no longer a marginal or transitional phenomenon. It is an immanent part of economic globalization. In the North, increasingly we see conditions of the "South," and in the South centers emerge that have much in common with the "North" (Group of Lissabob, 1997). New hierarchies of class, gender, and race emerge in the system of flexible accumulation. In the textile industry in Miami, for example, the producers are mostly Jewish men, the subcontractors are overwhelmingly Cuban men, and Cuban women fill the sweatshops (Ferrandez Kelly and Garcia, 1992). Globalization and the spatial dispersion of economic activities have thus created new gender hierarchies, which are intensified through class, ethnic, and national membership. Males overwhelmingly control the unregulated area of subcontracting while women (particularly immigrants) are found in the sweatshops of the "global factories" (Fernandez Kelly and Sassen, 1995).

Gender Regimes: From Fordism to Globalization

Methodologically, the argument presented here rests on the assumption that the transformations of specific historic regimes of accumulation go hand in hand with the reconfiguration of gender regimes and gender orders. With the concept of gender, the social construction of masculinities and feminities is emphasized rather the biological definition of the sexes. Linda Gordon (1993) defines gender as a series of meaning systems which are socially constructed as sexual differences within the context of systemic male domination. Gender thus refers to societal networks of hierarchical regulated social relations, which are ordered along a socially dividing line that places women on one side and men on the other (Kreisky and Sauer, 1995). The concept of gender regime is used here to refer to institutionalized practices and forms of gendered systems of domination that are constituted as social ordering principles in all societies. Social norms, rules, regulations, and principles are not gender neutral entities, but are continually reproduced through the organization or structure of practice that persists in its effects on subsequent practices. The process of institutionalization means, as Connell points out, to create conditions that make cyclical practice probable (1987: 141). The finally gender orders are the aggregate of these gender regimes at the level of macro-politics. The interaction between state powers that bear on gender relations, cultural definitions of gender and the historical possibilities in gender relations make up these orders. They are stabilized through the various micro-and meso-practices that ensure the reproduction of these macro-political orders. Stabilized means that gender regimes and orders become sufficiently institutionalized as a result of specific historic regimes of capital accumulation. At the same time, the ongoing gender practices stand in "reflexive relations" (Giddens, 1984) to the existing power structure of the sexes. Women and men continuously renegotiate the meaning of gender identity, struggling over the formation and dissolution of accepted categories, and the reconfiguration of institutional relations (Connell, 1987: 139). Gender regimes represent symbolic gender order that is at the same time an arena of power in which the boundaries are part of a struggle between the sexes to the define their contours. Given the dynamic process of gender regimes and orders, there is not only one historical "masculinity" or an unchanging a historic "feminity". Masculinities and feminities abound in their plurality in terms of both their spatial and temporal contexts. Gender regimes and orders are utilized in this study as heuristic devices to delineate and analyze the development and subsequent reconfiguration of these categories within specific historical contexts.

These conceptual tools will provide the basic building materials to explain the complex connection between the transformation of the Fordist regime of accumulation and the reconstruction of the new gender regimes and orders. In this context, I draw upon the theoretical insights of the French Regulation School, which stipulates capitalist modes of production as a series—but not necessarily a linear projection—of different historic regimes of accumulation and modes of regulation. The central question of this chapter is: how is the transition of the Fordist regime of accumulation to a flexible global regime of accumulation related to the reconfiguration of new gender regimes?

Gender Regimes During the Fordist Period

The Fordist phase of capitalism (1959-1973) has already entered the history book as "the golden age of capitalism." The particular compromise between capital and labour was surely "the golden age" if one was a white, male, industrial worker living in a western capitalist country. A look backward through the prism of a gender analysis tells a different story of the gender regimes and orders that accompanied the golden age. Beginning at the turn of the century,

Fordist industrialization replaced the extensive mode of production associated with agrarian capitalism, and transformed the existing gender regimes based on the unity of the private and reproduction and the public and production spheres. In contrast to the agrarian period, the Fordist production model elevated the white man to the center of industrial capitalism. Males entered this new production paradigm both as managers in the newly emerging vertical organizations of the multinational firms (Chandler, 1977) and as factory workers herded together in the places of mass production. The workplace and "his" family wage were tailored to the needs and interests of the male worker and "his" dependent family. The conditions for this Fordist "breadwinner model" were negotiated in the hierarchical, exclusionary, male-biased bastions of labour unions and employers, associations. These collective bargaining institutions possessed a monopoly in the formulation and implementation of wage-bargaining decision-making (Schmitter, 1979). The corporatist organizations are deeply male-biased in their organizational, membership, decision-making, and leadership structures. Women are rarely found in leadership position; they are absent from employers, associations, from the corporatist negotiations among labour, the state bureaucracies and ministries, and employers' associations; and from economic "think tanks". Decisions affecting the entire economy and just workers and employers are made in these para-statal organizations,[5] bureaucratic administrations, and economic interest groups. The male industrial worker is at the center of this production model. In this gender-specific arrangement capital and labour are quite united. While they stand on opposite sides on class interests, capital and labour share a common interest in reproducing the existing hierarchical Fordist gender order.

Yet the Fordist accumulation regime is not completely exclusive of women, but includes them in a specifically dependent role. Inclusion was achieved through the status of the husband and in women's assigned social role as "career housewives." Women were not completely absent from the labour market. Integrating women into the labour force was certainly functional for increasing consumer demand. As pointed out earlier, they key to the Fordist production paradigm laying the rising access of average citizens to mass consumption. One way to integrate women was via the expansion of the Keynesian welfare state. Women were hired for the care of the elderly and children, as nurses, teachers, and to provide other services for dependents. At the same time, women were hired for low-skilled jobs in the social service hierarchy as social workers. Women were thus tied to the welfare state through a three-tier chain: as social workers, clients and consumers of public services. In virtually all western industrial countries, public services expanded in the Fordist period and this proved beneficial for women. Yet this statement has to be qualified. The newly created social service jobs were in no way comparable to the well-paid industrial jobs of the male workers. The labour market remained highly segregated, replicating the sexual division of labour between production and reproduction. Elisabeth Hagen and Jane Jenson are right in pointing out that "... the stereotypes, based on the deeply rooted assumptions about proper gender roles and gender relations, shaped labour markets no less in 'progressive' and egalitarian countries like Sweden than elsewhere" (1988: 90). This is not surprising given that the Fordist production model produced a gender order that, despite some differences, shared the overall characteristics of the "breadwinner model." Feminists have shown that European countries can be categorized as strong, weak, or medium breadwinner models (Ostner, 1995). Despite these differentiations, none of the western industrial capitalist countries have developed a gender order that is outside of the breadwinner system. Aside from the job opportunities in the care-giving and social services, women also found new opportunities at the lower end of the production line. Gaining entrance onto the factory floors had to do with the fundamental economic restructuring that started in the 1970s. With the process of economic rationalization, male jobs were increasingly sacrificed at the expense of cheaper and less skilled labour. Highly-paid industrial workers became redundant and women were hired for the low-skill assembly line jobs instead. That they succeeded in entering the factories did not mean that the few remaining well-paid industrial jobs were open to them.[6] The labour market remained sharply segregated, and the jobs available to women were at the lower end of the occupational hierarchy, and were generally the worst. As in the public sector, the private sector seemed to replicate the sexual division of labour. The gender order reflected the social norms of a gender-specific separation between the public and the private. In this process, the non-monetarized housework of women became largely devalued; women, despite their integration in the labour market, were subordinated to the male breadwinner and their activities were regarded as a secondary earning source to be spent only for consumption purposes (Hagen and Jenson, 1988; Kurz-Scherf 1996).

The gender orders of the Fordist period can be summarized as consisting of three central elements:

1. The role of women, despite their integration into the labour markets, was tied to the reproductive and private sphere.
2. The role of women identified with the private arena corresponded with the male's role as the "breadwinner."
3. A gender-specific separation between the private and the public characterized the Fordist period.

In the geometry between class and gender, men were subordinated directly to the market. Women, on the other hand, were subordinated directly to men and only indirectly to market forces.

The present restructuring of the global economy and the increasing internationalization of capitalism has, as I will show in the next section, undermined the existing Fordist regime of accumulation and modes of regulation. The link between mass consumption and mass production has collapsed and we seem to face a new uncertain economic regime without an institutional structure to control to unfettered forces of the market. This fundamental restructuring toward a system of 'maximal markets' and "minimal states" has also weakened the male breadwinner model and the entire gender order that has been associated with the Fordist period. That global restructuring is occurring on a gendered terrain is largely forgotten in the mainstream accounts (Bakker, 1994), a point to which I will return in the subsequent section.

The New Gender Orders

Can we identify a new configuration of gender order(s) that is emerging in response to these dramatic changes in both the production paradigm and the social structure? I start with the assumption that the three central aspects of the Fordist gender order are being fundamentally transformed. To recall, the three elements of this order are: *(a)* the male breadwinner model; *(b)* women associated with reproduction and the private sphere; and *(c)* the gender-specific separation between the private and the public arena. The reconfiguration, which can only be inferred at this point and not tested as an hypothesis, seems to take place on many different levels. First, the Fordist model of the male breadwinner is a phenomenon of the past. Second, the stark gender-specific separation between the public and the private and the associated assignment to the reproductive and productive economy no longer reflect the reality of the situation. Third, while equality has increased among men and women depending on their racial, class, and national belonging (Friese, 1995). Finally, a new gender-specific social division is emerging between those (mostly male) who frequent the hypermobile "money society," and those (mostly female and unskilled) that remain bound to the national "work territory". These changes do not imply only negative consequences for women. They also have the potential of weakening and dissolving local, particular cultures and systems of male domination.

(a) *The Disappearance of the Fordist Family Breadwinner Model*

Globalization has eroded the material conditions for the male breadwinner and his dependent wife and family. The increasing rise of double wage-earners since the 70s is a by-product of this development. Double wage-earner families can be divided into two groups. On the one side are the relatively well-off professionals who are part of the formal economy. A much larger group can be found in the medium and lower level of the economy, who rely on the additional wage of women to maintain or improve their living standards. There is also the group of single parents (mostly female), whose numbers have increased dramatically. In the United States, 67 per cent of single mothers and 53 per cent of mothers with children under three years old worked for wages in 1998. Of the double wage-earner families, 53 per cent had children (Fernandez Kelly and Sassen, 1995; Ward and Pyle, 1995). The increasing "feminization of the labour process" has undermined the family wage system. Most wages in the informal economy are no longer adequate to support a family; nor do they any longer provide economic security.

The increasing integration of women in the labour market has promoted new definitions of gender roles and has led to changes in the social value structure. The Fordist norm of women dependent on the male breadwinner is being replaced by the increasing individualization of women. Women from Mexico, living in the United States, express this value change as follows. Previously when a woman worked outside the household, everybody knew that she only did this to help the man; it was his duty to support his family. Now it is women's duty. Women are expected to work outside the household whether they want to or not (Fernandez Kelly and Sassen 1995: 112 and 113).

(b) *The Reconfiguration of the Public and Private and Production and Reproduction*

The informalization of the labour market has greatly undermined the separation between the reproductive economy. This separation was once the hallmark of the Fordist gender order. Increasingly the processes of production and reproduction (also of social reproduction) are played out in a wide spectrum ranging from the informal, formal, and household economies.[7] The conceptual separation between the private and the public does not take into account that the daily work of many women is done in a 'triple shift' (Hossfeld, 1990) between formal, informal and family or subsistence activities.[8] Whether this work is done by women in the Caribbean, in Asia or in Silicon Valley, its concern feature is that women's work is a combination of activities in formal transnational production, informal sectors, and in the subsistence economy. The borders of this "triple shift" are quite fluid for women, but relatively rigid for men. In order to secure their survival, women often spend up to 16 hours in this 'tripe shift.' In contrast, males are rarely found in the household economy and work either as sub-contractors in the informal economy, or in the formal economy, or in the formal economy (Ward and Pyle, 1995).

In the 1970s, feminists pointed out that gendered opposition between markets on the one hand, and family on the other, express an ambiguity that is full of contradictions. Regina Becker-Schmidt has argued "that what we generally understand as public (*i.e.*, the social market economy) has a capitalist economy many private property characteristics, and *vice versa*, the most private institution, (*i.e.*, the family) carries out public function functions in education, reproduction of the labour force, care for the elderly among many other public activities" (Becker-Schmidt, 1993: 219).

The feminist expansion of the concept "work" to include the non-monetarized sector of the reproductive sphere remains, however, tied to the conventional idea of two complementary spheres. To the degree that the male breadwinner role is pushed more and more into the background, women are forced to earn their of the "feminization of work" Joan Smith and Immanuel Wallerstein pleaded in the 70s for a reconceptualization of "work" in the spheres of family, production, and the public. Instead of using the concept "family" and separating monetary production form non-monetarized reproduction, they use the concept of the "household." Households are groups of family members, unrelated members sharing the living quarters, and neighbourhoods that share resources. In this concept, no difference is drawn between the monetarized and non-monetarized economy, and between family members, friends, and neighbours. The notion of "income" is expanded to include such barter services as subsistence production and is extended to neighbourhood services and help (Smith and Wallerstein, 1992: 6-9).

These new forms of "work" are also redefining the existing gender identity. While the woman was identified with the family and subordinated to the male in the fordist period, she is "reduced" an individual in the global economy. The informal economy is only interested in "her" labour power. Reconciling the need to have a job and raise children at the same time is no longer issue. From an economic standpoint, reproductive activities are made "invisible." Any demands for child-care or other social services are silenced. Whether a sick child or an elderly parent hinders a woman worker from appearing at the doors of the Free Export Zone is her "private" concern. Her place is taken by somebody else (Lemoine, 1998). Women have finally reached the long awaited abstract equality with men! Not in terms of watds, but in terms of an abstract notion of individualism that is free at last from child-care. Despite its private seclusion, the reproductive work during the Fordist period was at least socially recognized. Now with the flexibilization of the labour market, child rearing has, once again, become an economic and social externality, and the dialectical relations between market and non-market activities has disappeared for the neoliberal discourse of the global economy (Elson, 1994; Mann, 1994)

(c) *The Increasing Inequality Among Women*

The rising integration of women into the labour force has also meant a greater disparity among women of different class, race, and national belonging. Although the new members of the new "club society" are mostly the "new boys," as Wendy Larner (1996) calls the new global players of the neoliberal New Zealand model, professional white middle-class women in the knowledge and information industries are no longer a rarity. Linda Mc Dowell (1997) has shown in her study of the male finance stronghold of the city of London that a slight crack did open for a new class of female professionals. As a result of the expanding international service economy, young, well-educated females succeeded in entering the middle and upper echelons of the finance and business world in the "global cities," although with the caveat, as Saskia Sassen has pointed out, "...that notwithstanding the growing number of top level women professionals in global economic activities and in international relations, both these worlds can be specified as male-gendered insofar as each in its distinct way has the cultural properties and power dynamics that we have historically associated with men of power, or least some power" (1996: 10).

Labour market segmentation into a high-paid "post-Fordist informational economy" and the expanding informal sector of the "labouring poor" has increased the disparity among women. Low-skilled service jobs are not just an important part of the infrastructure of the formal economy. They also permit socially privileged women in Europe, North-American, and in other countires access to a professional career. As long as women, independent of their social class, remain responsible for reproductive work, the conditions upon which women enter 'male' structures are gender-specific. Socially privileged females have the advantage of falling back upon mostly cheap, often illegal immigrants, to perform household tasks and the child-rearing. Without adequate public services, and without the fall-back position on women from developing and transitional countries, women whould not be able to climb the professional ranks that demand great personal mobility and flexibility. Whether these activities are performed by mostly over-qualified Polish Women in Germany, or African-American and Latin American immigrants in the United States, they lead to a new international division of labour at the household level. On the oneside is the "Mistress" and on the other stands the "Maid," separated by different racial, ethnic, and national backgrounds.

A professional woman's career of the European or American middle or upper class is thus possible only in the narrow confines of ethnicity, class, and gender (Friese, 1995; Mahnkopf, 1997).

(d) *Gender-Specific Social Divisions*

Globalization has led to social division between those who remain tied to a territorially bounded "work-society" and the "money society" that no longer is constrained by national boundaries. This opposition between the global money society and a national "work society" resulted from the "disembedding" of the monetary sphere from the productive economy (Alvater and Mahnkopf, 1996). Huge profits are now made in the sphere of financial circulation and not in material production. As result, finance capital has become dominant in the global economy.

The separation between finance capital and place-bound capital explains the present crisis of the welfare state. Despite a "borderless" global economy, the majority of women and men continue to depend on the solidarity and the "community of fate" of national societies. It was after all the nation-state that extended political rights to the working class and integrated them as citizens. The territory of the nation-state thus became to the "political and social home" of the working class. Within the boundaries of the national territory, the Keynesian full-employment guarantees provided the economic stability criteria for the Fordist model. The nation-state was also the vehicle for creating a national identity. I have already alluded that these political rights, as Carole Pateman (1988) pointed out, went hand in hand with a specific modern form of patriarchal welfare state.

Members of the money society, mostly white and male, do not depend on the solidarity of the national territory. They are members of a global "club society," in which the code of money is the medium for global identification. Voting in national elections is no longer an expression of national identity. Electoral politics is at best a vehicle to stop tax increases or programmes for social distribution. Financial elites are still proforma citizens of their respective states, but they do not depend on national solidarity and the "community of fate." They invest in the stock market now to provide for retirement later. For these members, the provisions of the Keynesian social state have outlived their usefulness. Their needs are fully met and bought on the free market. Formal rights of citizenship have thereby not changed. But the conditions for citizenship rights have been undermined by the "borderless" global economy. The basis of the "work society" has been the Keynesian social compromise between the haves and less well-off. Under the conditions of global competition and the push for the lowest "single price," the logic of the global economy is on a collision course with the logic of the Fordist social compromise.

In their triple dependence on the welfare state (as social workers, clients, and consumers), women are particularly hard hit by the social welfare crisis. As a result of the reduction of public services, they are "punished" in various ways. First, reducing social services means that these services once again become part of the non-monetarized private sphere. Cutting costs for the care of the elderly, in the health sector, and for education places these burdens again on the shoulders of women. Second, the present privatization of these social services destroys the very conditions that have made the integration of women in the labour market possible. Particularly for women in the lower skilled professions, publicly provided child-care services often make the difference between seeking employment or staying home. Finally, social service jobs generated by the Keynesian welfare state disappear with the dismantling of public services (Jensen, Hagen and Reddy, 1988).

Globalization has thus fundamentally challenged the very notion of what is public and what is private. In the process, it has worsened gender-specific social division. The neoliberal "reprivatization discourse" (Fraser, 1989) seeks to repatriate the economic and social to the former domestic enclave. Reprivatization of the domestic, as Janine Brodie argues, has elevated and revitalized the hetero-patriarchal family (Brodie, 1996: 57). It rests on the dubious assumptions that the family is responsible for social reproduction, and that a family still consists of the male "breadwinner" and his dependents. Aside from the conservative and ideological premise of these assumptions, they neglect to take into account the changing reality of the family. The Fordist gender order no longer exists. To day's reality is that women-even if they wanted to – no longer have the "luxury" to remains as caretakers in the home. In ever greater numbers, women have joined the labour market, while labour market participation rates for males has stabilized or even declined. How the reproductive issues will be resolved in this "borderless" global economy is the million-dollar question.

Finding a gender-conscious resolution of the tasks connected with human reproduction is made all the more difficult by the changes in the social structure and the reorganization of existing power relations. As pointed out earlier, the state no loner guided by a Keynesian logic, but is driven by the logic of competition. These changes have also produced fundamental reorganizations within the state apparatus itself. Departments associated with the Keynesian welfare states, such as labour and social and human services, have all been revalorized at the expense of the valorization of economic and financial departments. The reorganization has not weakened, hollowed out, or marginalized the authority of the state as is suggested by a majority of the globalization literature. True, the singular focus on the decline of public services may support such a view. However this one-sided focus on the welfare state has failed to take into account new power centers that have arisen in the state and are closely tied to the global financial and economic interests.

This reorganization within the state has produced tremendous battles between those who celebrate the unfettered workings of the global markets and those who are disillusioned by the destructive effects of the unregulated free market. Both sides invoke language that is a stark reminder of the ideological struggle of the Cold War. Not only is the battle fought over the superiority of respective economic models, the arguments are also very much about the moral superiority of "free trade faith" versus "regulated free trade faith." Whereas the former camp sees the Liberal Market Economy as "the Highest Stage of Making," (Martin, Le Monde diplomatique, June 1997), the latter invokes the Keynesian state as "the Highest Stage of the State" (Jessop, 1994). Absent from any of these studies is any awareness of the differential impact globalization has had on men and women.

A Feminist Agenda

Feminist scholars are now confronted with new challenges. The question is no longer whether the nation-state is in its very structure male-biased, or whether state structures and offices can be used to promote women's rights and interests. Feminists are now challenged to make visible the new centers of structural and strategic disparities in the network societies. Paradoxically, just as German feminists no longer reject the state outright as an apparatus of male control and domination[9] and even rally around the "patriarchal welfare state," the state is no longer the site of sovereignty and the exclusive subject for domestic and international politics (Sassen, 1996; Strange, 1996). The increasing acceptance of the state as vehicle for feminist activities in the 80s and the shrinking capacity of the state of control domestic economic activities are both closely tied to Thatcher and Reagan's neoliberal revolution of the late 70s and early 80s. The "neoliberal utopia," as Bourdieu (1988) calls the transformation toward a pure market-oriented economy, with its disregard for the values of collective solidarity and national belonging, ahs raised[10]—if not the level of general politicization of the feminist movement—the insecurity of feminists of all ranks. The neo-liberal "backlash" (Faludi, 1991) against the still mostly marginal and often symbolic achievements in political and economic equity between the sexes in western capitalist countries has signaled a more concentrated feminist interest in the properties of the nation-state being reconfigured in the light of global economic restructuring.

International feminist discourse on the state can be divided into two major theoretical strands: the widely cited Anglo-American and Scandinavian "state feminism"[11] on the one hand, and dominant discourse in the German-speaking countries on the structural characteristics of "male-bonding" in the state, on the other (Kreisky and Sauer, 1997; Kulawik and Sauer, 1996; Kerchner and Wilde, 1996). The concept of "state feminism" refers to the role of the state structures and offices in promoting women's status and rights. Adherents of this school start with the assumption that state structures can be used to promote the interests of women (Stetson and Mazur, 1995; Eisenstein, 1990). In contrast to these liberal notions of feminism, the goal of German research is to deconstruct the "maleness" of the state and through feminist intervention engender the very structure of the state.

Skepticism toward the state and the almost complete rejection of participation in political institutions is a particular feature of the German "autonomous feminist movement." Due to the authoritarian and undemocratic legacy of the Germany state, the feminist movement perceived these institutions as unchangeable. Only a politics outside of these political state institutions promised to reflect the interests of women. With the increasing institutionalization of the green party in the 80s the autonomous feminist movement redirected its strategy and became more open to established political forces (Young, 1999; Lang, 1997; Kulawik, 1991). Despite the differences in discourses, practices and strategies of "state feminism" and the classical concepts of the nation-state and the welfare state (Young, 1997; Demirovice and Puhl, 1997).

The continuing focus on nation-states can be explained in party by the increasing attack on public services and the rising degree of privatization since the 80s that hit women in particular as clients, state workers, and beneficiaries of the Keynesian social state. While the authority of the state has declined within its territorial borders, the nation-state is still the only placed and space in which the irreconcilable principles of the market and democracy can come together and citizens can achieve and share a common identity of a "national community of fate" (Held, 1991). These national communities of fate are the outcome of long and brutal struggles between the bourgeoisie and the monarchy first, and subsequently between capital and labour. The social democratic compromise between capital and labour did alleviate the worst economic inequalities, and the inequalities of the market were further minimized by the introduction of political equality among (male) citizens (citoyens), and by providing some minimal aspects of social equity (Altvater, 1997). That this political and social equality was deeply biased against women has received much attention from feminists scholars (Pateman, 1988; Nelson, 1990; Gordon, 1990; Fraser, 1990). That feminists continue to focus on the nation-state as an important transformative agent for achieving a gender-neutral "national community of fate" is thus quite understandable. Yet the question arises whether economic globalization and the resulting de-nationalization of politics has not made the focus on the nation-state an anachronism. Today feminists of all persuasions are being called upon to come to grips with the new realities of the spatial dispersal of global economic activities and the decline of the sovereignty and exclusivity of the nation-state.

Global actors sharing the power with the state include transnational corporations; financial markets; insurance, information, and rating agencies; international institutions such as the World Trade Organization (WTO), the World Bank, the International Monetary Fund (IMF), and the Organization for Economic Cooperation and Development (OECD); transnational trading and economic blocks such as MERCOSOR, ASEAN, NAFTA, and the European Union (EU); non-state actors (NGO's) as, for example, Amnesty International, the Olympic Sports Organization, and Catholic Church; and transnational associations and networks, including the Mafia and international speculators (Strange, 1996).

The expanding interconnection between state and non-state organizations, and among domestic, international, transnational, and supranational activities, can no longer be analyzed with the theoretical and methodological instruments available from such disciplines as political science sociology, or economics. The network society with its reorganization of social structure and power relations has fundamentally contributed to what Sassen (1996) calls the mergence of a "new geography of power." That economic activities have become global and the institutional encasement of the nation-state reconfigured means that feminist research reconfigure gender orders and power relations in the network society is both a theoretical and political challenge feminist face.

At the same time, globalization should not be looked upon only as a negative phenomenon for gender relations. The informalization and flexibilization of the labour markets has opened up new opportunities for women. In the export-oriented "global factories", it is women who are the preferred workers. That the price has been high is also no secret. On the average, the "feminization of labour markets" has expanded flexible labour market structures, replacing the life-long, secure Fordist (male) employment patterns. Despite the low wages and the exploitative conditions that are part of the Free Export Zones, studies also show that—in contrast to national firms-transnational corporations provide higher wages and better working conditions (Lemoine, 1998; Ward and Pyle, 1995).[12] Furthermore, the integration of women into the labour force has also helped to lessen dependence on husbands and families. Finally, women are by far not the passive victims in these "global factories," as the globalization literature seems to suggest. Newer studies show that women increasingly join labour unions in South Korea, the Philippines, and South Africa and actively fight against the practices of wage dumping, de-skilling, and other tactics of transnational corporations (Ward and Pyle, 1995). The picture of the passive working women is thus not only an ideological caricature; it also shows the contradictory process of globalization. Women are the preferred workers in the "global factories" because they are presumed to be passive and difficult to organize in labour unions. But the very experience with such exploitative working conditions also politicizes women to struggle against such conditions. That most labour struggle successes are only of a short-time duration addressing mostly local situations, and therefore have no long-term effect on transnational corporate behaviour is also no secret (Ward and Pyle, 1995).

The integration of women into the global market has another unintended side effect. It can also weaken local patriarchal structures. Once again this process is contradictory. Through integration in the global economy, women can resist male domination to some extent. They also lose in this process the protection that this local patriarchal culture offers. This loss of local protection can be redressed through international conventions on human rights, such as the Fourth World conference on Women in Beijing in 1995 and the official "Platform for Action and the Beijing Declaration." As a result of these international conferences, we are witnessing the ascendancy of new human rights regimes. Through these new legal mechanisms women can gain more representation in international law in matters involving human rights can challenge the exclusive authority of the State over its citizen. Since all residents, whether citizens or not, have the right to claim human rights, "human rights begin to impinge on the principle of nation-based citizenship and the boundaries of the nation" (Sassen, 1996: 33). This strengthens individual actors and non-governmental organizations to challenge the state as the sole subject of international law. These new legal regimes also have implications for the concept of citizenship. Women, either as individuals or as collective, can be recognized as subjects within international law. Human rights organizations and feminists have demanded for some time to redefine the anarchic conception of international relations and develop international mechanisms to intervene domestically if human rights are endangered. With the slogan, "Women's Rights are Human Rights," women have created in Beijing a basis from which to make claims for their protection overriding decision made by their own states. Skeptics may reply that this slogan is little more than a "tiger without teeth." But one should remember the Helsinki Declaration of 1975 and the adoption of the "77." It was this rather benign document that proved the basis for the Eastern European opposition to launch their "velvet revolution."

Globalization cannot be viewed only as rightmarish scenario. It is neither theoretically helpful nor does it promote political action for women to turn into frightened rabbits when confronting the "snake" of globalization. Undeniably, economic globalization has constrained the political scope of nation-states and narrowed the capacity of citizens to claim gender-neutral social rights from the state. However, one also has to recall that the reconfiguration of the Fordist gender order also offers an opportunity for women to develop new concepts and strategies to achieve equality on a global scale.

NOTES

Aglietta, M., 1979. A Theory of Capitalist Regulation. London; NLB.

Altvater, E. 1997. "Market und Demokratie in Zeiten von Globalisierung und okologischer Krise," in: Altvater, E., Brunnengraber, A., Haake, M., & Walk, H. Vernetzt und Verstrickt. Munster: Westfalisches Dampfboot, pp. 241-256.

Altvater, E. & Mahnkopf, B., 1996. Grenzen der Globalisierung. Munster: Westfalisches Dampfboot.

Bakker, I., 1994. The Strategic Silence. Gender and Economic Policy. London: Zed Books.

Bauman, Z. 1996. "Glokalisierung oder: Was fur die einen Globalisierung, ist fur die anderen Lokalisierung, " in: Das Argument, pp. 653-664.

Beck, U., 1997. "Heraus aus dem nationalen Politikbiotop," in: Die Tageszeitung, 13 Juni.

Becker-Schmidt, R., 1993. "Geschlechterdifferenz-Geschlechterverhaltnis: soziale Dimensionen des Begriffs 'Geschlecht, "' in:Zeitschrift fur Frauenforshcung, No. 2, pp. 37-46.

Bourdieu, P., 1988. "Die Sachzwange des Neoliberalismus," in: Le Monde diplomatique, March, p. 3.

Brodie, J., 1994. "Shifting the Boundaries: Gender and the Politics of Restructuring", in: Bakker, I. The strategic silence London: Zed.

Castells, M., 1996. The Rise of the Network Society: The Information Age: Economy, Society and Culture, Volume I. Oxford: Blackwell Publishers Ltd.

Chandler, A., 1977. The Visible Hand; The Managerial Revolution in America Business. Cambridge: Harvard University Press.

Connell, R.W., 1987. Gender and Power. Society, the Person and Sexual Politics. Stanford: Stanford University Press.

Demirovic, A. & Puhl, K., 1997. "Idemtitatspolitik und die Transformation von Staatlichkeit: Geschlechterverhanltnisse und Staat als Komplexe materielle Relation", in: Kreisky, E. & Sauer, B. (Hrsg.), Politische Viereteliahresschrift, Speical Issue, and in:Geschlechterverhaltnisee in Kontext politischer Transformation, 28, pp. 220-240.

Die Gruppe von Lissabon, 1997. Grenzen des Wettbewerbs. Munich: Luchterhand.

Elson, D. 1994. "Macro: Gender and Economic Analysis in the Context of Policy Reform," in: Bakker, I. Strategic Silence. *Gender and Economic Policy*. London: Zed Books.

Eisenstien, Hester, 1990. "Femocrats, Official Feminisam and the Uses of Power, in: Waston, Sophie (Hrsg.), Playing the State. Australian Feminist Intervention. London: Verso.

Faludi, S., 1991. Backalsh. New York: Crown Publishers.

Fernandez Kelly, M.P., 1989. "Broadening the Scope: Gender and International Economic Development," in: Sociological Forum, No. 4, pp. 11-35.

Fernandez Kelly, M.P. & Garica, A., 1992. "Power Surrendered, Power Restored: The Politics of Home and Work among Hispanic Women in Southern California and Southern Florida," in: Tilly, Louise & Guerin, Patricia (eds.), Women and Politics in America. New York.

Fernandez Kelly, M.P. & Sassen S. 1995. "Recasting Women in the Global Economy: Internationalization and Changing Definition of Gender," in: Bose, C.E., & Women in the Latin American Development Process, Philadelphia.

Fraser, N., 1990 "Struggle Over Needs: Outline of Socialist-Feminist Critical Theory of Late-Capitalist Political Culture," in: Gordon, L. (ed.) Women, the State and Welfare. Wisconisn: The University of Wisconsin Press.

Fraser, N., 1989. Unruly Practices: Power, Discourse and Gender in Contemporary Social Theory. Minneapolis: University of Minnesota Press.

Friese, M. 1995. "Modernisierungsfallen im historischen Prozeb, zur Entwocklung der Frauenarbeit im gewandelten Europa." In: Berliner Journal fur Soziologie, 2, pp. 149-162.

Giddens, A., 1995. Konsequenzen der Moderne. Frankfurt & Main: Suhramp.

Giddens, A., 1984. The Constitution of Society. Cambridge: Polity Press.

Gordon, L., (ed.), 1990. Women, the State and Welfare. Wisconsim: The University of Wisconsim Press.

Gordon, L. 1993. "Gender, State and Society: A Debate with Theda Skocpol," in: Contention, Vol. 2, No. 3, Spring, pp. 139-155.

Hagen, E. & Jenson, J., 1988. "Paradoxes and Promises. Work and politics in the postwar years," in: J., Hagen, E. & Reddy, C. (eds.), Feminization of the Labor Force. New York: Oxford University Press.

Harvey, D., 1989. The Condition of Post-Modernity. Oxford: Blackweil.

Haraway, D., 1997. Modest Witness @ Second Millennium: Female Meets Onco Mouse, New York.

Held, D., 1991. "Democracy, the Nation State and the Global System," in: Economy and Society, Vol. 20, No. 2, pp. 138-172.

Hirsch, J., 1995. Der nationale Wettbewerbsstaat. Berlin-Amsterdam: Edition ID-Archiv.

Hirst, P. & Thompson, G., 1996 Globalization in Question Oxford: Polity Press.

Hossfeld, K. 1990. Their Logic against Them: Contradictions in Sex, Race, and

Class in Silicon Valley," in: Ward, K. (ed.). Women Workers and Global Restructuring. Ithaca: Cornell University Press.

Jenson, J., Hagen, E., & Redy, C., 1988. Feminization of the Labor Force. Paradoxes and Promises. New York: University Press.

Jenson, B., 1994. "Veranderte Staatlichkeit," in: Grimm. D. (ed.), Staatsaufgaben. Baden-Baden: Nomos.

Jessop, B., 1988. "Regulation theories in Retrospect and Prospect," paper presented at the International Conference on Regulation, Barcelona, 16-18 June.

Kerchner, B. & Wilde G. (eds.), 1997. Staat und Privatheit. Opladen: Leske+Budrich.

Kreisky, E. & Sauer, B. (eds.), 1997. Das geheime Glossar der Politikwissenschaft. Frankfurt am Main: Campus.

Kreisky, E. & Sauer, B., (eds.), 1995 Feminisctische Standpunkte in der Politikwissneschaft. Frankfurt am Main: Campus.

Kulawik, T., 1991-92. "Autonomous Mothers," West German Feminism Reconsidered, in: German Politics and Society, Issue 24 & 25: 67-86.

Kulawik, T.& Sauer, B. 1996. Der halbierte Staat. Frankfurt & New York: Campus.

Kurz-Scherf, I., 1996. "Krise der arbeit - Krise der Gewerkschaften, "in: Weibblick, No. 25, pp. 20-29.

Lang, S., 1997. "The NGOization of Feminism," in: Scoot, J.W., Kalpan, C. & Keates, D. (eds.), Transitions, Environments, Translation. New York and London.

Larner, W., 1996. "The 'New Boys': Restructing in New Zealand, 1984-94," in Social Politics, 3, No. 1, pp. 32-56.

Lemoine, M., 1988. "Die Arbeiter Zentrakanerikas als Geinseln der 'maquilas', in: Le Monde diplomatique, die Tageszeitung, Marz: 14-15.

Lipietz, A., 1985. akkumulation, Krisen und Auswege aus der Krise: einige methodische Uberlegyngen zum Begruff 'Regulation,'" PROKLA, March, pp. 109-137.

Mahnkopf, B., 1997. "Die 'Feminisierung der Beschaftigung' - in Europa and Anderwo," on: Weibblick, No. 718, pp. 22-31.

Mann, P.S., 1994. Micro-Politics: Agency in a Postfeminist Era. Minnestora: Univeristy of Minnesota Press.

Martin P., 1997. "Liberale Marktwisrtshcaft als hochstes Stadium der Menschheit," in: Le Monde diplomatique, June, p. 14.

McDowell, L., 1997. Capital Culture: Gender At Work in the City. Oxford: Blackwell.

Messner, D., 1997. "Netzwerktheorien: Die suche Nach Ursachen und Auswegen aus der Krise Staatlicher Steungfahigkeit," in: Alvater, E., Brunnengraber, A., Haake, M., & Walk, H., Vernetzt und Verstricky, Munster: Westfalisches Dampfboot pp. 27-64.

Nelson, B., 1990. "The Origins of the Two-Channer Welfare State: Workmen's

Compensation and Mothers' Aid in: Gordon, L. Women, the State, and Welfare. Wisconsin: The University of Wisconsin Press.

Ostner, I., 1995. "Arm ohne Ehemann? Sozialpolitische Regulierung von Lebenschancen fur frauen Im internationalen Vergleich," in: aus Politik und Zeitgeschichte, Sept. 1, B36-37 & 95.

Pateman, C., 1988. The Sexual Contract, Standford: Standford University Press.

Polanyi, K., 1944. The Great Transformation. Boston: Beacon Press.

Sassen, S., 1996. "Toward a Feminist Analytics of the Global Economy," in: Indian Journal of Global Legal Studies, Vol. 4, fall, pp. 7-41.

Schmitter, P.C., 1979, "Still the Century of Corporatism?" in: Schmitter, P & Lehmbruch, G., (eds.) Trends Toward Corporatist Intermediation. Beverly Hills: Sage.

Smith, J. & Wallerstein, I., 1992. Creating and Transforming Households. The Constraints of the World-Economy. Cambridge: Cambridge University Press.

Stetson, D.M. & Mazur, A. (eds.), 1995. Comparative State Feminism. Thousand Oaks: Sage.

Strange, S., 1996. The Retreat of the State. Cambridge: Cambridge University Press.

Thurow, L.S., 1997. The Future of Capitalism. New York: Penguin Books.

Ward, K., & Pyle, J.L., 1995. "Gender, Industrialization, Transnational Corporations, and Development: An Overview of Trends and Patterns," in: Bose, C.E. & Acosta-Belen, E., Women in the Latin American Development Process. Philadelphia.

Wichterich, C., 1998. Die globalisierte Frau: Berichte aus der Zukunft der Ungleichheit. Hamburg: Rowohlt.

Young, B., 1999. Triumph of the Fatherland: German Unification and the Marginalization of Women. Michigan: The University of Michigan Press.

Young, B., 1997. "Politik und Okonomie im Kontext vaon Globalisierung,": Kreisky, E & Sauer, B., (eds.), Politische Vierteljahresschrift, Sonderheft: Geschlechterverhaltnisse im Kontext politischer Transformation 28, pp. 137-151.

REFERENCES

1. First published in: Rita Mae Kelly, Jane Bayes, Brigitte Young: Globalization, Democratization, and Gender.
2. Castells Introduces the Concept of "Information Capitalism" to differentiate this type from "industrial capitalism."
3. The informal sector consists of a vast array of work ranging from legal to illegal activities, including "home based" work; work in the Free export Zones; sweatshop activities, street vendors, maids, illegal farm labour, prostitution, and many other such activities that are precarious and unregulated (Mahnkopf, 1997; Ward and Pyle, 1995).

4. Women provide the majority of the labour in these "maquila businesses": 58 per cent in Mexico (1995); 60 to 62 per cent in Costa Rica; 70 to 75 per cent in Guatemala (1993); and 60 per cent in the Dominican Republic (1992 Lemoine, 1998).
5. Para-statal refers to a level of organizational structure to be found between the state and society. These organization, if not created by the state, are recognized by the state as sole representatives of societal interests. This para-statal level of organization is often associated with corporatist bargaining between the state, labour unions, and employers associations. In Germany, these institutions can also be found in many other areas such as the health system and other social systems.
6. Women workers had staffed factories since the beginning of industrialization. They also occupied the factories during World War II as the men were shipped to the front. With the beginning of Fordism and the emphasis on the male breadwinner model, women were increasingly excluded from the center of industrial work and only integrated selectively or temporarily.
7. These labour market conditions are still overwhelmingly restricted to the New Industrial Countries and the Transitional Societies. However, this form, as the America example increasingly show, has also expanded rapidly in western industrial countries.
8. Formal work is defined as regulated and socially insured; informal work is flexible and unprotected; and family and subsistence work is neither regulated nor paid.
9. Rejection of the state as a repressive force is not shared by all European feminist theorists. In contrast to the German anti-state tradition, Scandinavian and other European feminists were from the start more state-oriented and chose "the march through the institutions" (state feminism) as they strategy to change the social and political role of women (Stetson and Mazur, 1995).
10. Baroness Thatcher declared that, for her societies no longer exist; only individuals.
11. Hester Eisentein speaks of "femocrafts" in state bureaucracies and institutions, who try from within to attain political change for the equality of the sexes.
12. For example, the minimum wage in the Honduram maquila is an average 40 Lempiras per day versus 30 Lempiras in national industries (Lemoine, 1998).

3

New Family Patterns: Germany after Unification[1]

CHRISTIANE LEMKE, HANNOVER

The current crisis of the welfare state in Europe has many roots- demographic trends, rising needs resulting from high unemployment, an increase of migration, the weakening of labour unions, pressure to meet the Maastricht criteria for monetary union... The collapse of state socialism in east Germany and subsequent unification of West and Germany are additional factors contributing to the strain on the German welfare system. Although the crisis was not produced by unification, the merging of the two different systems and the vast deindustrialization of east Germany placed new burdens on the welfare state and the thus accelerated the structural crisis which was unfolding since the mid-1980s.

One crucial factor for the crisis of all European welfare states is the crumbling of the traditional gender order. Modern welfare states were based on the assumption of the male-worker provider. The male head of the household would be paid a family wage sufficient to support children and a full-time wife and-mother, who performed domestic labour without pay. In the "golden age" of post-war European welfare state development, unemployment decreased to close to zero, wages and income were rising, and social provisions were expanded. Of course, many lives did not fit the pattern of the male-headed nuclear families – think of the countless war-windows with children in Germany after the war – but the normative family-wage ideal inscribed in the structure of the welfare state shaped many of the key policies up to the present time. A changing labour market characterized by high unemployment, increasing job insecurity, and wages insufficient to support a family single-handedly, as well as changes in the meaning and practice of family life, render the traditional conception of welfare state support obsolete. Families are less conventional and more diverse: many people no longer prefer the traditional male-breadwinner/female home-maker model (never the norm in East Germany, anyway), as demonstrated not only by rising female employment, but also the quest for homosexual partnership rights. The sharp increase in solo-mother families (about one-third in East Germany) poses a particular challenge to traditional welfare provisions, since it is these families with children who are most often confronted with poverty.

Feminist research has challenged the normative assumptions underlying modern welfare state provisions, as well as the redistributive policies based on work, need, entitlement. (Fraser, 1997; Langan/Ostner, 1991; Orloff, 1993) Neo-liberal, so-called "reform" policies implemented in the United States, Great Britain and, to lesser extent, in Germany were rejected by women's groups in these countries. Central to the feminist discourse is a challenge to the market-oriented (male) breadwinner model. A new perspective has been generated, based on the importance of care-work for human well-being traditionally confined to female labour in the family. My paper will address some of the conceptual and theoretical aspects involved in this debate about the importance of care-work provided by families or family-like units. Since unification, Germany embraces two very different traditions of providing welfare which I will use to elaborate on some of the comparative issues involved.

Beyond the Breadwinner Model: Family Patterns in Comparative Welfare State Analysis

Oddly enough, care-work performed by families never received full attention in comparative welfare state analysis until very recently, despite the fact that families are key welfare suppliers. It is not only through some recent feminist writings, that the importance of family care work has become a focus of systematic, comparative welfare state analysis. (Lewis, 1997; Orloff, 1993; O'Connor, 1992) Analyzing the three possible bases for making claims on the welfare state–work, need, and citizenship–feminists have uncovered an important gender component. Historically, in the democratic welfare state, employment (rather than military service as in the pre-modern state) became the key to citizenship, since it bestowed the independence which were the central criterion for citizenship, a criterion historically associated with men. (Pateman, 1988) While men have made their claims to the state support services on the basis of their labour in the paid labour force, fewer women could do so. Their claims were either based on their role as full-time female home-makers and mothers, or based on need, as part of public assistance programs provided for poor and needy people. Only a few countries introduced some programs based on citizenship alone.

In one of the most influential works on comparative welfare state analysis incorporating the citizen-worker notion, Gosta Esping-Andersen delineates "three worlds" of welfare capitalism (liberal, conservative/corporatist, social democratic). Focusing on the question to what extent welfare states enable their citizens to lead an economically and socially agreeable life independent from the market, the analysis is confined to state-market relations ("decommodification"). Several researchers have questioned whether the clustering of regime—types generated on the basis of the dimension of state-market relations "decommodification" still holds up when one considers state interventions into gender relations. Ann Orloff rightly points out that the focus on de-commodification is misleading, since it ignores the gendered stratification of welfare benefits and rights. Moreover, it gives only passing attention to family services and it excludes power relations in the family. (Orloff, 1993) She convincingly argues that the relation of the welfare state to paid labour should not be divorced analytically from its relation to the organization of caring and reproductive labour, much of which is done by women in families. Historical analysis, moreover, reveals the important contribution of women to establishing welfare policies. From this perspective, the notion of citizenship goes beyond the de-commodification aspect of welfare rights.

Two approaches emerge from this critique: Some authors found that the clustering of regime types based on the power-resource approach is still useful when certain adjustments are introduced. Angelica von Wahl, for example, argues that welfare regime analysis can be related to employment policies for women, such as affirmative action, if the women's movement as power resource is included in the comparative analysis of labour markets. (Von Wahl, 1995) In re-examining the labour markets of welfare regimes, however, Julia O'Connor shows that the clustering introduced by Esping-Andrensen is inconsistent when gender is taken into account. Child care and parental leave, the two examples for caring work, are only consistent with the regime types in respect to the two extremes, the Nordic/social-democratic and the liberal welfare states. The first cluster of countries (social democratic) is built around maximal public responsibility, while the second (liberal) establishes maximal private responsibility. The conservative country group represents, however, a more diverse and complex picture. Moreover, in terms of part-time work (a typical employment pattern for women in many European countries) there is no clustering along the "three worlds" distinction.

These inconsistencies lead others to argue that comparative analysis requires a different starting point than the "de-commodification" approach applied by Esping-Anderson. Jane Lewis rightly points out, that there are many ways of constructing typologies of welfare regimes, one alternative way is to analyze "caring regimes." *E.g.*, the conditions under which people engage in family work. (Lewis, 1997) This would shift attention to the unpaid provision of welfare by families. The family is considered as an independent variable in this approach to comparative welfare analysis.

On a conceptual level, the main point of this new literature in the opening of the theoretical space for the inclusion of policies relevant to gender equity. Embracing the variety of paid and unpaid services, such as care within family units, this more sophisticated approach identifies a complexity of services and opens the field for a variety of potential policy changes in European welfare states.

"After the Family Wage"—Exploring A Conceptual Thought Experiment

In a recent article, Nancy Fraser develops an interesting thought experiment about the future political conceptions of the welfare state. According to Fraser's emancipatory vision for what she calls the post-industrial period, the goal of welfare should be gender equity, a complex concept moving beyond the statement of the equality-difference debate. Equity is defined along the lines of seven principles: anti-poverty, anti-exploitation, income-equality, leisure time equality, equality of respect, anti-marginalisation, and anti-androcentrism. While her main goal is to develop alternative visions for the Unites States, where the "Personal Responsibility Act" of 1996 dismantled major welfare provisions-Fraser's conceptual framework may well be applied to the European debate about alternative visions of welfare.

Nancy Fraser distinguishes two ideal-type models of welfare state policy, the "universal breadwinner" – model and the "caregiver-parity" model. The first aims to foster gender equity by promoting women's work. According to Fraser, this model reflects a vision implicit in the current political practice of most U.S. feminists and liberals. Women's own wage earning is conceived of as a crucial element. The "universal breadwinner" model is very ambitious scenario since it requires *(a)* state provision of employment-enabling services such as day care and other institutions of care, and *(b)* macro-economic creation of full-time, full-paying jobs for women to sustain a respectable standard of living. The "caregiver parity" model is a vision implicit in the current practice of Western European feminists and social democrats. Its goal is to promote gender equity mainly by supporting informal care-work. Women's life-cycles would be characterized by alternate time of work and care-giving. The main point is to enable women with domestic responsibilities to support themselves and their families either through care work alone or through care-work and part-time employment without loss of benefits and significant income. This, too, is an ambitious project, since it requires state provision for care-giver allowances. Different forms of insurance provisions would have to be integrated into one system to meet the needs of care-giving to children, partners, the elderly, or other family members.

Both models would cut poverty rates among women and reduce their dependency and exploitation. They fall short, however, in meeting all the criteria of equity outlines above. The universal breadwinner model fails to promote leisure time and to abolish androcentrism, while the caregiver parity model fails especially to promote income equality and to prevent women's marginalization. In addition, neither model promotes women's full participation on a par with men in politics and civil society. Finally, neither model values female-associated practices enough to ask men to share them on a parity level; neither asks men to change, as Fraser points out.

The two models described by Fraser are ideal-type models and part of a "thought experiment" designed to rethink the very foundations on which modern welfare systems are based. Therefore, the models do no provide policy programmes. Rather, they reflect the key paradigms of the feminist discourse on the equality-difference-problem that characterized much of 1980s debate among feminists.

Moving beyond this polarization, which was pitting equality feminists against difference feminists, Fraser suggests a third way out. Based on the assumption that care-work is crucial for the well-being of society and key element for providing welfare, the third possibility is to "*include men to become more like most women are now,* namely people who do primary care-work." (Fraser, 1997: 60) The goal should be to make women's life-patterns "the norm" for everyone. Today, women often combine gainful employment and care-giving, but this poses great difficulties and leaves women vulnerable to overburden, social marginalization, and poverty, especially in the side array of cases in which the traditional "male-breadwinner model" can no longer be applied. The third way would be the "Universal caregiver" model. "Unlike Caregiver Parity", its employment sector would not be divided into two different tracks; all jobs would be designed for workers who are caregivers, too; all would have a shorter workweek than full-time jobs have now; all would have the support of; employment enabling services. Unlike Universal Breadwinner, however, employees would be publicly supported and integrated on a par with paid work in a single social-insurance system. Some would be performed in households by relatives and friends, but such households would not necessarily be hetero-sexual nuclear families. Other supported care-work would be located outside the household altogether—in civil society. (Fraser, 1997: 61)

As utopian as this model may be, its merits are multifold. It invites us to rethink the welfare services provided by families—and here particularly by women. As long as paid work outside the family constitutes the most important basis for welfare rights and is this compensated by welfare benefits, care work will not be valued as part of services in society. Moreover, instead of defining the typical female labour in the family as "functional" and legitimize women's dependency on men, it shifts as the focus to men's dependency on women's voluntary (unpaid) work. The most important point in this "thought experiment," then, is the deconstruction of the opposition between bread-winning and care giving, coded as male and female activities. It thus dismantles the traditional gender order on which the modern welfare system rests. Viewed from this perspective of re-evaluating labour in both settings, work and family, it also deconstructs the traditional opposition between (bureaucratized) public and (intimate) private settings in which welfare is embedded. To be sure, the thought experiment is not a policy prescription, but it opens the horizon to conceptually rethink the starting point for new family and social policies. The most interesting feature is the restructuring of gender hierarchies. Under theses premises the key point is to allow for flexibility and change through welfare policies.

Family Care and Paid Work: Two Breadwinner Models in Germany

Comparative analysis places Germany in the group of corporatist/ conservative welfare states. The emphasis on standard employment patterns and traditional family roles is the basis of the male breadwinner model. Placing family patterns into the broader context of the postwar construction of different welfare systems in the two German states, the old FRG and the former GDR (both of which no longer exist), I suggest re-reading the story of German unification as the story of a clash between two models of welfare provision. A different ascription of gender roles and family patterns is essential elements of this story. The traditional male breadwinner model was conceptual basis on which the West German welfares state rested (as Ilona Ostner has convincingly argued), whereas the east German social policy arrangement came close to the universal breadwinner model, described so elaborately by Nancy Fraser. (In fact, Fraser eludes to the experience of communist rules countries in her article).

The dependency of women on men's income has long been a major point of critique among West German feminists. (Lemke, 1994) Searching for alternatives, parts of the new women's movement rejected the marriage contract altogether, while other activists pushed for incremental reforms. Major changes in the family law were passed in the mid-1970s. The "Reform of Marriage and Family Law" in 1977 discarded the so-called "housewife-marriage," and women were to receive social security in case of divorce. More radical approaches, such as the early demand by feminists to grant a "salary" for housework ("Lohn fur Hausarbeit"), did not enjoy wide support in the women's movement and faded from the agenda. Opposing the ideology of difference and the claim of women's "natural" abilities for care-work, the women's movement subsequently focused on improving women's access to education and the labour market. Income inequality and discrimination in the work place became a main target of policy change, promoted by social democrats, the Green Party, and equal rights activists.

The strategies to improve equality between women and men generated some results, such as the introduction of equal opportunity offices ("Gleichstellungsstellen") in public and state administration in firms and universities. Anti-discrimination legislation, proposed by feminists and introduced in a few states in the late 1980s remains, however, highly contested. As Angelikavon Wahl has shown, equal employment policies are limited to constitutional norms or have been instituted rather late and through outside pressure. (Von Wahl, 1995)

By the time the new East Germany states joined the Federal Republic in 1990, the concept of equality had replaced the traditional rigid notion of different spheres of life, and women could claim some success in respect too incremental policy changes removing the discriminatory mechanisms built into the male-breadwinner-model welfare state.

Problems remained; however, as seen when one applies the seven criteria developed by Fraser. In terms of avoiding poverty, the welfare state was biased towards supporting married women, while poverty rates among single mothers were high. Therefore, it did a poor job in respect to anti-exploitation. The dependency on men was most visible in men's resistance to declare rape within marriage illegal (the law was only passed in 1996). Income equality was poorly developed; compared to other European countries; West Germany showed a rather high discrepancy between men's and women's income. Because of the traditional division of labour, leisure time equality was good for non-working women as was the equality of respect. The latter, however, was based on the notion of difference. In terms of avoiding women's marginalization and reducing and androcen-trism, the male-bread-winner model performed only poorly.

The east German path was quite different, in as much as the state promoted women's work and provided for child care facilities. Wages were generally low, and there was still a segregated employment structure, but women could draw their (modest) welfare rights and benefits from their won work. With the exception of elderly women, poverty among women was generally low. The employment rate of women steadily increased, and with 83 per cent of all women working outside the home, the country ranked among the highest in terms of women's employment (West Germany: 57%). On the average, women contributed 40 per cent to the household income (West Germany: 18%). Women's dependency on men decreased, as the high divorce rates and the rising numbers of children born out of wedlock illustrate, and the anti-exploitation effect was thus high judged by Fraser's criteria, income equality between women and men was only mediocre, since women often accepted positions well below their qualification in order to combine their work with caring for children ("Vereinbarkeit Von Berufstatigkeit and Families"). In respect of leisure time, the east German model was poor; the "dual burden" for women is extensively treated in the literature about East Germany in the 1980s. In terms of equality of respect, the bias of Marxist-Leninist ideology towards "productive" labour never gave full credit to the "unproductive" labour of the care-giver at home equality of respect was therefore biased towards the standard of the working citizen. The East Germany model, moreover, performed poorly in overcoming androcentrism; both welfare provision and the politics of "patriarchal state socialism."

(Irene Dolling) were highly andocentric, *e.g.* promoting traditional masculine norms and values. The most severe shortcoming of the universal breadwinner model, though, was that women's (and men's) participation in civil society and politics was severely hampered by rigid political structures.

Both states were worlds away from what Fraser envisioned as a "universal care giver" model and did not allow for flexible gender roles when it came to welfare benefits and rights. While politics in West Germany was geared towards enforcing the traditional male breadwinner model, East Germany measured women in terms of the male norm. By not allowing for a flexible gender system, both states failed to adjust to the changing realities of the crumbling gender order to crucial to welfare state development at the end of the this century.

While many families no longer fir the traditional "male-breadwinner model" today, the current crisis of the German welfare state forecloses the possibility of through reforms of the gender order. Well-qualified generations of younger women find it difficult to continually pursue their career given the insurmountable difficulties of finding child care facilities and adjusting women's work schedules to old-fashioned school schedules. Recognition for women's care-work was even harder to come by. A rather modest improvement was the recognition of three years spent for raising child "Kindererziehungszeiten" in the pension system since 1995 (three "functional" years). (Mushaben, 1997) however, in 1996, women's earlier retirement age (60 years) was abolished (now 65 years). To be sure, not all women were "losers" of unification. In fact, elderly women saw a modest improvement in their standard of living, due to the introduction of the West German pension system based on years of employment. The hardest hit by unification are, however, single mothers and women with several children. Poverty rates among single mothers are increasing. In 1994, 42 per cent of Germany's 1.5 million single parents had monthly incomes less than DM 1,400; about 23 per cent of all welfare recipients ("Sozialhilfeempfanger") are single mothers.

The pillars of the West German welfare state based on the male-breadwinner model, basically carried over into unified Germany. Innovation with flexible gender arrangements is therefore difficult to achieve. Politics has neither a found a solution for coping with the crisis of the welfare state, nor has the state acknowledged the changed in family patterns. This leaves it up to women and men to individually cope with their changing life aspirations under post unification conditions. Families have to rely on private arrangements and initiatives to adjust to the challenges. New family have not yet received full credit in the welfare system.

LITERATURE

- Dolling, Irene, 1991: "ber den Patriachalismus staatssozialistischer Gesellschaften" Die.
- Geschlechterfrage im gesellschaftlichen Umbruch, "Wolfang Zpf, ed., Die Modernisierung moderner Gesellschaften. Verhandlungen des 25. Detaches Soziologentages 1990, Frankfurt; New York: Campus Verlag, pp. 407-417.
- Esping-Andersen, Gosta, 1990: The Three Worlds of Welfare Capitalism, Princeton: Princeton University Press.
- Fraser, Nancy, 1997: "After the Family Wage. A Post-industrial Though Experiment."
- Justice Interrupts: New York, London, pp. 41-66.
- Klausen, Jytte, Lousie Tilly, eds., European Integration in Social and Historical Perspective from 1850 to the Present, Boulder Col.: Row and Littlefield, 1997.

- Langan, Mary, Ilona Ostner, 1991: "Gender and Welfare: Towards a Comparative Framework", in: G. Room, ed., Towards a European Welfare State, Bristol SAUS.
- Lemke, Christiane, 1994: "Women and Politics: The New Federal Republic of Germany," Barbara Nelson, Najma Chowdhury, eds., Women and Politics World Wide, New Haven: Yale University Press, pp. 261-284.
- Lewis, Jane, ed., 1997: "Introduction" Family policies and the role of the family, "Comparing Social Welfare Systems in Southern Europe, Florence Conference, Vol. 3 (France Southern Europe), Paris: MIRE, pp. 305-314.
- Mushaben, Joyce Marie, 1997: "Restructuring the German Sozialstaat: Internal and External Forces for Change," paper delivered at the 1997 Annual Meeting of the American Political Science Association, Washington D.C.
- O'Connor, Julia, 1992: "Citizenship, Class, Gender, and the Labor Market: Issues of De-Commodification and Personal Autonomy", paper presented at the workshop on comparative welfare state analysis, Zentrum fur Sozialopitik, Universal Bremen.
- Orloff, Ann, 1993: "Gender and the Social Rights of Citizenship: The Comparative Analysis of Gender Relations and Welfare States." American Sociological Review 58, No. 3, pp. 303-28.
- Pateman, Carole, 1988: "The Patriarchal Welfare State," in: Democracy and the State, ed. by Amy Guttmann, Princeton: Princeton University Press.
- Von Wahl, Angelika, 1995: Gleichstellungspolitik in der Bundersrepublik und den USA im Vergleich, PhD Dissertation, Freie Universitat Berlin.

REFERENCE

Paper prepared for presentation at the conference "The Future of the Welfare State", Humboldt Universitat Berlin, Center for British Studies, 17-18 November, 1997, published in: Weber, Helmut, ed.: The Future of the Welfare State, British and German Perspectives, Trier: Wissenschaftlicher Verlag 1999 (shorter version).

4

Feminist Theory of Democracy and the Dispute of Difference

CHRISTIANE LEMKE AND KATRIN TONS, HANNOVER

In recent years, the rise of postmodern thought has presented a major challenge for the notion of difference within feminist theory. At the same time, feminist theory is confronted with charges of being too theoretical and politically remote. The erosion of political utopias, accelerating since the early 1990s, as well as the increasing demand for group-specific cultural recognition and the reduction of social inequalities in both east and west, raise new questions about the political perspectives of the dispute of difference. What are the implications of various conceptualizations of difference for a feminist theory of democracy, given the complexity of current social changes? How do these concepts influence feminist analysis of administrative power, democratic participation, the public sphere, and social and cultural distinctions? Can these approaches to difference contribute to realizing, framed by historical and cultural conditions; influence the–possibly different—assessments of the political fruitfulness of this discourse?

Debating feminist post-modern theory highlights the contextual dependence of feminist theorizing in a more general way. For example, in comparing the feminist debate in the US and in Germany, it is noteworthy that the debate about the political implications of post-modern theory began in Germany at a much later point in time (cp. *e.g.* Klinger, 1997). While American feminists included impulses from post-modern theory relatively early in their work, German theorists remained critical. The post-modern critique of basic assumptions of feminism resulted in a defensive reaction here in Germany. Deconstruction poses a particular challenge for a more politically oriented feminism, because of its implicit deconstruction of the empirical-epistemological subject "woman" (Dolling/Krasis 1997: 7). Academic feminism, as sociology Hildgard Maria Nickel (1998) recently commented, is increasingly losing its "socially critical bite" in the depute of difference, as it moves away from the empirical reality of the life of women and men.

The following article reconstructs the course of the debate about difference in American political theory. On the one hand, this discourse has been influenced by intellectual traditions and concepts of European social theory, which is evident, for example, in the growing reception in the last years of the work of Jargen Habermas or the French Post-structuralists. On the other hand, the theoretical debate has taken specific turns and produced syntheses, which are rather unusual here in Germany. For example, American political philosophers, which are rather unusual here in Germany. For example, American political philosophers Seyla Benhabib and Nancy Fraser, both drawing on the work of Habermas, express an openness towards feminist post-modern theories, although the discourse ethics on both sides of the Atlantic poses a sort of antipode to post-modern lines of thought. However, while Benhabib sets strict boundaries for the acceptance of deconstructivist methods in feminist theory building, Fraser pleads for a feminist theory of democracy which would combine elements of Post-structuralism and the critical social theory of Habermas.

The following analysis is based on the assumption that we still need to carve out carefully the contribution which postmodern theory can make to political science and politics in general. As Seyla Benhabib has observed, it is part of the irony of history that the project of modernity with its, "meta-level tales of liberal democracies" (Richard Rorty) has become suspect to the intellectuals of the late-capitalistic Western World, while these ideals witness a powerful renaissance in the post-communist transformation societies of Eastern and Central Eastern Europe (Benhabib, 1995: 7). Current social theory debates, therefore, center around the conflicting approaches of the liberal political tradition with its notion of universal rights and values, the post-modern critique of instrumental reason, and the positioning of critical feminism within this dispute.

Our discussion of the critiques of the liberal model of democracy follows a distinction between three stages. This distinction has a heuristic function. It should not in any way suggest a homogeneity, which would not be justified given the coexistence of varying approaches during specific time periods. The first stage begins approximately at the time of the formation of the new women's movement at the end of the 1960s, beginning of the 1970s. It is characterized by the critique of liberal contract theory which had acquired dominant intellectual position in American political thought with its strong liberal tradition. It included a first re-examination of central themes of the classic liberal model, such as universal citizenship, equal rights, and boundary drawn between the private and public spheres, which continue to deeply influence feminist theories up to this day.

The dispute about difference has its origins in this first stage, but controversies intensified with the inclusion of post-modern theories, which begun in the United States in the mid-1980s. In this second stage, at least three varying paradigmatic conceptions of difference can be distinguished. The first approach sees gender differences as a theoretical construction of identity and the essence of being. Carol Gilligan's work on moral psychology, which represents the first of these positions, hypothesized a specifically feminine moral approach to care-taking, which has been in the center of feminist ethics discussions in recent time (*see* Nagl-Docekal/Pauer-Studer, 1993). Gilligan's work became one of the most important starting points for theoretical reflections in political science. Joan Tronto, a New York political scientist, for example, has elaborated on the connection between ethics and politics in modern democracy (1987; 1993; 1996). By politically reformulating the care-taker's ethics, Tronto lays claim to overcoming the conservative core of Gilligan's moral psychology. Does her analysis truly lead to new evaluation of gender difference, which departs from Gilligan's interpretation? This question will be discussed further on this text.

Already with Tronto, who elaborates extensively on the difference among women, a second approach to conceptualizing difference appears. This approach is based on the internal heterogeneity of gender. It is most emphatically represented by Irs Marion Young. In her *Justice and the Politics of Difference* (1990), Young calls for new democratic rules of representation, which could account for differences in the cultural and social context.

Finally, in Judith Butler's work, constructions of difference as identity are criticized from the deconstructive perspective. Butler renounces all forms of identity politics. What effect does this "anti-foundationalist" critique have on a feminist reconceptualization of democracy? This question has been discussed in great length since the beginning of 1990s, and it marks, in our opinion, the start of a third stage. Nancy Graser, for example, calls explicitly for a methodical eclecticism, focusing on the critical potential of varying theoretical approaches to develop a political feminist theory. She takes the position that feminism should no longer be perceived as a separate field of research, but as a critical perspective leading the analysis of democratic institutions and policies (cp. Fraser, 1998).

Three Stages of Critique

1. *The Critique of Political Liberalism in Early Feminist Debate*

Common to both, the American and German feminist discussion during their formative years, is the intent to publicly themes have been excluded from politics as "private" issues. "Recapturing the private for the political discourse (...) situates politics increasingly outside the spheres of activity of the institutions designated for this purpose. This trend corresponds to approaches in women's studies toward violence, sexuality, health and the body", writes the sociologist of knowledge, Theresa Wobbe, about new research in the field of women's studies. She shares another important observation regarding the fields of this research in Germany: "It is interesting, that those themes related to privacy and to sexuality are closely inked to the American research on women, while those themes grouped around work, the job market, gainful employment, and housework are oriented at German theoretical traditions, such as Marxism and critical theory." (1995: 75) This comment refers to the varying political and cultural context of the formative conditions of recent women's research in both countries.

(1) While the autonomous women's movement in Germany unfolded in close connection to the new left, and gained its theoretical profile in critical consideration of Marxism, in the U.S., feminist theory and practice were based on radicalized political Liberalism. In contrast to the German discussion, the American new women's movement was influenced by the civil rights movement, which took up the concept of civil rights as individually actionable rights of historically discriminated groups, thus achieving potentially greater political success (cp. Von Wahl, 1995). The women's movement draw explicitly on the tradition of Liberalism, emphasizing the universal

idea of justice, so integral to the American political culture. Politically, this becomes especially visible in the demand for equal opportunity in education and in career choices, which were legally defined by the "affirmative action" policies, as well as in the demand for constitutional protection of equality through the Equal Rights Amendment.

(2) On the theoretical level, the feminist critique started with the tradition of classic liberal contract theory, thus attacking the "downside of power" (Holland-Cunz 1996: 375), which underlines the universal promise of freedom within liberal contract theory. In her work The Sexual Contract (1988), now considered a classic, Carole Pateman criticized classical political Liberalism most succinctly. The tradition of social contract theory, on which modern Western democracies rests, includes, according to Pateman, a second, quasi non-public contract, the marriage contract, which secures the domination of men over women. Since in modern democracies, private and public spheres are so divided to begin with, that the declared private "marriage contract" remains excluded from the public, the gender hierarchy therein established remains to be a taboo theme in politics over periods of time. Thus, Pateman argues on a level which puts the liberal concept of democracy, based on the contract model, very much in question.

While Pateman challenges a key concept of liberal democracy based on her theoretically substantiated critique of the patriarchal rule, another stand of theory concentrates on the separation of private and public spheres characteristic for modern democracy, and the resulting codes of femininity and masculinity. As one of the first political theorists, Jean Bethge Elshtain, in her work public Man – Private women published in 1981, elaborated on the origins of this discrimination and separation of the two spheres within the history of political theory: On the one side is the sphere of the private, centered around female relationships of family and housework, a sphere in which bonding, care-taking and intimacy form basic experiences; on the other side, is the public, a politically defined sphere with its structure of impartiality, impersonality, and distance, out of which women, as the embodiment of privacy, have been historically excluded and declared to be a political persons. A powerful discrimination within politics was thereby constructed and the historical inheritance reaches into the present controversy about the character of politics. Elshtain's work already centered on the fundamental question for the republican tradition, of how civic virtues and citizenship can be realized in modern democracy, given the legacies of gender separation and hierarchy. This question is also taken up, for example, by Mary Dietz ("citizenship with a feminist face") and Jane Mansbridge ("democratic community").

(3) Elshtain's concept for a solution consists of, first, a demand to sustain both spheres to protect the privacy of women's life, and, second, the incorporation of female values of nurture, protection, and preservation into politics, in order to build the political community on a new, non-hierarchical political-moral organizing principle.

Elshtain's path-breaking work has–despite her concept of femininity–led to important theoretical insights for the critical reflection about the separation of the two spheres, public and private. It became especially clear, how theory itself (here: classical political theory) contributes to the continual reconstruction of the gender divisions through theory formulation. From the perspective of an increasingly self-reflective feminist theory, which is evident in the 1990s — this critical finding must, indeed, also be applied to Elshtain's own position. The counterproductive consequences of her approach are especially apparent in some of the political-practical implication. In the present debate about the welfare state, for example, Elshtain warns against the decline of the nuclear family, which she to quickly–without critical reflection on the real situation of women–considers (cp. Elshtain, 1996). In the context of the welfare debate, standardization of social relationships leads not only to the stigmatization of single mothers, but suggests a problem setting, which indeed conceals the true structural causes of poverty.

As in Jean Elshtain's work, Carole Pateman's position implies — although in somewhat lesser form–essentialist connotations. In the collected volume *Beyond Equality and Difference,* edited by Bock and James in 1992, Pateman presents the view point that women should demand special citizens 'rights, which would take into account their specific "roles" (motherhood and care-taking) (Pateman 1992: 27ff.). This shows that, while theoretical positions on difference in the early American-feminist debates were productive inasmuch as they produced a critique on Universalist positions, they themselves often continued those same rigid contrasts of equality difference, which they strove to overcome, when moving to formulating political goals.

2. *The Second Stage: "The Dispute of Difference"*

In the second stage of the American feminist discussion, it is Carlo

Gilligan's thesis of a specific female moral development that provoked the strongest essentialist critical reactions. Gilligan's research was triggered by Lawrence Kohlberg's model of the psychological development of children and juvenile. Based on his empirical findings, Kohlberg came to the conclusion that particularly male interviewees were able to ground their arguments in universal moral principles–which in his view signify the highest step of cognitive development.

(4) However, according to Gilligan it seemed obvious that only one dimension of moral orientation towards rights and justice had been taken into consideration. Her own empirical research seemed to demonstrate especially for the female teenagers a second context-related moral development defined by concrete relationships and the acknowledgement of specific needs. Gilligan perceived the different the different patterns of moral insight as the expression of early childhood experiences, according to which the identification with the care-giver role of the mother is unproblematic for girls but stands in the way of the formation of male identity. However, the concept of gender difference to which Gilligans's studies gave rise to has become the target of widespread criticism that emerged from the empirically grounded debate on her scientific method and data base (Nunner-Winkler, 1991; cp. Also Horster, 1998). Based on their own findings German social scientist Getrud Nunner-Winker and colleagues concluded that not gender but rather the problem in question and the specific moral dilemma it raised for the interviewees is responsible for the context-related argumentation. While the problem of abortion evoked questions about the context of the decision mostly in women, men tried to resolve this moral dilemma by the application of universal principles of justice. The pattern of moral interpretation reversed itself when the interviewees were confronted with the issue of draft avoidance; now the female interviewees utilized universal principles of justice as a point of reference for their reflection.

The relevance of the ethics of care for democratic theory has been recently pointed out by Joan Tronto. According to Tronto the advocates of the ethics of care should challenge the narrow but often presupposed perception of "care" as a private and therefore politically irrelevant moral orientation. The precondition for this, Tronto argues, is that issue of care transcends the interpretative framework of developmental psychology. Politically speaking, the question must be raised "how social institution might be arranged to expand these conventional understandings of boundaries of care" (1987: 661). In her study *Moral Boundaries* (1993), Tronto unfolds her own ideas in regard to a political theory of care. The conceptual thoughts Tronto develops in this study are based on the discussion of the political power context of Gilligan's findings that had been predominantly drawn from the moral conceptions of white American middle-class girls. Tronto's study follows the impetus to challenge Gilligans's focus on gender difference by shifting orientation. ..Amore telling finding is that the differences Gilligan found between men and women may also describe the differences may not be prominent among other groups in the population besides the relatively privileged people who have constituted Gilligan's examples." (*ibid:* 82). According to Tronto, certain social groups possess a more differentiated moral understanding, with helps to overcome the false dichotomy between differentiated moral understanding, with helps to overcome the false dichotomy between justice and care. The experience of discrimination and/or the closeness to a specific Afro-American mentality and culture are in her view responsible for this understanding.

The reference to the relationship between an Afro-American or African culture and the ethics of care is not particularly new (cp. *i.e.* Collins, 1990; Harding, 1987). In our view, Tronto's attempt to politicize this line of argumentation by turning it to the advantage of marginalized social groups must fail. The assertion that these groups "are closer to the real world of care" (Tronto, 1993: 117), demonstrates a moralized version of the standpoint theory, which question of inequality into play, the moralizing undertone of her study seems to stand in the way of her aim to challenge the sociological complexity behind the concept of difference. The question is not even posed whether a lower-middle-class worker experiences the same form of disadvantages as the long-term unemployed women and mother from the underclass. What is the difference between discrimination due to race, sexual orientation, ethnicity, gender, or class? And, to what constellations of conflict does the interface of various forms of social inequality point?

That these questions remain relatively unconsidered in Tronto's study in further illustrated by her almost reductionist and sociology under defined perception of violence. Tronto is very sensitive towards physical and more subtle (psychological) forms of violence that proceed from the privileged and point at socially disadvantaged minorities, for instance when she speaks about the devaluation and privatization of "other" culturally and/or sexual orientation or the more direct and physical "anti-Black, anti-Gay, or anti-Semitic violence" (1993: 95). Forms of violence which occur within a social class or minority group, are not taken into account. The members of a so-called underclass are characterized in a one-sided manner as the victims of a more powerful violence from the outside without even questioning the possibility of a violence that comes from the truly disadvantaged and is directed towards their own family and peer.

Tronto's study reveals a second problem related to her attempt to clarify the public relevance of the ethics of care. Here, she writes that Gilligan is not able to challenge the boundaries between private and public morality due to her development psychological frame of argumentation (*ibid:* 87ff). Accordingly, her own concept of care-taking makes a point of including institutionalized public forms of "care-work."

(5) But this seems to be a double-edged move. While Tronto is now able to challenge problems of distributive justice and democracy is made dependent on the symbolic and institutional re-evaluation of care-work (*ibid:* 162) – the question arises whether the conceptual expansion of the notion of care in terms of all reproductive activities – from comforting a loved one to professional cleaning work – blurs the original character of the ethics of care as defined by Gilligan.

A third and last point of critique regards Tronto's own positioning within the feminist debate. That Tronto is not only concerned about the "gender" – dimension of the unjust distribution and evaluation of care-work becomes clear when considering her description of a "feminist nightmare", which marks an attack of a specific, liberal version of the white middle-class feminism. Who is taking care of these children as Mother rushes off to be the corporate counsel for an insurance company in Hartford, Connecticut? Not a well paid, highly professional woman, but an illegal immigrant, paid substandard wages and no social security benefits (...) while some women are now permitted into the elite, many more women, and for that matter, many more men, are now pushed further down into the servile class (*ibid:* 20). But given Tronto's demand, that the conservative core of Gilligans's ethics of care (which implies the view that women are by virtue of their sexual identity privileged to care) should be dissolved, the question arises: Why should feminist scholars make themselves the defendants of the morality of care taking whether it is expressed in its traditional or in Tronto's politically reformulated version. Should the ethics of care even be in the center of feminist politics? In regard to this question, Tronto's study reveals a normative "over-stretch" and she tends to fall back one exactly the concept of gender difference based on identity and attribute which she wanted to overcome in the beginning.

A theory of democracy that redeems its promise to consider social inequality and difference based on ethnicity, sexual orientation, race, and gender without reducing the one to the other would have to deal with the difference of redistribution and social recognition. Iris Marion Young's Justice and the Politics of Difference (1990) presents a good example. Her demand for group-specific rules of representation aims for an institutionalized form of political cultural recognition that empowers various disadvantaged social groups to effectively take part in democratic politics without undermining their differences. Young argues against a universal model of citizenship and democratic public, which according to her always implies the danger to level differences. For example, she criticizes liberal interest group pluralism because due to its privatizing and competitive character it supposedly fails to offer enough room for the articulation of suppressed groups. According to Young, even left-liberals concerned with the social integration of marginalized groups run the danger of suppressing differences. This supposedly accounts for Rawls 'Theory of Justice' (1971), because it is based on the universalist ideal of impartiality, as well as for the tradition of the democratic republicanism in its historical and current communitarian for. Young states that it also can be applied to Habermas' and, in a certain sense, even to Benhabib's version of discourse ethics, according to which the transcendence of particularity should lead to consent. According to her, a concept of participatory democracy based on the recognition to differences must be defined in terms of a complex model of citizenship and group implying institutional mechanisms and public resources for the support of policy consulting functions and veto-rights as well as strategies of empowerment for the purpose of democratic organization: "A democratic public should provide mechanisms for the effective recognition and representation of distinct voices and perspectives of those of its constituent groups that are oppressed or disadvantaged."(1990: 184)

Young defines social disadvantage primarily in terms of the disregard of differences. The problem with this perspective is that there is an indefinite number of differences, the recognition of which could be used for. Politically, this gives rise to the question what forms of difference deserve institutional representation. Some differences, such as specifically class or gender-related inequalities, are structurally conditioned; they rather deserve the abolishment by redistributory means than cultural and political recognition. Hence, it is questionable whether Young's model of representation really makes sense in regard to her attempt to do justice to various forms of difference.

In our view, Nancy Fraser argued convincingly that Young leaves a certain tension between economic and cultural forms of oppression unresolved. Her analysis is based on a model of the social group that insufficiently differentiates between conscious and unconscious or unwanted forms of difference. According to Young, the formation of a social group depends on depends on affinity and shared characteristics based on similar experience and a mutual sense of identity. However, as Fraser (1997: 189ff) pertinently points out, this concept can be applied to new social movements, ethnic groups, and inequalities due to sexual orientation while important economic inequalities remain relatively unconsidered. In regard to class-related forms of inequality. Young can be criticized for her concept of class neither applies to the objective structurally defined position of class (class in itself) nor the collective effort to dissolve class as defined by the subjective consciousness of its members (class for itself). Instead, Young proceeds from the premise that these forms of inequality will be automatically resolved once her concept of cultural and political recognition is put into practice. Nancy Fraser objects by arguing that various forms of differences according to sexual orientation and ethnicity should not be eradicated but recognized. Various strategies follow from this distinction.

How important it is to clarify the defining relationships of class, race, gender and sexuality in sociology terms becomes obvious when dealing with differences according to gender and ethnicity. In both cases the possible interrelation of culturally defined difference and economic inequality is exemplified (cp. Fraser *ibid:* 195).

Judith Butler presents currently the strongest criticism of forms of "identity politics" that not only have a viable tradition in the United States but continuously influenced feminist concepts of the political such as those of Iris Marion Young.

(6) Butler argues that politics based on group identity must lead to fractionalization, because it assumes a group homogeneity which never exists in reality: Every attempt to assign a universal or specific content to the category "women" and thereby presumes that such a prior guarantee of solidarity is necessary (will) inevitably evoke fragmentation (...) "Identity" as a point of origin can never from the stabilizing ground for a feminist movement, for categories of identity are not only descriptive; they always imply a normative and thereby exclusive character" (1993: 49). According to Butler, the listing of "features of membership" beyond gender (such as: sexual orientation, age, ethnicity, etc.) presents the hopeless attempt to fight very fragmentation implicit to the category "women". The "etcetera", which often stands as a sign of exhaustion at the end of such a listing, illustrates the imaginary space of the signifying processes, which should be made the point of origin of new feminist political theory (cp. Butler 1991: 21off).

A differentiated consideration of the questions raised by Butler presupposes in our opinion the acknowledgement of what Butler calls the difference between the abolishment of the term subject and the "anti-foundationalist" critique she would prefer. It is not so much the disregard of terms such as subject, but rather the conscious reflection of the excluding moments, which come into play, whenever one relies on these terms as a foundation. A political theory, characterized by the awareness of this danger, must never stop to reflect on its presupposition in order to identify their possible underlying exclusions (cp. also Knapp, 1994; 1996). Butler seems quite aware of the fact that it could be a political necessity in our societies to speak as and *for* women. But, in her opinion, a feminist political theory should avoid fixing substantial attributes to the electorate for whom feminism speaks by labeling it as "women" (1993: 48). What is needed instead is a new understanding of the political capacity to act that is not based on identity but rather on the ability to change the interpretations of identity-establishing signifying practices. The category women become a scene of constant openness and reinterpretation" (Butler, 1993: 55). Since there is no prior materiality, and "sex" and "gender" are rather being seen as contingent figures, the binary heterosexual system of gender identity could and should be permanently redefined and changed.

If one regards identity as a "signifying practice" and subjects as the "effects of a rule-bound discourse", it makes sense to make the capacity to act dependent upon the ability to redefine the constituting terms of the subject. But where are the boundaries of such a deconstructivist perception of the political? Are there not again certain dimensions of inequality that remain in the dark because they cannot be grasped without a thorough understanding of social theory? Where exactly lies the critical potential of Butler's approach for a feminist democratic theory?

The possibility of a combined application of critical theory and Butler's post-structuralist approach to questions in democratic theory is examined by Seyla Benhabib and Nancy Fraser in the dispute on difference. In what follows we argue that their different evaluation of Butlers approach can be traced back to their respective perception of Habermas' discourse ethics.

The Usefulness of the Dispute of Difference for Democratic Theory

Seyla Benhabib and Nancy Fraser share the view that the work of Jurgen Habermas provides an important starting point for a feminist redefinition of concepts in democratic theory. However, the apply different aspects of Habermas work to these conceptual questions. While Fraser refers to the political and theoretical significance of the Habermas theory of the public, Benhabib is more interested in the philosophical problem of the normative foundation of critique. For Benhabib it is specifically the inter-subjective turn introduced by Habermas discourse ethics that provides a fruitful reorientation of critical theory when it comes to feminist reading of concepts in democratic theory. However, given the extensive feminist critique of universalism, she cannot adopt Habermas's universalist pragmatic argumentation without revision. Hence, Benhabib does not choose the rational person of justice (the generalized other) as the starting point for her own philosophical conception of universalism. Her model "interactive universalism" is based instead on the (re-) contextualization of the subject of justice that should become recognizable as the "concrete other". The other becomes "concrete" when we keep in mind that she is not only a right bearer, but also an emotional and physical being bound by a specific historical and cultural context and her/his own identity establishing psychological and physical abilities and needs.

With the introduction of this paradigmatic chance from the "generalized" to the "concrete" other (Benhabib, 1995a: 161ff), Benhabib diverts the moral-philosophical emphasis from a Kantian focus on rights, distributive justice and eligibility to a Hegelian preoccupation with solidarity, recognition and dignity. Compared to Habermas' strict formal grounds for reason, Benhabib's version of the discourse ethics implies stronger normative assumptions about both, the preconditions and content of discourses. According to her, discourses are not only procedural regulations for the determination of generally valid answers to questions of justice. Benhabib does not deny that discourses motivated by a participatory understanding of democracy are institutionally and formally confined by the Universalist tradition of justice. However, she argues that the moral substance of discourses depends on a model of interaction, which must be placed outside the legal-juridical community of recognition. A more complex model of discourse is rooted in the "community of needs and solidarity" where the conciliatory power is based on the will and ability of the debaters to take into account the standpoint of concrete others. The defenders of discourse ethics cannot afford to consider evaluative questions of the good life: "Practical-moral discourses flow into aesthetic-expressive ones; autonomy is not only self-determination in accordance with just norms but the capacity to assume the standpoint of the concrete others as well" (Benhabib, 1986: 334).

Benhabib's notion of the community of needs and solidarity is two-fold in character. It is utopian in the sense that it should support the full unfolding of the normative-critical potential of discourse ethics. And it implies an empirical point of reference in order to make constructive change comprehensible on the motivational level. In Gilligan's ethics of care and the political struggle for recognition of new social movements, Benhabib suspects the reciprocal pattern of interaction that enables the single person to become aware of "difference" as a positive moment (Benhabib, 1986: 350ff). Hence, Benhabib's model of "interactive universalism" implies the specific feminist interpretation that we described in the beginning as a concept of gender difference based on identity and attribute. In her view, the marginal treatment of ethics of care in Habermas' theory of communicative action points to the consideration of a specifically female moral understanding as peripheral and meaningless for the public discussion of politically relevant questions—and not least for the formation of theory. By opening the moral discussion for ethical questions the de-historicization of the private sphere and the resulting exclusion of women from the public arena should be finally put to an end (cp. Benhabib, 1995a: 193ff).

Benhabib places her feminist ethics in the context of the "female" ethics of care; she adopts the given relationship between biological sex and social gender as a frame of reference for her won proposals for feminist social critique and democratic theory (cp. *ibid:* 166). In her view, the ability to participate in public discourses does not only depend on supportive institutional arrangements (cp. 1995b); it is also dependent on the possibility to bring in the ones specific identity defined by the consequential relationship of sex and gender. In this respect, Benhabib invites feminist theorists to take constructive advantage of their gender specific experiences for the rearrangement of democratic theory and practice. Thus, her ideas must conflict with Bulters approach, who focuses on the deconstruction of the epistemic-normative point of reference for heterosexual gender relations. Benhabib's approach is only compatible with a "weak version of post-modernity", which is based on her thesis that the feminist fascination with the post-structural critique of "identity-thought" is due to the specifically female experience of a lack of possibilities for meaningful intervention in the conditions of ones individual existence (Benhabib, 1995a: 27). With this in mind, feminists should be able to resist the temptation of radical deconstructivism (*ibid:* 235ff.). What this temptation exists in becomes clear when considering Jane flax's three theses about the deconstruction of the subject, the historical narrative, and metaphysics (*see* Flax, 1990: 32ff.). While the "strong" version of Flax's theses is incompatible with the emancipatory idea of the feminist movement because it radically questions all substantialist interpretations of man, nature, and history; the "weak" version could provide an important starting point for the feminist reformulation of the political project within the tradition of the enlightenment. From a feminist perspective, the thesis of "the death of man" should be seen as the de-mystification of the male subject of reason. Benhabib writes that "the death of history" could be interpreted in terms of the entry of gender difference in written history. Finally, the feminist reading of "the death of metaphysic" represents the skepticism towards the claims of transcendental reason.

If it is intention of Seyla Benhabib is give expression to the hidden normative potential of discourse ethics. Nancy Fraser tests the applicability of Habermas' social theory from the gender perspective. The question "what's critical about critical theory" (1989), which aptly characterizes Fraser's reception of Habermas up to her current contributions of democratic theory, focuses on the uncovering of the critical tools that are actually available to Habermas (1997). The result of these tests, which frequently lead to the accusation of a lack of gender sensitivity, will then be used in pragmatic ways for the development of her own categories for critical analysis. Compared to Benhabib's Habermas critique, his approach not only allows for greater methodic flexibility, it is also requires a greater distance to the philosophical—normative programme of the discourse ethic. Fraser's historical ideology-critical method abstains from a philosophical foundation (Fraser/Nicholson, 1990); as we will argue on the following pages, this will allow her to integrate Butler's post-structralist approach into her won position.

The significance of Habermas' concept of the public is already evident in Fraser's early critique of his conceptualization of "system" and "life world" as two contrasting societal spheres, that are ruled by different logics of integration and action (Fraser, 1989). Fraser argues that from the gender perspective, this central argument of Habermas' theory of society is not only empirically questionable, but also leads to inconsistencies on the analytical level. Even though Habermas manages to show that the life world is colonized by administrative and regulative procedures of modern welfare states, his critical view fails to take into account that the needs and interests of women are already disciplined and cut back on a level of self-perception through a normatively protected interpretation of femininity and the public (cp. Fraser, 1989: 134f.). The feminist fight for decolonization (the substitution of normatively protected contexts of interaction by patterns based on communication), Fraser always stresses the democratization of access to discursive resources and the control over the interpretation of needs: "we are (...) struggling for women's autonomy in the following sense: a measure of collective control over the means of interpretation and communication sufficient to permit us to participate on a par with men in all types of social interaction, including political deliberation and decision making" (Fraser, 1989: 135). Therefore, Habermas' rejection of a feminist public sphere as a particular mistake in the fight for universal justice (cp. Habermas, 1979: 29; 1987: 579) is deficient. According to Fraser, his position shows not only a lack of consideration for the historical relevance of a feminist counter public, but also a tendency to conceal the subtle mechanisms of exclusion, which are set in discourses outside of formal procedure of access: "The question of open access cannot be reduced without remainder to the presence or absence of formal exclusion. It requires us to look also at the process of discursive interaction within formally inclusive public arenas" (Fraser, 1997: 77). In the transformation from "I" to "us" it can happen that particular points of view are neglected without consideration, or that subordinate groups cannot "find the right tone" to express themselves, or that their words are interpreted as "yes" although they meant "no", and that they are ignored and thereby encouraged to conceal their interests and needs (Fraser, 1997: 77ff.; cp., also Mansbridge, 1994).

Therefore, a feminist theory of democracy cannot simply adopt the quest for one comprehensive public arena Politically, it must insist on an additional institutionalization of multiple, sub-and opposing public spheres. Theory building must be inspired by discourse analysis to cross the borders of the existing public. In the same vein, it is not enough to publicly establish an awareness for specific forms of gender discrimination, rather, it is necessary to develop strategies to detect subtle mechanisms of exclusion. Recently, Fraser demonstrated this claim in her analysis of the prominent hearings involving Clarence Thomas and Anita Hill, and charges of sexual harassment (cp. Fraser, 1997: 99ff). In the summer of 1991, when a charge was brought by Anita Hill, a professor of law, against Clarence Thomas, nominee for the seat of Chief Justice of the Supreme Court, this charge made the headlines, and the issue of sexual harassment became a major theme for the American Public.

(7) According to the us constitution, the Senate hearings precede the seating of the Chief Justice. In this case, they were not merely reported live in the media; newspapers and radic stations extensively gathered the opinion of various social groups and tried to come up

with a cross-section of opinion within America society. The case was especially explosive in that, not only the witness (Anita Hill), but also the accused (Clarence Thomas) were of Afro-American descent; both had worked themselves up to the upper-middle class. Thus in this case, those facets of inequality dealing with race, class, and gender converged. Fraser's discourse analysis shows, how Clarence Thomas was able to exploit all three factors, sex, race, and class of origin, against Anita Hill in the hearings. While Thomas skilfully brought racial stereotypes of bear on his behalf in these hearings–for example, through manners of speech, as in electronic "lunching" — Hill became on a symbolic level, a white upper-class American, because she took it up herself to accuse an Afro-American of sexual harassment. Thomas eventually emerged as the victor in these conflict — the Senate confirmed him as Justice of the Supreme Court — due in part to restrictive legal and procedural mechanisms. Based on these mechanism, the debate was limited to the conflict between Thomas and Hill — so that, for example, no other witnesses were permitted in the hearings who asserted that they had been sexually harassed by Thomas. The private sphere of the accused was carefully protected, while Hill had great trouble defending herself against the intrusiveness of the public and the media, and to define her private space.

(8) Moreover, in the judgment of the case, the Senate avoided consulting an expert opinion about psychological effects and typical reactions of a victim of sexual harassment. Through these means, the responsible politicians strove to delegitimize the accusation against Thomas, and to block any further challenges which might have had far-reaching political consequences.

According to Fraser, the real problem in this dispute lay in the question as to who had the power to draw the line between the private and the public. Fraser suggested that the lack of an Afro-American feminists theoretical approach to the public sphere posed an additional difficulty for defending Anita Hill. She calls for such a theory which should not only conceptionalize the problem of some possessing more to defend the borderline of the public than others; it also should address the uneven balance of powers between different spheres (*e.g.* governmental offices, media, informal publics in every day life, counter publics) (Fraser, 1997: 118).

Therefore, in debating the boundaries of democracy, feminist theory should acquire more insights. From a methodological point of view, however, it cannot afford to manage without new analytical tools when arguing about difference. According to Fraser, especially Judith Butler's insightful perception of the politically relevant mechanisms of exclusion and legitimization provides important analytical tools for a feminist theory of democracy. Fraser shares Bulter's approach to Foucault's knowledge-power analysis. Accordingly, Fraser and the social historian Linda Gordon developed a methods of "critical political semantics", in which they applied Butler's critique of the constitution of the subject to the discursive process of establishing social policy.

(9) Historically, women and Afro-Americans (male or female) were perceived as "dependants". Thus they became the negative counter image of the independence of the Caucasian wage earner and family bread winner. This artificial upgrading of wage earning, and simultaneous down grading of all non-paid family work, child rearing and care-taking characterizes the structure of the American social system, which stigmatizes single mothers as undeserving and marginalizes them. Institutionally and culturally, the polarization between the legitimate, wage-related social security system, and the stigmatizing welfare system based on criteria of need, is in no other western society as apparent as in the United States (cp. Lemke, 1998).

The discursive practice of (negative) attribution proceeds all the way into present post-industrial society. Especially in the context of social cutbacks which factually push women and mothers into the cheap wage sectors of the service industry, dependency has as negative a connotation as a disease in need of therapy (*e.g.* "co-dependency"), a loathsomely depicted "Culture of Poverty" and specifically feminine weakness of cowardice when faced with the toughness of the job market (Fraser/Gordon in Fraser, 1997: 121ff.), Critical political semantics aims at foiling a discourses like this one with opposing interpretations and thereby thwarting strategies of responsible politicians.

(10) Social injustice is constructed within a complex matrix of factors of gender and social conditions. Political strategies will have to start from this multi-layered context. Current feminist research shows persuasively that theories of democracy claiming to do justice to the complex conditions of power and policy-making, without taking into account the discursive forms of practicing power, will be incomplete. The third stage of theoretically reflecting the meaning

of difference, which is characterized by a politicization of the feminist dispute of difference, is taking up this necessity more seriously.

An earlier version of this article first appeared in German in: Gudrum Axeli Knapp, ed.: Kursokorrekturen. Feminismus Zwischen Kritischer Theorie und Postmoderne, Frankfurt a. M.: Campus, 1998.

REFERENCES

1. An example for this may be Catherine Mckinnon's provocative theory, in which she puts forth the assumption that sexuality takes the same position for feminist theory, as work does for Marxism. Her radical critique of power, which finds the root of the oppression of women in their sexual subordination, illustrates Theresa Wobbe's observation, that sexual difference, rather than the social division of labour, dominates the American feminist discourse. Mckinnon argues that when it comes down to it, entire justice and social systems are based on this context of oppression (sexuality) and serves to justify it.
2. The proposed amendment to the U.S. Constitution would have made discrimination on the basis of sex unconstitutional. However, due to a growing neo-conservative backlash in several states, there was no majority to be found to ratify the amendment (cp. Mansbridge, 1985)– the American liberal tradition is most visible in the abortion regulation. In 1973, the Supreme Court in "Roe vs. Wade" made abortion legal based on the "right to privacy", *i.e.* the individual and personal right to decide about a pregnancy. This rule is the basis for abortion regulations until today.
3. An excellent summary of current American political theory can be found in the two volume book of Susan Moller Okin and Jane Mansbridge (1994).
4. Kohlberg's theory is based on a model of stages of moral development, according to which adolescents go through different levels of moral maturity. The highest level of maturity in this model, which is based on universal ethics theory, is the orientation on the basis of laws and principles (cp. Kohlberg, 1981: 409-412).
5. "On the most general level, we [note from the authors: Berenice Fischer and Joan Tronto] suggest that caring should be viewed as a species activity that includes everything that we do to maintain, continue and repair our "world" so that we can live in it as well as possible. That world includes our bodies, our selves, and our environment, all of which we seek to interweave in a complex, life-sustaining web" (Tronto, 1993: 103). This definition of care-work is not only based on the inner circles of family and/or friends. It also refers to the institutionalized forms of care-work (*e.g.* child day-care organized as a business, and cleaning work) (cp. Tronto, 1993: 114).

6. Young's approach is influenced by the theory of identity politics, since her concept of groups depends on mutual perceptions of identity. However, this is a weak version of identity politics, which takes into consideration important points of critique from the feminist post-modern discussion, especially in respect to political agency. Young's concept of "seriality" (1994), which is based on the work of Jean-Paul Sartre, tries to avoid strong politics of identity by grounding the ability to act collectively of minimal forms of mutual references depending on the situation.
7. In the 1980s, Clarence Thomas worked for the "Equal Employment Opportunity Commission", Anita Hill, who was just starting her career, was his assistant. Hill accused Thomas of having sexually harassed her massively at this time. Repeatedly, he pressured her into having a date with him, ignoring graphic material that he had seen, and so on. Anita Hill did not press charges against him at time. However, in 1991, when President Bush nominated Thomas for Chief Justice of the Supreme Court, she went public in the Senate hearings, hoping at the same time to keep her name secret in order to protect her privacy.
8. The invasion of privacy was part of a planned strategy in order to de-ligitimize Anita Hill's charges, as openly admitted by the Republican Senator Simpson: "Anita Hill will be sucked right into the maw, the very thing she wanted to avoid most. We will be injured and destroyed and belittled and hounded and harassed, real harassment, different from the sexual kind." (Republican Senator Alan K. Simpson, quoted in Fraser, 1997: 105).
9. Butler writes about the constitution of subjects: "In a certain way the subject constitutionalizes itself in a process of exclusion and differentiation, may be even repression, that thereafter gets masked and covered up by the effects of autonomy. In this sense autonomy is the logical consequence of dependency. This means that the autonomous subject can only keep up its illusion of autonomy by covering up the fault from which it constitutionalizes itself."(1993: 44). In their analysis of the "keyword" of American debates on welfare (dependency), Fraser and Gordon show that the subject-building processes of exclusion also apply to politics, especially welfare policy.
10. See Nancy Naples's discourse analysis (1997) of the congressional hearings for the Family Support Act of 1988.

NOTES

Benhabib, Seyla (1992), Kritik, Utopie. Die normativen Grundlagen der kritischen Theorie, Frankfurt a.M. (engl.: Critique, Norm and Utopia. A study of the Foundations of Critical Theory 1986).

Benhabib, Seyla (1993), "Subjektivitat, Geschichts-scheribung and Politik. Eline Replik", in Benhabib, Seyla/Judith Butler/Drucilla Cornell/Nancy Fraser, Der Streit um *Differenz Feminismus,und Postmodern in der* Gegnewart, Frankfurt a.M., pp. 105-22.

Benhabib, Seyla (1995a), Selbst im Kontext, Kommunikative Ethik in Spannungsfeld zwischen *Feminismus Kommunitarismus und Postmoderne, Frankfurt a.M.* (engl.: Situating the Self, 1992).

Benhabib, Seyla (1995b), "Ein deliberatives Modell demokratischer Legitimitat", in: Deutsche Zeitschrift fur Philosophie, Vol. 43, No. 1: 3-29 (engl.: Deliberative Rationality and Models of Democratic Legitimacy, in: constellations, Vol. 1, No. 1, April, 1994).

Benhabib, Seyla (1996), "Uber das zeitgenossische Unbehagen an der Demokratie", Vortragsmanuskript der Veranstaltung des Kulturforums zur Sozialdemokratie zum Thema "Philosophie und Politik", Oct. 4, 1996 (see also: "Frankfurter Rundschau", Sept. 12., 1996).

Butler, Judith (1991), Das Unbehagen der Geschlechter, Frankfurt a.M. (engl: Gender Trouble, 1990).

Butler, Judith (1993), "Kontingente Grundlagen: Der Feminismus und die Frage der Postmoderne", in: Seyla Benhabib/Judith Butler/Drucilla cornell/ Nancy Fraser, Der Streit um Postmodern in der Gegenwart, Frankfurt a.M., pp. 31-59;

Collins, Hill Particia (1990), Black Feminist Thought, Boston.

Dietz, Mary (1985), "Citizenship with a Feminist Face. The Problem with Maternal Thinking", in: Political Theory, Vol. 13, No. 1, pp. 19-37.

Dolling, Irene/Beate Karis (eds.) (1997), Ein alltagliches Spiel. Geschlechterkonstruktion in der sozialen Praxis, Frankfurt a.M.

Elshtain, Jean Bethge (1981), Public Man - Private Women. Women in Social and Political Thought, Princeton.

Elshtain, Jean Bethge (1996), "Why end Welfare as we know it?", in: Stanley W. Carlson-Thies/ James W. Skillen (ed.), Welfare in America. Christian Perspectives on a Policy in Crisis, pp. 3-20.

Flax, Jane (1990), Thinking Fragments. Psychoanalysis, Feminism and Postmodernism in the Contemporary West, Berkeley.

Fraser, Nancy (1989): "What's critical about Critical Theory? The Case of Habermas and Gender", in: Unruly Practices. Power, Discourse, and Gender in Contemporary Social Theory, London, New York: pp. 113-44.

Fraser, Nancy and Linda J. Nicholson (1990), "Social Criticism without philosophy: An Encounter between Feminism and Postmodernism", in: Fraser/Nicolson (ed.), Feminism/Postmodernism, London, New York, pp. 19-39.

Fraser Nancy (1997), Justice Interptus. Critical Reflections on the "Post-socialist" Condition, London, New York.

Fraser Nancy (1998) , "Es geht darum, Frauenz zu Mannern zu machen", Das Gesprach (Interview), "Frankfurter Rundschau" February 9, p. 7.

Gilligan, Carol (1982), In a Difference Voice. Psychological Theory and Women's Development, Cambridge, Mass.

Habermas, Jurgen (ed.) (1979), Stichworte zur geistigen Situation der Zeit, Vol. 1, Frankfurt a.M.

Habermas Jurgen (1987), Die theorie des kommunikativen Handelns, Vol. 2, Zur Kritik der instrumentalistischen vernunft, Frankfurt a.M.

Hardin, Sandra (1987), "the Curious Coincidence of Feminine and African Moralities: Challenges for Feminist Theory", in: Eva Feder Kittay/Diana T. Meyers (ed.), Women and Moral Theory, Totowa, pp. 296-315.

Holland-Cunz, Barbara (1996), "Politische Kritik Patriarchaler Herrschaft", in: Franz Neumann (ed.), Handbuch Politische Theorien und Ideologien, Vol. 2, Opladen, pp. 357-388.

Horster, Detlef (ed.) (1998), weibliche Moral - ein Mythos? Frankfurt a.M.

Klinger, Cornelia (1997), "Liberalismus-Marxismus- Postmoderne. Der Feminismus und seine glucklichen oder unglucklichen Ehen mit verschiedenen theoristromungen im 20 Jahrhundert", in:Politische vierteljahresschrift. Special edition: Transformation des Politischen und die Politik der Geschlechterverhaltnisse, edited by Eva Kreisky and Birgit Sauer.

Knapp, Gudrun Axeli (1994), 'Politik der Unterscheidung", in: Geschlechterverhaltnisse und Politik, edited by Institut fur Sozialforschung, Frankfurt a.M., pp. 262-87.

Knapp, Gudrun Axeli (1996), "Traditionen-Bruche:Kritische Theorine in der feministischen Rezeption" in:Elvira Scheich (ed.), Vermittelte Weiblichkeit. Feministische Wissenschafts-und Gesellschaftstheorie, Hamburg, pp. 113-51.

Kohlberg, Lawrence (1981), essays on Moral Development, volume I, the Philosophy of Moral Development, San Francisco.

Lemke, Christiane (1990), "Women and the Welfare State", in: Leviathan 2, pp. 239-54.

Lemke, Christiane (1998), "Zwischen Markt und Staat. Geschlechterpolitik im 'liberalen' Wohlfahrtsstaat der USA", in: Ilona Ostner (ed.), Mutter, Ehefrau, Erwerbstatige. Sozialpolitik als Geschlechterpolitik im internationalen vergleich, Frankfurt a.M. (in print).

Mansbridge, Jane (1985), Why we lost the ERA, Michigan.

Mansbridge, Jane (1994), "Feminism and Democracy", in: Mansbridge,/Susan Moller Okin (ed.), feminism. Schools of thought in Politics, Cambridge, Mass., Vol. I, pp. 435-49.

Nagl-Docekal, Herta (1993), "Jenseits der Geschlechtermoral", in: Nagl-docekal/Herlinde Pauer-Studer (ed.), Jenseits der Geschlechtermoral. Beitrage zur Feministischen Ethik, Frankfurt a.M., pp. 7-33.

Naples, Nancy A. (1997), "The 'New Consensus' on the Gendered 'Social Contract". The 1987/88 U.S. Congressional Hearing on Welfare reform". In: Signs, Vol. 22, No. 4.4, pp. 907-945.

Nickel, Hildegard Maria (1998), 'Gesellschaftskritischer Bib ware vonnoten. Akademische Profilierung und politischer Handlungsdruck: Frauen – und Geschlechterstudien in der Zwickmuhle" in: "Frankfurter Runschau", Forum Humanwissenschaften, January 20, p. 10.

Nunner-Winkler, Gertrud (ed.) (1991): die Kontroverse um eine geschlechts-spezifische Ethik, Frankfurt.

Okin, Susan Moller und Jane Mansbridge (ed.) (1994) Feminism, Schools of Thought in Politics, Bd. 2, Cambridge, Mass.

Pateman, Carole (1988), the Sexual Contract, Cambridge UK.

Pateman, Carole (1992), "Equality, difference, subordination: the politics of Motherhood and Women's citizenship', in: Gisela Bock/Susan James, Beyond Equality and difference, London/New York, pp. 17-31.

Pauer-studer, Herlinde (1993), "Moraltheorie und Geschlechterdiffernz. Feministische Ethik im Kontext aktueller Fragestellungen", in: Pauer-Studer/Herta Nagl Docekal (ed.), Jenseits der Geschlechtermoral. Beitrage zur Feministischen Ethik, Frankfurt a.M., pp. 33-69.

Rawls, John (1971), A Theory of Justice, Cambridge, Mass.

Tronto, Joan (1987), "Beyond Gender Difference to a Theory of Care", in: Signs, Vol. 12, No. 4, pp. 644-63.

Tronto, Joan (1993), Moral Boundaries. A Political argument for an Ethic of care, New York.

Tronto, Joan (1996), "Where to Place the Blame: Or, The Reform tool Kit revisited', Tagungsmanuskript, Annual Meeting of the American Political Science Association, San Francisco, 29 August–1 September, 1996.

Von Whal, Angelika (1995), "Traditionlinien, thematische Felder und theoretische Motive der deutschen Frauenforschung' in: Frauen-Prisma, Wissenschaftliche Beitrage zur Frauenforshcung, Postdam, pp. 67-84.

Young, Iris M. (1990), Justice and the Politics of Difference, Princeton.

Young, Iris M. (1994), "Gender as Seriality. Thinking about Women as a Social Collective', in: Signs, Vol. 19, No. 3, pp. 713-738.

5

Gender-Specific Division of Labour in Hungary Since the Regime Change

KATALIN KONCZ, BUDAPEST

Introduction

This study on the lack of equal opportunities for women and men in Hungary presents an overview of the main development affecting the gender-specific division of labour since the transformation of our society from a dictatorship and planned economy to a democratic market economy. Because the social position of women spans across a range of areas, the analytical framework of the gender-specific division of labour should include cross-cultural and inter-disciplinary aspects. Due to the significant role tradition plays in the gendered division of labour, a historical point of view is also vital. I will therefore use a three-dimensional approach to examine the situation and position of women in Hungary as post-communist country.

(a) The different fields of the division of labour within society are: politics, the labour market and the family. Women and men participate in both the public and private sphere. The "public sphere" includes politics and the labour market, where women and men are productive members of the paid labour force. In the "private sphere" people are active as members of groups (families) and also as individual; here, it is women who are primarily responsible for the care of the husband, children and parents. The social position of women can therefore be characterized by their position in politics, the labour market, and within the family.

(b) Past and present tendencies possible future solutions. Because of the active role tradition and the socialization process play in shaping attitudes of gender, identifying

problems and offering solutions, it is necessary to take an historical point of view, apply an interdisciplinary approach (considering social, economic, cultural, geographical and psychological elements), and make international-intercultural comparisons.

(c) Analyzing the facts reveals causes for phenomena, and consequences and future strategies can be determined from these causes. In line with this concept, I will analyze the position of women in Hungary since its transition to a democratic market economy.

Transitional Period in the East and Central European Countries

Hungary and other countries in the region have been faced with a task unparalleled in history. Changes in the political and economic systems are taking place simultaneously. This has made it necessary to introduce these countries to political simultaneously. This has made it necessary to introduce these countries to political and economic requirements radically different from their former ones. And these radical changes are taking place under unfavorable internal conditions and disrupting foreign economic and market conditions. The tension, both overt and under the surface, which has been accumulating for decades now combines with catharsis of the political change-over.

After 1989, Hungary entered a trying and difficult period: the transformation of society:

- From a communist dictatorship to a democratic society.
- From a state-centralized economy to a market oriented economy.

This transformation fundamentally rearranged the political, economic and family conditions of the country, the human relations behind them, and through these the position of individuals, in particular the possibilities and opportunities for women. It is difficult to estimate the effects of the transformation partly due to the complexity, variety and inextricability of the interrelations, and partly due to the often contradictory and limited information available to the researchers.

The only thing that can be stated with absolute certainty is that these radical changes deeply affect the situation of women (and men), their role in public life, in labour relations and in the family.

They make the social and individual roles of gender practiced in the past useless, which creates uncertainty and makes people feel defenseless. Depending on their social position and personality, individuals cope with this shock differently The extent and the speed with which they adapt themselves to the new conditions are different, as are their coping strategies. Through the balance of rearrangement, the separation between winners and losers is not located primarily along lines of gender; rather, several markedly obvious consequences affect women and men in a different manner.

The most important elements of the transformation are:

- the democratization of society.
- the transformation of ownership relations from public control to private property.
- the adoption of the rules of market economy, which has taken place in a very short and historically unparalleled period time.

(a) The pre-condition for democracy is ensuring equal opportunities for both gender and developing the institutional system necessary to achieve this.

(b) Private property is motivated by profit, which relies on cost sensitivity for the efficient use of resources. The requirement of efficiency leads to the elimination of superfluous resources, including "unstable" labour resources, such as married women with small children.

(c) The most important characteristic of the market economy is competition. Although in principle the labour market is by nature open to men and women alike, women are if fact at a disadvantage because of their different social roles and levels of training. This weakens their position and increases their discrimination in the labour market.

The Position of Women in Political Decision-making Processes

The precondition of the assertion of democracy is to ensure equal opportunities for both gender and to develop the institutional system required to achieve this. One of the phenomena of Hungarian society, which is the process of pluralization and democratization, appears paradox at first glance, namely that women are being pushed into the background in political decision-making processes.

Women's involvement in policy-making occurs through various institutions: through legislative and executive power, through political parties, and through organizations such as trade unions and women's movements. Following the comprehensive political change, women were pushed into the background in every form of political representation in Hungary as well as in the surrounding region.

Women in the Different Politics Forums

The share of women in Parliament is strikingly low. The first free election (1990) ensured seats for 27 women (7%). In June 1991, there were only six other European countries in which participation by women was lower.[1] The second elections (1994) resulted in increasing the number of seats occupied by women to 43 (11.2%), but in 1998 this declined substantially (32 women = 8.3%, Table 1). There are only several women holding an office in Parliament. However between 1994 and 1998 there were two female Deputy Speakers of the House; at present there is only one.

Table–1
The Proportion of Women in Parliament by Mode of Obtaining Mandates 1990, 1994, 1998 (%)

Mode of Obtaining Mandates	*1990*	*1994*	*1998*
From individual constituencies	2.8	8.7	6.8
From territorial party lists	8.3	12.7	10.2
From national party lists	15.5	14.1	8.5
Total	7.0	11.2	8.3
Women and men = 100%			

Source: Parliamentary Almanad, 1990, pp. 72-272; Central Statistical Office, 1994, pp. 11-20; and Election 98, pp. 197-203.

It was not until 1945 that women obtained the right to vote. From then on the number of female Members of Parliaments (MPs) grew steadily until 1980, when they constituted nearly one-third of the National Assembly, amongst the highest proportion in the world. Female MPs began to reduce in number in 1985, and this tendency continued after the political transition to democracy (Table 2).

The ousting of women to that extent is not typical of today's developed democracies. North European countries have the highest (one-third and more) parliamentary proportion of women. There is only one country (Greece) in the European Union where the proportion of women is lower than that of Hungary (Table 3).

Table–2
The Proportion of Women Among MPs from 1945 to 1998

Date of Elections	*Number of MPs*	*Proportion of Women (%)*
1945	357	3.1
1947	372	4.0
1949	402	17.2
1953	453	11.0
1958	338	17.5
1963	340	18.2
1967	349	19.7
1971	352	23.8
1975	352	28.6
1980	352	30.1
1985	387	20.9
1990	386	7.0
1994	386	11.2
1998	386	8.3

Source: Inter-Parliamentary Union, 1992; Parliamentary Almanad, 1990, pp. 72-272; Parliamentary Edition, 1994, pp. 5-172, and Election 98, pp. 197-203.

Table–3
Participation of Women in the National Parliamentary Assemblies of the European Union Member States, Norway and Hungary, and in the European Parliament in 1997 and as of September 30, 1999 (%)

Countries	*Proportion of Women*	
	1997	*1999*
Austria	23.5	26.2
Belgium	16.7	23.3
Denmark	34.9	37.4
Germany	25.9	30.9
Greece	6.3	6.3
Finland	33.5	37.0
France	8.6	10.9
Ireland	14.2	12.0

Contd...

Countries	Proportion of Women	
	1997	1999
Italy	10.2	11.1
Luxembourg	18.3	16.7
Netherlands	29.5	36.0
Portugal	13.0	13.0
Spain	18.5	21.6
Sweden*	44.0	42.7
United Kingdom	12.0	18.4
European Union 15	17.1	....
European Parliament	26.6	....
Norway	36.4*	36.4
Hungary	11.2	8.3

* Parliament includes 15 substitutes for Ministries.

Source: European Commission, 1998, p. 97, http://www.ipu.org./wmm-e/classif.htm. pp. 1-5.

The "statistical approach" prevalent in the former communist era was not wrong because of its political window-dressing role or because it did not achieve effective results, as is often assumed by many today. It was wrong because it forcibly interfered in an organic development process (as did the communist system as a whole) without the given preconditions of development (*e.g.* a strong women's movement). Prior to the change in the political system, the women's movement had no real involvement in women's policy-making or the enforcement of equal rights. The interpretation of female emancipation was based in Marxist-Leninist ideology and was incorporated into the political machinery serving to perpetuate the system. This explain the emergence and formal entitlements of women (and other segments of society including the young and working class) in the sphere of politics. This process resulted out of economic necessity (*i.e.* efforts to realize full employment) rather than a female endeavour to gain genuine equal rights. In other words, Hidden in an ideological guise, emancipatory efforts were backed for purely economic reasons–the demand of an expansive economy for unlimited, cheap, unskilled labour. Along with its seamy sides, however, this peculiar emancipatory policy also produced definite results often forgotten by the present possessors of power. Women

WERE there. Were **PRESENT** and **DID TAKE PART.** And experience gained in Norway justify that this is not insignificant as beginning (Likestillings, 1990).

The hypothesis and expectation of many who assumed that women's opportunities would improve in the new democracies have proven to be false. The change in the political system made no difference in terms of handling women's issues or increasing the numbers of female MPs. In the communist era, women were and under the new system have remained – more active only within the scope of movement assigned to them by society, never overstepping the boundaries. And the boundaries have remained the same. Based on current reality, the cause of this phenomenon has also become obvious. For Hungary and the other countries in the area, the present position of today's developed democracies cannot serve as a grounds for comparison. The building up of a democracy constitutes a long historical process. The proportion of women participating in parliament is currently in those countries in which their right to vote and to be lected was realized already in the first decades of 20th century (Table 4). The initial parliamentary involvement by women in these countries was extremely low; however, embedded in social progress, it continued to strengthen.

Table–4
The Date Women were Granted Full Rights to Vote and to be Elected, and the Proportion of Women Among MPs in Some Countries as of September 30, 1999

Countries	*Female Proportion*	*Date Grated Full Rights to Voted/be Elected*
Austria	26.2	1918
Denmark	37.4	1915
Finland	37.0	1906
Germany	30.9	1918
Netherlands	36.0	1919
Norway	36.4	1907-1913
Sweden	42.7	1918-1921

Source: IPU, 1992; European Commission, 1998, p. 97; http://www.ipu.org./wmn-e/clssif.htm. pp. 1-5.

After the change to democracy, Hungarian women had a disadvantageous position from the outset: a mere 8.5 –11.2 per cent of the individual candidates were female, with an increasing tendency (Table 5). During the elections their chances further worsened: while 14.4 per cent of the male candidates were elected, only 11.8 per cent of women candidates obtained mandates in Parliament.

Table–5
The Distribution of Candidates for MP by Gender 1990, 1998 (%)

Date of Elections	*Distribution of Candidates*		
	Women	*Men*	*Total*
1990	8.5	91.5	100
1994	10.0	90.0	100
1998	14.2	85.8	100
Share of Candidates who Obtained Mandates			
1990	11.7	14.4	14.2
1994	15.5	13.8	14.0
1995	85.3	9.7	9.0

Source: Calculations on the basis of Parliamentary Almanad, 1990, pp. 72-272; Central Statistical Office, 1994, pp. 11-20; and Election '98, pp. 197-203.

The 1994, elections saw an advance in women's positions, with more (10%) female candidates representing the parliamentary parties. The number and percentage of women elected increased substantially, and the chance of a women being elected was better than that for men. Seats were won by 15.5 per cent of the female, but only 13.8 per cent of male candidates. In an international comparison, with 11.2 per cent female MPs Hungary's position has improved. However, this improvement suffered a setback in 1998 and today, within the European Union there are only less female MPs in Greece than in Hungary.

At the beginning, more women gained access to Parliament through party lists, especially national lists, than through individual constituencies. While in 1990 four-fifths of the women won their seats through party lists, this figure dropped to two-thirds in 1994, where it remained in 1998 (Table 6).

There was a substantial increase in voter confidence towards female candidates during the second and third elections. The proportion of women directly elected in individual constituencies

Table–6
The Distribution of Women in Parliament by Mode of Obtaining Mandates 1990, 1994, 1998 (%)

Mode of Obtaining Mandates	*1990*	*1994*	*1998*
Individual constituencies	18.5	34.9	37.5
Territorial party lists	29.6	37.2	40.6
National party lists	51.9	27.9	21.9
Total	100	100	100

Source: Calculations on the basis of the Parliamentary Almanad, 1990, pp. 72-272; Central Statistical Office, 1994, pp. 11-20; and Election '98, pp. 197-203.

was one-fifth in 1990, while more than one-third of them received votes as individual candidates in 1994 and 1998.

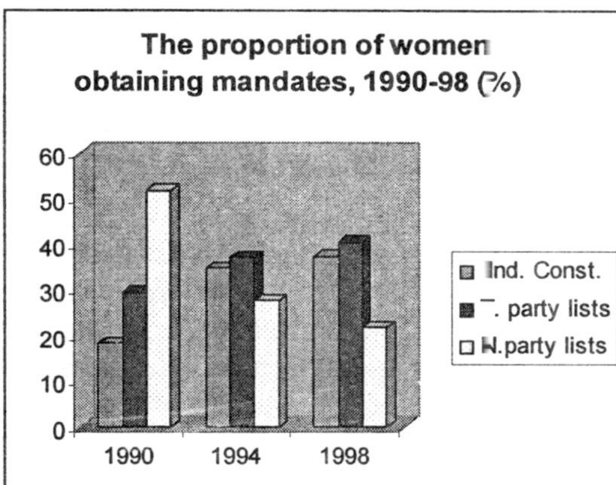

The Proportion of Women Obtaining Mandates, 1990-98 (%)

Source: Calculation on the basis of Parliamentary Almanad, 1990, pp. 72-272; Central Statistical Office, 1994, pp. 197-203.

Because of the high proportion of women entering Parliament through lists, the responsibility of the parties is extremely important. Individual party alignment with women's issues and female candidates varies. According to international standards, the progressive and newly created parties are more open towards women's issues and requirements for equal opportunity. In 1998, the proportion of women was highest within the Association of free Democrats (12.5%) and the coalition of Hungarian Democratic forum and Association of Young Democrats Hungarian Bourgeois Party (11.8%).

Since its inception, only few women have held an office in Parliament. However, from 1994 until 1998 there were two female Deputy Speakers of the House: there is currently one woman in this office. During the entire period, there has been only one woman among the presidents of parliamentary commissions. Female MPs have a strong presence in the Parliamentary Committees on social, family and educational issues, as is generally the case in all countries. Women's issues have not been, and are still not, on the agenda of any of the committees. As result of an initiative launched by the women MPs of all parliamentary parties, a join subcommittee on women's issues has been set up as part of the Committee on Human Rights, Religious and Minority Issues, which is an important development towards a policy of equal opportunity. International organizations and agreements usually relegate the women's issues to the authority of his committee. The subcommittee examines bills submitted to Parliament from women's perspectives, bearing in mind their specific interests.

There is a wider scope of movement at a local; municipal elections present greater possibilities for women everywhere in the world. Women stand a better chance of overcoming prejudice and becoming successful through their personal contacts. In the eighties, 27-32 per cent of local and regional council delegates were women. In and after the 1990 local elections, their proportion both among candidates and later in municipal assemblies dropped to 14-16 per cent. Women were more successful winning seats in municipalities in small settlements than in major cities (receiving 16% and 13%, respectively). In running for high-profile offices, women are at a disadvantage compared with men. In 1985, 6 per cent in 1990 only 3 per cent and in 1998, 5.1 per cent of mayor's offices were filled by female candidates in towns. In smaller settlements, in 1990, 10 per cent of the mayors elected were women as were 12.8 per cent in 1998. The pyramid principle can be observed here as well: women have less of chance of obtaining prestigious posts, *e.g.* as members of national assemblies, than being elected members of local governments. The situation for women improved during the last municipal election (1998). Of Budapest's 23 districts, three of them have a woman as mayor.

The under representation of women in Hungary's government is obvious. The government—who by the way has inherited serious burden from the past—has no women's policy, and women's issues have not been included in its programme. There was not a single female minister in 1990. Today, one ministry (the Ministry of Justice) is headed by a woman, and there are two state secretaries and three undersecretaries of state.

With the exception of a few North European countries, women's representation within the government is very modest in the majority of the developed market economies (Table 7). The survey quoted also points out that a close relationship exists in the developed market economies between the parliamentary ratio of women and their representation at the ministerial level.[1] In the past decades, government agencies for the protection of women's interests have been established in the developed market economies. In these countries—and in several developing ones (!)—these are either a special ministry, ministerial department or some other state agency or independent agency supported by the state. Following the Forth International UN Conference of Women held in Beijing, the Equal Opportunity Office was launched within the framework of the Ministry of Labor (today: Female Representation Office within the framework of the Ministry for Social and Family Issues, which is responsible for women's issues within the government and had limited power).

Table-7

Proportion of Women within the Government in the European Union Member States and in Norway as of October 1999 (%)

Countries	*Proportion of Women*
Austria	25.0
Belgium	11.8
Denmark	26.3
Finland	33.3
France	29.6
Germany	15.6
Greece	18.6
Ireland	13.3
Italy	21.4

Contd...

Countries	*Proportion of Women*
Luxembourg	25.0
Netherlands	28.6
Portugal	10.3
Spain	26.7
Sweden	50.0
United Kingdom	22.7
Norway	36.4

Source: http://www.dhdirhr.coe.fr/equality/Eng/Table 1. htm, pp. 1-2.

The absence of women in the Hungarian Government is surprising even in comparison with other East European countries (Table 8).

Table–8
Proportion of Women within the Government in the Post-communist Countries October 1999 (%)

Countries	*Proportion of Women*
Slovak Republic	22.2
Bulgaria	18.8
Croatia	12.5
Albania	11.1
Lithuania	11.1
Ukraine	11.1
Macedonia	10.0
Russian Federation	8.3
Czech Republic	7.1
Estonia	6.7
Hungary	6.3
Poland	0.0
Latvia	0.0
Romania	0.0
Slovenia	0.0

Source: http://www.dhdirhr.coe.fr/equality/Eng/Table.htm, pp. 1-2.

The proportion of women within the various parties is generally lower than that in the population. In Sweden, Norway and the United

Kingdom, 40-50 per cent of all party members are women. The proportion of women within different parties is 30-40 per cent in Austria, Belgium, Finland, Ireland, Luxembourg and Japan (IPU, 1992: 65-68). The female representation in progressive parties and the Greens is higher than in traditional ones everywhere in the world. In Hungary, the proportion of women in the different parties was 24-37 per cent in the early nineties (IPU, 1992: 66).

From the point view of practicing power, the role of party leaders is more important than numerical representation within the party. For lack of data for Hungary, based on the international average I estimate the female proportion in the governing bodies of parties to be an average of one to five women (IPU, 1992: 74). In the parties of the countries who participated in the above-mentioned survey, female sections are common. According to my information, in Hungary the HDF (Hungarian Democratic Forum), HSP (Hungarian Socialist Party), CDPP (Christian Democratic People's Party) and ISHP (Independence Small-Holders Party) have female sections. I have come across somewhat complex but clear and unambiguously formulated programmes in the case of CDPP and HSP.

Of the countries answering the questions put to them in the survey conducted by Inter-parliamentary Union[2], 56 political parties from 34 countries apply positive discrimination within the party and in parliamentary elections. This positive discrimination has three forms: the quota system, appointment and reserving seats for women. The last two are usually applied in developing countries. (IPU, 1992: 100-122) The evaluation of the Quota system is accompanied by repeated disputes.[3] It is difficult to measure its effect in numbers, but many examples can be cited for and against it. The unparalleled ground women have gained in Norway is often explained by the introduction and application of the quota system. In Finland, where the parliamentary ratio of women was the highest in eighties, quotas do not exist. (IPU, 1992: 98) Norway, quotas are more and more being replaced by affirmative action in the developed market economies.

Trade Unions and women's organizations are currently playing a decisive role in supplying a basic framework for political participation by women. In most countries of the world, the female ratio among members of the trade unions is generally higher than in the parties, but women are less organized than men. As in the case in political parties, the female ratio is low in the governing bodies of the trade unions, though the chances of women are better here than in parties. Women made up 45 per cent of trade union leaders prior to 1990, but the statistics hide the fact that female leaders worked at lower-ranking levels (55% of shop stewards were women) while their participation on the top leadership was negligible. In the multi-party system, the new independent trade unions are seeking their place, but there are still few women (2-3) in the top ranks. In the current situation in Hungary, the ousting of the trade unions from the political arena reduces women's possibilities for participation. In the developed market economies, the female sections of the trade unions play an important role; their deputies represent women's Board of the National Association of Hungarian Trade Unions, the Female Section of the Steel and Iron-workers' Union and the Democratic League of Independent Trade Unions are the only organizations worth mentioning that actively protect women's interests.

Female organizations play an important role in recognizing, representing, publicizing and protecting women's interests. The waste of the women's movement in the "socialist" era is a decisive factor in the slack demand for and the limited interest in women's political participation. The revival and strengthening of the women's movement may be the future political for making the parties and the government aware of the necessity of women's policy and of developing the protection of female interests.

In the developed market economies, the strengthening of the women's movements dates back far before the establishment of women's sections within the parties—a product of the period succeeding the Second World War. In Hungary, following the abolition of the women's movement and the political parties, we can witness that as part of, and parallel to, the overall change in the political parties, we can witness that as part of, and pluralized and the parties established their respective female sections one after the other. Initially, the motivation and willingness to cooperate was limited (*see* Women's Union), which is the result of the period full of spite. From the point of view of the goal—the protection of women's interests—this is definitely. A good counterexample of effective cooperation is the Polish women's movement, which ideologically speaking also divided and has similar historical precedents.

Participation in the various parties, protectionist organization and women's interest groups, in particular in their governing bodies, is of decisive importance from the point of groups, in particular in their governing bodies, is of decisive importance from the point of view of moving women, in part because it implies a period of preparation in which the methods of obtaining power and practicing it can be learned. Moreover, it is also important because they are the channels leading to the highest spheres of political decision-making, to Parliament and the government. In this respect an important role is also played by the various professional organizations and associations, who lobby their causes. Because they are not centrally organized, female society is locked out from these formal and informal networks leading to power, which aggravates both their incoming to power and successfully practicing it.

Causes for the Limited Participation of Women in Political Decision-making Processes

In the process of government transition, women have been forced to the periphery of political decision-making processes in Hungary as well as in the other East and Central European countries, which is a symptom of their underprivileged position in society. An explanation for this handicap can be found in history, more concretely in the traditional practice of the division of work between the two genders. Within this context, and given the lack of social aid, a contradiction results between women's social roles, namely between

- their role in the family, and
- their desire to participate in decision-making processes.

This contradiction prevents the women from participating on equal footing with men in political and economic decision-making processes.

Aside from the general causes for the inferior position of women in society, insufficient participation by women in political power can be explained by the factors determining political participation at all, which are

- the intention of political leaders to eliminate discrimination against women;
- the social, political, economic and cultural conditions needed for their participation;
- women's attitudes and their demand for participation.

Women are ensured juridical equality in Hungary. However, genuine equality men and women has not yet been attained despite the existence of constitutional, legal and regulatory provisions. Inequalities continue to exist in practice, in political, economic and cultural life, and within the family. There is a contradiction between de jure and de jure facto position of women. In the new democracy, the women's issued have been pushed into the background. Never has there been such silence surrounding women's issues as since after the change of regime.

The most important social and cultural conditions required for more extensive participation in policy-making are the following:

- improved education and qualification measures,
- higher employment rates,
- social assistance to help reconcile women's various tasks,
- a more democratic division of labour within the family,
- the transformation of cultural traditions that stand in the way of achieving equality between men and women.

Some of these questions will be presented and treated later in this study.

Quantitative Labor Market Characteristics of Female Employment

The labour market position of women can be characterized quantitatively by the level, structure, and by the forms of employment and unemployment.

(a) The Level of Female Employment

During state socialism, economic and social policy aimed at full employment, which was achieved within a historically short period of time. In 1980, 82.0 per cent of female and 87.9 per cent of male labour force were either employed or associated with cooperatives. The number of active wage-earning women grew continuously associated until 1989. The expansion of female employment levels was forced from both the supply and the demand side. Generally low income levels compelled members of the active-aged population and pensioners to find jobs, which was also a precondition for their entitlement to welfare. Due to these conditions, within a short period of time the two-income family model became the standard in both Hungary and the other East and Central European countries. On the other hand, the unrestricted demand for resources–derived from the interest of employers insensitive to running costs (soft budget/cost limits, Kornai, 1980) —

led to overstaffing and kept productivity low. This two- sided economic process led to a maximum allocation of available human resources, leaving no room for alternative forms of employment. The result was maximum level of female economic activity (85.8%), exceeding the male employment level (84.7%), which was unprecendented even by international standards (Table 9).

Since the regime change in 1989, the labour market has been undergoing dramatic changes, and the employment conditions for women have become unfavorable. Employment levels have decreased in line with the steady increase in unemployment. Between 1986 and 1997, the number of active wage earners dropped by 1.281 million; 52 per cent of the reduction affected women. Women represented 44 per cent of those in employment relations in 1998. The substantial decline in female employment applies both to active-aged women and those past the retirement age. At the beginning of the transformation, 85.7 per cent of those women eligible for work were active wage earners (including those on maternity and childcare leave). This figure fell to 72.2 per cent by 1995, and had dropped as low as 69.1 per cent by 1998. Generally high unemployment does not solely account for this tendency: it includes several measures aimed at encouraging labour force outflow since the transformation. For instance, early retirement plans have been introduced, mothers with three or more children are able at home and receive a modest income, the child care allowances plays a role in protecting women from unemployment, an increasing number of young people are staying longer in the educational system (Labor Ministry, 1995).[4]

Table-9
Activity Rates by Gender in Hungary from 1980 to 1998 (%)

Year	*According to Concept Used*			
	Until 1998	*Since 1998*	*Until 1998*	*Since 1998*
	Female		*Male*	
1980	82.0	75.2	87.9	86.5
1981	83.3	75.4	86.5	86.5
1982	83.6	76.1	87.0	87.0
1983	83.9	76.6	86.7	86.7
1984	84.1	77.0	85.8	85.8

Contd...

Year	*According to Concept Used*			
	Until 1998	*Since 1998*	*Until 1998*	*Since 1998*
	Female		*Male*	
1985	84.2	77.4	85.3	85.3
1986	85.1	78.2	84.8	84.8
1987	85.6	78.5	85.3	85.3
1988	85.1	77.8	85.2	85.1
1989	85.8	78.1	84.7	84.7
1990	85.7	77.9	84.8	84.8
1991	83.8	75.7	84.3	84.2
1992	82.8	74.3	80.8	80.7
1993	79.7	71.2	79.3	79.2
1994	75.8	67.5	76.3	76.2
1995	72.2	64.0	73.8	73.6
1996	69.9	62.4	73.8	73.6
1997	68.9	60.9	73.4	73.3
1998	69.1	61.3	73.4	73.4

According to concept used until 1998: includes persons on maternity and childcare leave. According to concept used since 1998: does not include persons on maternity and childcare leave.

Source: Central Statistical Office, 1998b, pp. 20-31.

One of the major factors influencing the rate of women's employment is the displacement of female pensioners from the labour market. The number of female pensioners in employment relations was 223.000 in 1986; by 1997 this number had dropped to 66,500. (The situation of employed male pensioners is worse than that of women: while 245,000 male pensioners were employed in 1986, in 1997 there were only 50.000 in employment relations.) (Central Statistical Office, 1998b).

In the meantime, there has been strong growth in women's employment activity rates in the European Union, where women continue to account for an increasing proportion of the labour force and for the majority of new jobs being created in members State. In 1996, 57 per cent of the labour force in the European Union was composed of women (Table 10), and women have accounted for all of the labour force growth over the last two decades. (European Commission, 1998:55)

Table–10
Activity Rates of Women and Men Aged 15-64 in the European Union 1991-1996 (%)

Year	*Women*	*Men*
1991	55.8	79.8
1992	55.7	78.7
1993	55.9	78.1
1994	56.4	77.9
1995	56.7	77.4
1996	57.2	77.5

Source: European Commission, 1997, pp. 108-110.

Employment levels among women below 25 and over 50 years of age is significant lower in Hungary than in the highly industrialized countries. (Table 11)

Table–11
Employment Rates by Age and Gender in the Highly Industrialized Countries and in Hungary, 1997

Age Groups	*Europe 15*	*US*	*Japan*	*Hungary*
		Women		
15-24	32.4	50.1	41.4	30.6
25-54	61.9	73.6	63.7	67.2
55-64	25.9	49.5	47.7	16.2*
Total	50.5	67.5	60.7	61.3*
		Men		
15-24	39.4	53.8	45.6	43.6
25-54	84.5	88.4	95.3	84.9
55-64	46.6	65.5	80.6	44.2*
Total	70.6	80.8	88.5	73.3*

*Age group of 55-59.

** Cannot be compared, because of the different working age groups.[5]

Source: European Commission, 1999, p. 11, and calculation on the basis of the Central Statistical Office, 1998a, pp. 20-31, 75.

Hungary has applied for membership to the European Union. In view of the alignment of the European Union towards equal opportunity for the genders, it will be a definite disadvantage that the activity rates of women (25-49 years) is less in Hungary than among the other candidates countries for access to the European Union (European Commission, 1998: 43). A lot of effort has to made in order to fulfill the EU criteria, especially in regard to mainstreaming strategy.

The Structural of Female Employment

The period between 1990 and, a very positive structural reorganization took place in Hungary. The tendency of the employment structure by sector was similar to the European Union average (Table 12).

Table–12
Composition by Sector of Employment in Hungary, 1990 and 1998, and in the European Union, 1997 (%)

Sectors	*Hungary Female*		*Male*	*Total*	
	1990	*1998*		*Hungary 1998*	*E15 1997*
Agriculture	14.8	4.4	10.6	7.9	5.1
Industry	30.2	25.0	39.5	33.1	30.1
Services	55.0	70.6	49.9	59.0	64.8
Total	100	100	100	100	100

Source: Calculation on the basis of the Central Statistical Office, 1998a, pp. 76-78 and the European Commission, 1999, p. 15.

In the agricultural sector, the proportion of women dropped from 14.8 per cent to 4.4 per cent mainly because of the privatization process: small agricultural business rely on limited labour. Female employment in industry also dropped in comparison with all female wage earners, but to a lesser degree than in agriculture. Similar to the international tendency, the employment rates for women has increased in the service sectors. Nearly three-quarters of all active female wage earners work in different service industries. The feminization process in the tertiary sector has strengthened in the course of the transitional period.

Forms of Female Employment

In Hungary, employment structures have remained inflexible for both women and men. Full-time employment dominates, while part time employment continued to be neglected; and other alternative forms of employment, *e.g.* job sharing, are limited. The proportion of partime employees among active working age wage earners has always been marginal in Hungary. In the eighties, when the labour shortage was most extensive, at under 3 per cent the part-time employment rate was at highest. The majority of part-time workers were pensioners; the overall of all part-time employees (including pensioners) was less than 9 per cent of all active wage earners (Koncz, 1984).

When compared with countries of the European Union, one of the most significant differences in Hungary's employment characteristics is the low proportion of part-time workers. While in the European Union nearly one-third of women work part-time (Table 13), in Hungary only 7.6 per cent of active women wage earners work less than 35 hours a week (Frey, 1997: 15).

Table–13
Women Employed Part-time: Average of Countries of the European Union 1991-1996 (%)

Years	*% of*	
	All Employed Women	*All People Employed Part-time*
1991	27.7	82.7
1992	28.9	82.5
1993	29.6	82.3
1994	30.5	81.7
1995	31.2	80.9
1996	31.5	80.5

Source: European Commission, 1997, pp. 120-121.[6]

In the member states, 24 million people worked part-time in 1995. The majority of new jobs created over the last several years have been in the part-time employment sector: Seventy-one percent of newly created men's job and 85 per cent of those for women were part-time, a form of employment that continues to be primarily reserved for women (only 5% of men work on a part-time basis) (European Commission, 1998a: 67).

According to one study made on part-time jobs and the motivation of employment in Hungary cannot be found in legislation, nor in the demand or supply side (Frey-Gere, 1994). The results of the study point out that employer and employee responses went beyond the importance of part-time jobs. The causes for the gap between intention and reality can be only explained by the real attitudes of respondents, which was emphasized in research conducted in France in the early eighties. Employer decision-making in Hungary is influenced by an excessive labour market supply: they can satisfy their demand by drawing on cheap and easily attainable labour. Part-time jobs require a certain amount organization. Which employers are reluctant to perform? The low income levels influence women's attitudes towards part-time jobs: Because of the high inflation rate and the low real wages, women need full-salary jobs in order to maintain even a low standard of living. Due to the especially high unemployment rate of men in some regions of Hungary, in some households. Women are the sole wage earners. This throws some light on the fact that women choose (compulsory) part-time employment only if there are no other possibilities available to them. Workplace flexibility is an issue that needs to be solved in the near future in order create better conditions for combining work with household duties in Hungary.

A New Phenomenon: Unemployment

In the past four decades, large-scale unemployment was a phenomenon unknown in Hungary. It began emerging parallel to the transformation of the economy. In January, 1990, the number of unemployed was insubstantial; it continued to increase, and by 1994 the trend had begum to change.

Table-14
Unemployed Rates in Hungary by Gender from 1986 to 1998 (%)

Year	*According to Concept Used*		
	Until 1998	*Since 1998*	*Until and Since 1998*
	Female		*Male*
1986	0.0	0.0	0.0
1987	0.1	0.1	0.1
1988	0.2	0.2	0.2
1989	0.2	0.2	0.3

Contd...

Year	*According to Concept Used*		
	Until 1998	*Since 1998*	*Until and Since 1998*
	Female		*Male*
1990	0.4	0.4	0.5
1991	1.5	1.7	2.2
1992	6.6	7.3	9.0
1993	11.2	12.6	5.1
1994	11.1	12.5	15.2
1995	9.9	11.2	12.7
1996	10.0	11.3	12.0
1997	9.6	10.9	11.7
1998	9.7	10.9	11.1

According to concept used until 1998: includes persons on maternity and children leave.

According to concept used since 1998; does not include persons on maternity and children leave.

Source: Central Statistical Office, 1998b, pp. 20-31.

In 1998, 11.1 per cent of the labour force were unemployed. This rate is lower than that in countries of the European Union. On average, unemployment data for these countries continue to show a substantially higher unemployment rate among women than among men (Table 15). An unusual trend can be seen in the unemployment rate for women in Hungary: women's unemployment rates are lower than that of men. In November 1998, 44 per cent of all registered unemployed were female.[7] An explanation for this a typical phenomenon can be found primarily in the special features of the structural reorganization that has place since the regime change: Employee reduction was carried out in those sectors where the proportion of women is likewise not typical among young women seeking first-time employment: the female share is 45.5 per cent. In some regions, the proportion of women looking for their job exceeds that of men, *e.g.* in Budapest (52.2%) and in Fejer Country (54.8%).

Compared with men, the difference in unemployment benefits for women is not as high as their respective wage differences would indicate. Women receive an average monthly benefit payment equal to 96.5 per cent of that for men. Amongst the long-term employed (over 180 days), the share is 95.7 per cent. The gender gap can be attributed to income differences which are much higher.

Table-15
Unemployment Rates for Women and the Men in the European Union 1991-1996 (%)

Years	*Women*	*Men*
1991	10.3	7.0
1992	10.9	7.9
1993	12.0	9.6
1994	12.8	10.3
1995	12.5	9.6
1996	12.5	9.9

Source: European Commission, 1997, 108-110, p. 9.

Qualitative Labour Market Characteristics of Female Employment: Position of Women in the Labour Market

The most important social preconditions for the widespread employment of women (education, day-care facilities) have been created in the past decades, and the introduction of social policy has contributed to an improvement in the labour market position of women. Despite these measures, however, their labour market position continues to be inferior to that of men. Objective socio-political facts–among them the labour market mechanisms—prevent women from achieving equality in society and within the family, sphere which are also considerably influenced by tradition. The conditions of the market economy continuously perpetuate the influenced by tradition. The conditions of the market economy continuously perpetuate the foundation for discrimination. Under these circumstances, the role played by women in the reproduction of the labour force and of the population, as well as their resulting functions, are transformed into disadvantages. The transition to a market economy aggravated the social position of women: the demand for labour has decreased, unemployment has risen, social assistance has been pushed into the background.

The current democratic constitution—as did the previous communist constitution—stipulates that women and men shall have equal opportunities and prohibit any discrimination based on gender membership. However, these provisions have not been enforced in practice, and there are no penalties for discrimination. Theoretically, women may petition the constitutional court for redress, but not one has done so to date.[8] In practice adverse circumstances for women still continue to be recreated in both overt forms in the spheres of politics, the economy, culture, and the family. This duality perpetuates the contradiction between legally stipulated equal rights and lack of genuine equal opportunity.

The labour market position of women has always been more unfavourable than that of men, and it has worsened in the course of the transitional period. The disadvantage women are subject to manifest in different ways.

- Female labour plays a secondary role, acting only as a reserve in the labour market. This is why the employment of women is linked very closely to the prevailing economic situation and why there is extensive hidden unemployment amongst women. The secondary role of female employment has been reinforced over the course of the transitional period.
- Women are often forced to interrupt their careers for child-birth and child-rearing.
- Their chances for promotion are more restricted than those for men.
- Labor market segregation lowers the prestige of women's jobs and leads to an unfavourable counter-selection.
- Women's wages and incomes are generally less than those of men, and they are employed at the lower levels of the income hierarchy.
- The opportunities for women to defend their interests are weaker and have worsened in the course of the transitional period.

Hiring Discrimination: Unfavourable Entrance Conditions

Women are at a disadvantage the moment they first enter the labour market: nevertheless, the educational level of active women wage earners is better than that of men. One explanation for this phenomenon is that the labour market does not grant as much recognition to educational levels as it does to professional training and qualifications. Women are less qualified than men despite the fact that they have completed general schooling requirements. Compared with men, this circumstance lessens their chances for finding or changing jobs.

Women are often compelled to interrupt their careers because of their dual role. Child-rearing primarily remains solely the responsibility of women. When children are ill, women are the ones who stay home to tend them. Women take advantage of the possibility of receiving a child-care allowance or child-care assistance. Employers are reluctant to hire women because of the increased likelihood of interruptions and limited working hours in comparison with men, even finding a job are much worse than those for men. If will be virtually impossible to integrate women over 40, older women and women returnees into the labour market if employers continue to practice discrimination based on age and gender.

Promotional Discrimination—The Glass Ceiling Effect

Women are at a disadvantage when it comes to leadership positions both in the spheres of politics and economy. They are overlooked for promotion in favour of men. The interruption of paid work, insufficient remuneration for household duties, the traditional division of labour within the family prevents achieving equality for women in the sphere of gainful employment. In any number of cases, promotion barriers prevent the vertical mobility of women. They enter segments of the labour market that offer unfavourable conditions and as a rule find jobs at the lower levels of the employment hierarchy. The female employment structure can be characterized by a pyramid: the proportion of women is high at the lower level of the employment hierarchy and low on the top. In 1988, only one-third of women (compared with one-half of men) in white–collar jobs occupied a supervisory position. The proportion of women is higher in the lowest positions. Of all the high–level mangers in Hungary, less than 3 per cent are women.

Women in Business

Women's contributions and the specific skills they bring with them can prove to have a very positive effect on society as a whole. Setting up their own business enables women to access employment as well as contribute to job creation. There are no reliable up-to-date statistics (some of them contradict each other) on the minority of female entrepreneurs in Hungary; however, according to my own estimation, approximate 38 per cent of the 734,000 SMEs are run by women (Table 16).

The small business sector is securing is women's livelihoods to an ever growing extent. In 1993, over 20 per cent of all income earners

Table–16
Number and Proportion of Female Entrepreneurs

Enterprises	*Number of Women (Thousands)*	*Proportion of Women (%)*
Companies and partnerships	42	16
Sole proprietors	237	51
Total	279	38

worked in small business, including self-employed retailers. The female share of small business enterprises is rising. A statistic from 1988 showed that their proportion among full-time businesses was under one-third in the competitive sector, by 1993 this number had risen to nearly two-fifths (Ministry of Labor, 1995[9]).

In 1993, there were 213,000 women working as self-employed retailers. Another 37,000 women were registered as joint proprietors. The proportion of women in sole proprietorships was higher (over 40%) than in partnerships, where female owners represented only 30 per cent. Most of them, however, are in business as a second job, and so the proportion of women among those involved in second jobs is relatively high. While only 37 per cent of all full-time self-employed retailers are women, at 56 per cent of all retired sole proprietors they are in majority (Ministry of Labor, 1995).

Characteristics of Female Entrepreneurs

Women typically run business in quite a different way than do their male counterparts. They tend to establish very small enterprises in sectors generally considered, such as the service sector. They prefer areas requiring limited capital investment and hence involving reduced risk, such as renting out property to retail trade, an area in which they out-number men. They are also active in the catering business, where family resources can be used efficiently. They also operate as shop-keepers, though to limited extent. In general it can be said that women prefer setting shop reduced risk and growth—areas that ensure a livelihood rather than high profits. According to survey conducted in 1998 by the Hungarian Small Enterprises Society on the situation of Hungarian entrepreneurs, women are more cautious than men with regard to investments and the size of business enterprises. They are also more pessimistic about the future of the Hungarian economy as well as that of their company (Kallai, 1998: 7).

According to a study on the development of female entrepreneurs (Gere, 1997[10]) business enterprises established by women–mainly in the service sectors and for the development of local potential–facilitate the combination of professional with family life. Creating or expanding a business is very labour-intensive. The educational level of female entrepreneurs is higher than that of the average active wage earner. The majority of the women were formerly employed in the state sector, a status that they exchanged for entrepreneurship. The hypothesis that entrepreneurship is the most important means in fighting unemployment proved to be unreal. But the shock of job loss was one of the most important motivating factors of employees to become entrepreneurs. More than 50 per cent of all women wage earners became entrepreneurs in the wake of the high threat of unemployment (Gere, 1998:7).

One of the largest problems facing potential female entrepreneurs is their lack of resources. Between one-third to two-fifths of the respondents did not have the means available required for running a business (Table 17). The majority of female entrepreneurs established their business based on their professional skills and with a minimum of capital and tools.

Table–17

The Main Conditions for Starting Business (%)

Conditions	*Means*		*Means not Necessary*	*Total*
	Available	*Not Available*		
	To Respondent			
Capital	66.2	21.4	12.4	100
Space	52.9	39.0	8.1	100
Machines	40.2	42.4	17.4	100
Professional skills	83.8	11.6	4.6	100
Entrepreneurial skills	58.3	38.3	3.4	100
Orders	35.1	44.6	20.3	100
Clients	45.9	49.0	5.1	100
Suppliers	34.2	35.5	30.3	100
Others	12.1	31.5	56.4	100

Source: Gere, 1997, p. 7.

Ilona Gere presented the study in the course organized for female entrepreneurs within the framework the Match Project (Budapest University of Economic Sciences), 20-21 November, 1997.

Results from different surveys confirm the difficulty in gaining access to sources of credit. Women encounter specific difficulties on this issue. According to my survey of female entrepreneurs, the largest obstacle to the establishment and development of businesses is financing. This results in problematic relations with banks reluctant to grant women credit reserved for what they consider to be high-risk projects. One of the problems facing small and medium-sized enterprises is the unacceptably high amount of security required to cover a business loan the difficulty of obtaining even a small amount (500.00 fornits is equivalent to about 3.800 DM). Women have more of a problem receiving credit as they cannot use family assets as collateral. Companies established by women are therefore undercapitalized, lacking both working capital and bank support, although the respondents thought that the key to success is a high level of capital (40.5%) and a good network of personal contacts (11.2). The majority of women (51.9%) asked for and received support from their families, more than one-fourth (27.9%) from friends (Gere, 1998:14, 10).

Many of female entrepreneurs surveyed had no specific strategy or business plan despite the fact that the majority of bankruptcies are due to insufficient financial planning. Their lack of marketing knowledge makes competitiveness even more difficult (Table 18) Members of partnerships were in a better situation in the respect.

Table-18
Distribution of Women According to Marketing Activity (%)

Marketing Activity	*Sole Proprietors*	*Partnerships*
Thoroughly weighed the business chances	14.4	27.4
Investigated what is expected	28.2	29.8
Did not because of confidence in success	25.0	23.7
Did not think it would be necessary	16.2	9.3
Did not because this was the sole possibility	16.2	9.8
Total	100	100

Source: Gere, 1998, p. 8.

According to 82 per cent of the respondents, their lives completely changed after starting up a business. However, 60 per cent of the women surveyed claimed that the division of labour within the family had not changed. One-fourth of the women said that they had sole responsibility for households chores (Gere, 1998: 15, 16).

Needs of Women-owned SMEs

In Hungary there is no affirmative action programme for either women or men entrepreneurs, despite the fact that affirmative action contains formal efforts to enable women and ethnic minorities to overcome past patterns of discrimination. This lack of protection of entrepreneurial interests, especially with regard to women and minorities, limits their opportunities for equality in society and in the business world. The American affirmative action model could serve as a good example to decision-makers on how to assist women and minorities (Knzma-Koncz, 1999).

There are different means and methods for assisting female business owners and women starting up their own business.

- It is essential that they gain access to financing: through special grace periods, though better information, through networks of banks willing to finance small entrepreneurial projects.
- It is important to develop a system of specific allowance, loans, or starting capital for companies set up by women. Special grants and loan guarantee facilities should be created.
- It is necessary to set up a network of women entrepreneurs supported by government funding.
- The administrative paperwork required to establish new enterprises and run them has to be simplified and made more efficient.
- Information and training and should be promoted by providing businesswomen with better information on financing and counseling. Special instruction should be offered on self-employment.
- It is indispensable to strengthen the influence of institutions who represent entrepreneurial interests to policy-makers.

Education Level and Qualification of Women

In recent decades the educational level of women has increased significantly all over the world: in Hungary it approaches that of men. In 1996, 27.4 per cent of all women and 23.6 per cent of all men and aged 18 and older had completed secondary school (Table 19).

Table–19
Distribution of People by Educational Qualification and Gender as of January 1, 1996 (%)

Population	*Women*	*Men*
Of the population		
– 10 years old and older with no schooling	0.5	0.7
– 15 years old and older, completed at least eight grades of primary school	67.7	64.9
– 18 years old and older, completed at least secondary school	23.6	27.4
– 25 years old and older, completed third-level education	8.2	7.0
Total	100	100

Source: Central Statistical Office, 1998, p. 38.

The picture is even more favourable when the employed segment of the population is taken into consideration, since here women achieve higher levels of education than men. In 1997, 40.3 per cent of employed women and 27.3 per cent of employed men had completed at least secondary school (not including three-year apprenticeship schools). More women in the workforce had third-level degrees (16.4) than men (14.1%) (Table 20). However, there is a large discrepancy between the proportions of active women income earners with a college degree (54.4%) and university graduates (38.7%). There were significant differences by generation: the educational level of young women exceeded that of men.

Table–20
Distribution of Active Income Earners by Highest Qualification and Gender, 1997 (%)

Qualification	*Women*	*Men*
Less than eight grades of primary school	0.9	1.0
Primary school	24.2	19.1
Apprenticeship school	18.2	38.6
Secondary school	40.3	27.3
Third-level education	16.4	14.1
Total	100	100

Source: Central Statistical Office, 1998, p. 38.

Their relatively solid educational background could be expected to create favourable conditions for women in the labour market. But educational achievements do not readily translate into skilled or professional occupational achievement and economic security for Hungarian women. The majority of blue-collar women are semi-skilled and unskilled workers (Table-21).

Table-21
Composition of Employees by Status in 1997 (%)

Status	*Women*	*Men*
Skilled worker	16.3	47.3
Semi-skilled worker	17.2	17.6
Unskilled worker	11.4	8.1
Non-manual worker	55.1	27.0
Total	100	100

Source: Central Statistical Office, 1998, p. 79.

According to my calculation, more than three-fourths of the men possess some kind of skill compared with only 44 per cent of the women. Girls typically choose to attend grammar schools (two-thirds of all grammar school students are girls), while boys tend to continue their education in apprenticeships schools (nearly four-fifths of those enrolled).

There is a marked segregation by gender within the various occupations. In 1997, 91.3 per cent of the students of textile manufacturing in the apprenticeship schools were girls; of those, 98.1 per cent were studying wearing apparel manufacturing. Of the male students, 77.5 per cent were learning a trade. At the vocational secondary schools, girls composed 91.9 per cent of those studying nursing, 80 per cent of those studying to become postal workers, and 74.2 per cent of those studying to receive commercial qualifications. At the third level of education, women occupied the following courses of study: primary school education (96.4%), special education (92.7%), elementary school education (87.8%), secondary education (71.0%), and nursing (92.2%). (Central Statistical Office, 1998: 229) The segregation by gender in the school system follows the segmentation of the labour market and lays the ground for and reinforces the feminization process.

Income Differences

Women receive 50 to 80 per cent of men's wages everywhere in the world. Earning and income differences can be analyzed from two different points of view:

- where women are situated in the income hierarchy.
- the amount of the income difference for persons occupying the same position and performing comparable work.

Most women hold jobs at the lower levels of the income hierarchy. While the earnings of three-quarters of women are below average, this is the case for only one-third of men. In 1989, white-collar women in the textile industry earned 55 per cent if the salaries of their male counterparts, for blue-collar women the rate was 67 per cent. The gender gap tended to decrease, and by 1998 women's gross incomes were 73.3 per cent of those of men in manual jobs, and 63.6 per cent in non-manual jobs (Table 22).

Table–22
Income Differences by Gender in Hungary
(by Average Gross Income), 1998 (%)

Enterprises by Size	*Less than 30,000 HUF*		*More than 100,000 HUF*		*Avg. Gross Income % of W/M*
	W	*M*	*W*	*M*	
Less than 11 employees	72.3	67.6	5.4	5.3	90.8
Less than 51 employees	65.0	60.1	4.8	5.0	91.1
More than 51 employees and public sector together	24.0	14.6	5.4	13.9	76.5
More than 300 employees	13.9	6.51	7.3	28.5	79.9
Public sector	37.8	35.1	3.6	10.4	83.7
Total	32.1	28.5	5.1	11.1	82.3
Manual workers	52.9	33.4	2.2	9.7	73.3
Non-manual workers	17.3	16.1	17.0	40.5	63

Source: Calculation on the basis of the Central Statistical Office, 1998c, pp. 12-70.

Owing to their objective position, their restricted possibilities and to the persistence of tradition, women's wage and incomes lag behind those of men throughout their professional careers. In addition, the differences become more pronounced with the time spent working. Both objective factors—such as the quantity of the work performed and its requiring vocational skills, the structure of female employment—and subjective factors—such as discrimination against women, the value placed on jobs–find expression in this discrepancy in income. The current wage scale system place higher value on men's capabilities, and wage differences compensate them for their undoubtedly poor working conditions and acknowledge their knowledge and experience. However, trraces of earlier distinctions still survive in public opinion and workplace collectives, and often even women themselves are inclined to overestimate men's work-in their role as breadwinners–compared with women's work.

The Feminization of Professions

The expansion of women's employment is accompanied in the long term by two opposing tendencies. On the one hand, women are taking on increasingly more jobs previously reserved for men (masculine jobs), while on the other hand, more and more professions are becoming feminized (feminized jobs) as a result of women's mass inflow into the workforce. In the end, the scale of feminization depends on when which tendency becomes dominant in female employment and with what force (Koncz, 1987).

Segregation by gender and by profession is a significant characteristic of the labour market. Most of the typical women's and men's professions are closed, which means that entry is limited for members of the opposite gender. Professional mobility between labour market segments is primarily a one-way process: while women are moving towards masculine careers, the opposite rarely occurs. This phenomenon creates and stabilizes the feminization is a counter-selective mechanism, which finds expression in prestige loss and the relative wage disadvantage of feminized jobs. This repels those with a better labour-market position, *i.e.* men, giving further momentum to the feminization of employment.

The proportion of women employed in feminized sectors[11] has increased since the beginning of industrialization (the first stastic stems from 1891: 88.1%) when in 1949, the trend changed (42.8%), after which the scale of feminization rose until 1990 (65.5%).[12] At this income earners worked in feminized sectors, 76.9 per cent of their male counterparts worked in masculine sectors (Knoz, 1994).

The equilibrium-creating function of female employment is not confined to the fact that the female labour supply adjusts itself to the prevailing demand for labour, as is usually assumed and discussed in the relevant literature. Female labour plays a significantly more important role in the transformation process of the employment structure.

Technical, economic and social development is accompanied by the continued transformation of the employment structure. In this process, which continuously renews itself, new skills and new occupations are born and old ones are transformed or cease to exist. Professions are assigned modified levels of prestige. Working people in better labour-market positions (men) can apply–with a chance for success—for jobs associated with higher social prestige.

Males and females are regrouped in part by new entrants to the workforce, in part by the reallocation of employees. The better average possibilities encourage the more mobile workers-men-to change jobs. The preconditions for mobility are better for men than for women. A greater proportion of men are skilled and usually possess specific job qualifications, enabling them to meet the higher requirements of modern technologies. Many of them participate in on-the-job training, further education and retraining measures; they are less burdened with household obligations, are less reluctant to take on work farther from their place of residence, and are more inclined to break away from what they are accustomed to and adjust to new circumstances. Women, however, few of whom have professional qualifications, often enter the world of paid employment directly from the household and do not take on work far away from thir homes; it is professions with less favorable working conditions that offer the highest opportunities for employment. This is why for lack of a better solution, women move towards such jobs.

Changes in the employment structure are transmitted through labour market mechanisms. As a result, the sectors employing a relatively large proportion of women offer less than average wage and income conditions. And the other way around: The feminization of a profession begins when following technical, economic and social change, the social prestige of a given profession begins to fall. It can be proven that the deterioration in the quality of occupations offering less favorable conditions and losing their prestige begins to make itself felt, which is also noticeable in the long run.

Occupational segregation is maintained by the labour market mechanisms transmitted and reinforced by socialization processes. Occupational employing a large proportion of women-feminized careers—are conceived and fixed in social consciousness as occupation destined for women from the outset. Socialization transmits and reproduces the values established in the course of the divison of labour, which are realized in practice by the career orientation of girls. Hungarian and international experience show that even despite intensive promotional efforts and vocational guidance, the majority of girls tend to choose occupations traditionally considered feminine.

Up to until the transformation of the former communist countries, feminization was a one-way process: as a consequence of the expansion of female employment, more and more professions became feminized. These professions lost their prestige and failed to attract male employees. After the regime change, with the extension of the market economy the demand for some professions increased significantly (*e.g.* professions in the financial and banking spheres), which led to the retaking of their prestige. The salaries and prestige of this profession began to rise and men began to become attracted to these—formerly feminized—professions. This tendency confirms the functioning of the labour market mechanism discussed above.

Combining Work with Household Duties

In past decades, the mechanisms of the economy provided incentives for the unlimited expansion of employment with the consequence that within a brief period of time, the dual-income family model became the norm. The socially organized sphere coerced full-time employment, shaped into reality by the need to earn money. With that, both adult members of the nuclear family were removed from the household for the major portion of the day.

Neither the socially organized nor the domestic sphere has adjusted to the altered conditions. Even today, workplaces operate as though there were in "invisible infrastructure" continuing to uphold the functioning of the household in an unchanged way. Organizations are still structured according to the needs of the male laborer working full time, with complete energy subordinated to the requirements of workplaces. The operating hours of the service sector are also not adjusted to demand, but operating according to a uniform scheme with an eight-hour workday. Organizations have not adjusted to the concrete circumstances and requirements of the dual- income family.

Under such circumstances, the balance between the social and household spheres, which had supported one another in the past, has collapsed, the result of which is that neither sphere can fully satisfy the demands made upon it by the other. The most important consequences have been that with the increased tension involved in the coordination this dual task, the socially organized sphere has become inefficient, family relations have become disharmonious, numerous social functions are unsolved, and disturbances to the socialization processes are increasing.

Women play a primary role in reproduction and for this reason, the spread of female employment is doubling their work burden. To enable them to adequately perform both the work required by reproduction and paid employment, society must create conditions that permit them to be reconciled: child-care facilities, mechanized household and organized services to facilitate housework. The social division of labour, which requires that women play two roles, means that most women carry too great a burden to participate actively. Considering they spend communting between home and their jobs, many women work 12 to 14 hours a day. The two roles– both of which require being, "on the job" full–time can only be accomplished at the expense of a woman's free time and by her neglecting the role she plays outside the home.

Hungary does not provide women with the adequate support system necessary for them to fulfill their double social role. The economic necessity to full-time work ties women to the workbench or the desk for more than eight hours a day. Other conditions that hinder women from reconciling their two roles include the lack of choice between paid work and domestic work, the lack of flexible working hours for women with small children, the lack of assistance with household chores, and high prices. Although the mechanization of households has greatly increased over past decades, the decline in living standards has meant that people cannot readily replace outdated appliances.

The most important precondition for female employment is help with child-rearing. Mothers are entitled to 24 weeks of maternity leave at full salary. After this period, in accordance with a system introduced in 1985 and later withdrawn by the former government, women were able to take advantage of a wage-adjusted (65-75% of their salaries) child-care allowance if they remained at home. The new government is reintroducing the system. Following a child's second birthday, a mother drew a flat-rate child-care allowance that varied according to the number of children. The second allowance was significantly lower than the first. Either the mother or father was eligible for both allowances after the child's first year. The former government transformed this into an income-dependent system.

After a child reaches three years of age, the role of the institution becomes more important. In 1997, 9.6 per cent (1980: 14.8%) of all very young children went to a crèche; 87.4 per cent of those children eligible spent the day a pre-school. The conditions of institutional child-care are worsening: crèches and pre-school are being forced to close down for financial reasons. For school-aged children, afternoon day-care centers for the hours parents are still at work play an important role, especially for young school-children. By age 14, however only 27 per cent of all school-children attend day-care center after school; 39 per cent are without supervision–latchkey children, alone at home or gathering in the streets or in subway stations. The decreasing living standard prohibits some families from paying for their children's mid-day meal at school. Milk actions sponsored by the SOROS Foundation or local communities are temporarily helping to alleviate this problem.

Over the past decades, the entry of women into labour market has been a particularly asymmetrical process. Although the majority of women joined the labour force, their responsibilities within the family were not reduced proportionately. Men did not assume as equal share of the work required in the family and the household. Women spend three times more time each day looking after their children and working in an around the home as men do. In the past, tradition has inhibited the transformation of the division of labour within the family. A large part of female work—according to my calculation: 40 per cent of their work cannot be measured, is not the remunerated, and is not reflected in statistics. The slowly developing democratization of the family was later halted due to economic stagnation and the deterioration of living standards. Because of decreasing incomes, men have recently been compelled to work overtime—that is if they are even given the opportunity to do so. Household work and child-rearing have consequently again become the primary responsibility of women. This situation has been reinforced by the conservative view of Hungarians regarding the division of labour within family. Public opinion still holds that the traditional division of labour between the genders is related to differences in women's and men's abilities.

Consequences: The Perspective of Female Employment

It can be seen from the nature of the tasks listed that employment policy can only succeed within a coordinated system of social, demographic, education and family policy, the focus of which must be the social reproduction of the population and efficient use of available labour potential. In a market economy, the employment of women (and of men) is first of all determined by the labour demand. In order for employment to adjust to the demands made by the economy and not come conflict with equal opportunity for the genders, a flexible employment system is required, one which is capable of adjusting with the least amount of tension.

This requires the bi-directional development of female employment.

(a) It is crucial that the possibility and conditions for choosing between work within and outside the socially organized sphere are created through the development of a system of diverse sources of income and social benefits, which will result in a redistribution of labour between the social and the household sphere.

A real possibility of choice assumes-ensuring the possibility for socially organized work for those who want it and a more co-ordinated system of conditions required for these job possibilities (schooling, retraining measures, child-care facilities, service network), depending on the number of children in the family, alleviation of the material pressure to seek paid work through welfare policy measures that provide effective support to families with children than is done currently, approaching a true possibility of choice.

(b) The extension of flexible forms of employment (for both genders) will help in the redistribution of labour in keeping with the demand of the economy and the family. This requires flexible forms of employment, an elimination of prevailing barriers, and satisfactory interest on the part of both employers and employees. It is necessary to emphasize the discriminatory nature of part-time jobs: they reinforce

the segregation of the labour market and are generally characterized by low status, low levels of remuneration, limited promotion opportunities, and low levels of social security.

(c) Unemployment is an inevitable concomitant phenomenon of the market economy, and labour market policies should continue be made to alleviate unemployment. It is important than the trend towards early retirements is halted.

Creation of the pre-conditions for making alternative choices between employment and household, as well as between concrete forms of employment, along with the flexible shaping and regulation of conditions in line with economy demand make it possible for employment to simultaneously adjust to the current labour market and family demands, thus creating an objective basis for the coordination of women's double task.

NOTES

Central Statistical Office (1994): Kepviselojeloltetek 1994-ben. (Candidates for MPs in 1994.) Budapest, p. 84.

Central Statistical Office (1998a): Magyar Statisztikai Evkony, 1997. (Statistical Yearbook of Hungary, 1997), Budapest.

Central Statistical Office (1998b) Magyarorszag munkermerlege. (Labor account of Hungary), Budapest, p. 42.

Central Statistical Office (1998c): Jovedelmaranyok a nemzetgazdasagban. (Ratio of incomes in national economy.) Budapest. August, p. 145.

European Commission (1997): Eurostat Yearbook '97. A statistical eye on Europe 1986-1996, Office for Official Publication of the European Community, Luxembourg, p. 512.

European Commission (1998): Equal Opportunities for Women and Men in the European Union. Annual Report 1997. Directorate-General for Employment, Industrial Relations and Social Affairs, Office for Official Publications of the European Community, Luxembourg, p. 140.

European Commission (1999): The Future European Labor Supply, Office for Official Publications for the European Community, Luxembourg, p. 56.

European Commission (1999): Employment performance in the Member States. Employment Rates Report 1998. Office for Official Publications of the European Community, Luxembourg, p. 28.

Employment 2002. The Future for Women. A documentation of the EU-Conference September 3-4, 1998. Ars Electonica Center Linz, 1481.

Frey, Maria (1997): Nok a munkaeropiacon. (Women in the labour market). In: Szerepvalitzasok-jelentes a nok helyzeterol. (Change of roles. Report on the situation of women, 1997). TARKI, Equal Opportunity Office, Ministry of Labor, Budapest, pp. 13-34.

Frey, Maria and Gere, Ilona (1994): Reszmunkaidos foglalkoztatas -a kihasznalatlan lehetoseg. Part-time employment -the unutilized possibility. Kozadasagi Szemle (Economic Review) No. 9. pp. 784-800.

Gere, Ilona (1998): Vallalkozo nok a mai Magyar tarsadalomban. (Female entrepreneurs in the resent Hungarian society.) Manuscript. 17 p. Management Training Co-operation in Hungary: Training course for female entrepreneurs. Budapest, 20-21 Novembern 1997.

Inter-Parliamentary Union (1992): Women and Political Power. Survey carried out among the 150 National Parliaments existing as of 31 October, 1991. Series "Report and Documents" No. 19, Geneva, 191 1

Koncz, Katalin (1984): A reszmunkadidos foglalkoztatas elmelete es gyakorlata. (The theory and practice of part-time employment.) Budapest, September 1984, Karl Marix University of Economics, Department of Labor Economics, p. 338. (Manuscript).

Koncz, Katalin (1994a): Hungarian Women's Political Participation in the Transition to Democracy. In: Barbara J. Nelson and Najma Chowdhury ed. Women and Politics Worldwide. Yale University, New Haven & London, pp. 347-360.

Koncz, Katalin (1994b): A bovulo noi foglalkoztatas ara: a palyak elnoiesedese. (The price of increasing female employment: the feminization of professions.) Tarsadlmi Szemle (Social Review), Vol. XLIX. No. 8-9, pp. 122-132.

Koncz, Katalin (1999): Nok a mumkaero-piacon a rendszervaltast kovetoen, (Women in the labor market after the regime change.) Munkaugyi Szemle (Labor Review) Vol. XIII. No. 1. pp. 22-27.

Kornai, Janos (1980): The economics of shortage, Publisher: Kozagazdasagi es Jogi Konyvkiado, Budapest, p. 658.

Kozma, Blanka-Katalin Koncz (1999): Pozitivi diszkriminacio tapasztalatai as Egyesult Allamokban. (Experience with affirmative action in the United States.) Munkuygi Szemle (Labor Review) Vol. XLIII. No. 7-8 pp. 24-30

Likestillings Radet (1990): Women's Status in Norway, Oslo p. 15.

Ministry of the Interior (1998): Valasztas 98'. (Election '98.) National Office of Election, Budapest, p. 203.

Ministry of Labor (1995): National report of the Republic of Hungary. United Nations Fourth World Conference on Women, 4-15 September, 1995, Beijing, Budapest, p. 72.

Parlmenti Almanch, 1990: (Parliamentary Almanac, 1990.) Publisher: Idegenforgalmi Propaganda es Kiado Vallalat, Budapest, p. 272.

Palamenti Kaidvany, 1994: (Parliamentary Edition, 1994.) Budapest, p. 172.

Roman, Zoltan (1998): Az EU csatlakozas es a kis-es kozepvallalati szektor. (The joining to the European Union and the sector of small and medium-sized enterprises.) Kozgadasagi Szemle (Economic Review), Vol. XLV. No.1. pp. 69-83.

REFERENCES

1. Albania (3.6%), Romania (3.6%), Liechtenstein (4.0%), Greece (5.3%), France (5.7%), United Kingdom (6.3%) (IPU, 1991: 1).
2. The Pearson's correlation coefficient is 0.76 (UN, 1989: 9).
3. Ninety-seven of the Parliaments of 150 countries have filled in the questionnaire compiled by the IPU (IPU, 1992: 3).
4. In the Symposium of the Inter-parliamentary Union of 1989, in which I also personally took part, it was precisely the application of quotas that gives rise to the most heated debate (IPU, 1989).
5. I participated in the elaboration of the report.
6. In Hungary, until 1998, the female working age group was composed of women from 15-54 years; since 1998 this figure 15-56 years. The male working age group is composed of men from 15-59 years. Because the ages are lower than in the Western countries, the comparable activity rates are lower than those of these countries.
7. After the research of Daniele Baroin, 1982.
8. The number of unemployed women is always inaccurate because of their special social role and its effect on their activity. If woman loser her job or completes school, she can stay at home or take maternity/ children leave. This is why a large proportion of women are not included in unemployment statistics.
9. The Equal Opportunity Office brought action against a firm's discrimination practices. The action was successful in principle but not in practice.
10. I took part in the elaboration of this report.
11. Ilona Gere presented the study in the course for female entrepreneurs with the framework of the MATCH Project (Budapest University of Economic Sciences), 20-21 November, 1997.
12. The proportion of women with this sector of these profession is more than 50 per cent.
13. There are no recent data.

6

Women at the Labour Market in Russia

ELENA Y. MESHCHERKINA, MOSCOW

With the lack of stability in the social and economic sphere, gender-related asymmetry of the labour market is becoming more and more evident in post-reform Russia in the late 1990s. As in many other nations, the gender-related inequality in Russia's employment sphere stems from both long-term movements and current trends.

The situation of females in the Russian labour market seems to be made up of a combination of existing objective trends in the domains of employment, unemployment, labour mobility, occupational skills and experience, income, and, to a greater degree, of more specific factors, such as employment motivation, reproductive issues/behaviour, social and psychological adaptation to new labour relations, and finally, gender stereotypes.

Objective Trends Characterizing the Situation of Women in Russia Society

Social and demographic data (if no other reference, in this chapter all dates from: Bulletin, 1998): The population in Russia in 1997 totalled 147.1 million, women making 78.1 million, or 53.1 per cent Birth-rate dropped between 1991 and 1996 by 26.5 per cent. At the same time, the share of women in their fertility age increased by 2.6 per cent (1991: 36.0%), representing worsening demographic reproduction processes as the population responds to the general bundle of social and economic problems.

About 31 million women are employed at the labour market, that is 47 per cent of the total number of employed. Employable women (16 to 54 years old) make ca. 40 million. Women from 30 to

49 years old (86% of the total) account for the highest level of employment[1]. The number of employed women of this group increased steadily from 1992 to 1995, while the total number of employed women fell slightly (Table 1).

Table-1
Percentage of Employed Women and Men in 1992, 1994 and 1995

	Women		*Men*	
Year	*Total*	*Age 30-49*	*Total*	*Age 30-49*
1992	48,6%	57,1%	51,4%	54,7%
1994	47,2%	61,8%	52,8%	56,6%
1995	46,7%	62,4%	53,3%	57,4%

The level of education of working women in higher than that of men: 52.3 per cent of all employees with a higher education are women. They make up 57.5 per cent of those with a secondary vocational training. 14 per cent of employed women, compared to 20 per cent men, do not have a complete secondary education.

It is difficult to estimate the exact number of unemployed in Russia because different agencies measure with different methods, which are additionally influenced by their ideological attitudes about the basic problems of the labour market. The statistics for the second quarter of 1997 indicate that 9.5 per cent of the total number of employees in the national economy are unemployed, 3.2 per cent of them officially registered as such (Statistical Revue, 1997, p. 69).[2] In 1997, the number of officially registered jobless women came to ca. 1.3 million, which is 13.3 per cent less than in 1996 (1.5 million). The ratio of registered unemployed women compared to the total amount of officially unemployed, however, has increased from 63 per cent to 64 per cent.

The rate of unemployment growth rural females exceeds that of women in urban areas. Within the total number of registered jobless women in 1997, the per cent of rural females has increased from 28 per cent to 28.2 per cent. The percentage of unemployed women in rural areas is estimated at: Bouriatia (78%), Tratrstan, Adygeha (76%), Bashkortostan (74%), Karachaevo-Cherkessia (70%), Kalmyika (67%), Tyva (65%), Lipetsk oblast (74%), Stavroprl and Altai regions (73%), Primorsky region, Novosibrisk and Omsk oblasts (71%), Kemerova oblast (70%).

As of late 1997, the larger part of rural female unemployed was composed of women with children under age (less than 16 years old[3]) and disabled children (58.2% *versus* 49.9% in town), and mothers of large families (18.9% *versus* 3.1%). Besides the number of children, the major difference between rural and urban registered female unemployed lies in their level of education:

Table-2
Education of Unemployed Women in Rural Areas and in Towns 1997

Education	*Women in Rural Areas*	*Women in Town*
Higher Education	4,1%	13,2%
Secondary Vocational Training	21,6%	28,9%
General Secondary Education	38,0%	32,9%
Secondary Education not Finished	21,2%	9,6%

Female unemployment in rural areas has a more long-lasting nature. As of the end of 1997, the average out-of-job period in Russia was 7.3 months, while for women it was 7.5 months, and 8.2 months for women in rural regions. Those on the dole over eight months made 42.2 per cent of unemployed in Russia as the whole, and exceeded 49 per cent in rural areas.

Nevertheless, the total number of those given employment has gone up. In 1997, for example, the agencies assisted 1.24 million women (52% of the total number of those provided with a job) in finding employment, versus 1.17 million (51%) in 1996. In 1997, with assistance of the employment agencies, 110,000 women participated in retraining schemes. 58 per cent of them have been employed. In 1997, the number of people who turned to employment agencies decreased to 12.9 per cent, but in case of women, this figure made 14 per cent. Over 1.5 million people, including 1 million women, were receiving doles in 1997; an average subsidy per one unemployed made 269,000 roubles versus 170.000 roubles in 1996.[4]

Labour Market and Women's Employment

Recent changes of the women's situation in the labour market occurred against the generally hostile background of the economy in transition. This transition is characterized by drastic drops in production yields, re-conversion process (transformation of the military industry to production of consumer goods), forced economic migration, lack of balance in assessment of labour of different complexity or quality, poor regulation of relations between work force and employers at private enterprises, etc.

One of the key problems of an economy in transition is the need for members of the work force to switch from old jobs to new ones. This turned out to be one of the major market bottlenecks of the 1990s. There was a trend to cut old jobs under the pretext of commissioning new ones, which appeared to be too scarce. The general drop employment continued, primarily in traditional industries. Nevertheless, this was not accompanied by a massive release of human resources. Although worker's wages had been cut subsequently, only few were forced to leave from 1992 to 1996, the per cent of those workers forced to leave, and were registered as unemployed, rose from 25 per cent to 26 per cent (Prokopov, 1998, p. 38). The majority started seeking new jobs and succeeded in finding them through transfers before becoming unemployed. According to experts' estimations, 14 to 17 million people joined the labour market annually in search of a job. Only one-third of them remained unemployed (Prokopov, 1998, p. 38). Those remaining at their factories were limited in their choices due to the absence of alternative jobs. They also faced limitations because of a lack of skills or professional requirements. Some relied on a rapid revival of the enterprises. All these trends were accompanied by under-employment or hidden unemployment. At some light industry factories (so-called "female" sectors) idle periods sometimes exceeded eight months.

Primarily due to a financial inability to carry out employment policies and the consequently ineffective ongoing programmes, some unemployed drafted from the category of officially-registered to informal groups. Another consequence of this trend is that, among the registered long-term unemployed, the number of those unemployed over eight months grew the most. The process of squeezing out people for the labour force and curtailment of employment programmes aggravated the situation of those who encountered major problems finding a job independently and were force to rely on the government for intermediary support at the labour market. As we know, women make up the majority of this category, thus shaping the image of official unemployment. Some analysts believe that it is not so much economic factors that form the level of registered unemployment, but social (*i.e.* mentality, expectation of paternalistic help or support) and demographic (*i.e.* gender-specific) ones (Simagin, 1998, p. 74).

One of the key issues of the employment policy is the reduction of the category of officially registered unemployed, many of whom are being concentrated into a group of long-term jobless. This presents a serious concern for the social group of female unemployed as the real economic situation threatens to freeze the existing women's unemployment and turn women into outcasts at the labour market, even though they have a higher educational level than men. Why does the duration of unemployment and dynamics of inflows and outflows of the unemployed present the special danger of pressing women into marginal positions? Lower outflows from the category of unemployed (due to, for instance, cuts in demand for work force) leads to a higher level of unemployment and longer periods of its duration. At the same time, the inflow of new job-seekers will also result in higher unemployment, although first shortening the average duration of unemployment. Gradually, however, the average duration of unemployment will grow due to a lack of job offers and demand for new jobs, and concentration of jobless in the group of long-term unemployed will become greater. Thus, from 1993 to 1995, the percentage of those women unemployed for over four months grew and finally reached 16.4 per cent-especially in the category of those unemployed over one year, where the amount increased form 9.3 per cent in 1993 to 15.0 per cent in 1995 (ISPEN, 1997, p. 144).

Will women be able to look for jobs independently, with the help of media, private employment firms, or directly through governmental employment offices? Is their employment potential equal to that of men's especially considering those who are long-term unemployed a facing major challenges finding re-employment? If we take as an example the regional experience, *e.g.* Kemerova oblast (Women in the Kuzbass labour market), the answers will not be in support of women.[5] Thus, in 1997, 31,000 women were registered at the Employment Center, including 28,000 with unemployed status, making 70 per cent of the total number of the unemployed; 31 per cent of registered women had been seeking jobs for at least eight months. And although the level of women's unemployment was higher than that of men (3.4% *versus* 1.3% in 1997), women could get access to only one-fourth of vacant jobs and position. The employment officers who review resumes would prefer a man with a university diploma, under 35 years of age, and well behaved. The principle reason given to refuse women so far has been their age—not the age close to retirement, but an age of 35-37, the blossoming time for creative and intellectual talents (Grigorjewa, 1998, p. 38).

The above situation in typical of the converted military industries, as well as of textile and clothing industries and sectors which are mostly female dominated—administrations staff, health-care, culture, education, trade and catering sectors. Territorial immobility in regions such as Ivanovo or Vladimir oblasts[6] only aggravates the unemployment situation. Actual and hidden unemployment found its reflection in the nation's daily life, as people expected close-downs, massive dismissals and loss of jobs. All this resulted in a new kind of labour mobility—that is, layoffs caused by fears that a factory might be closed and personal fired (Kuprijanowa, 1998b, p. 15). The trend took its shape as early as 1993 and became statistically significant: over 50 per cent of the National Institute of Public Polls responders admit a possibility of dismissal and ¼ of them volunteer to change jobs. The highest level of potential labour mobility belongs to the private sector workers. Among the national economy sectors, the above-mentioned female dominated trade and services are leading, followed by social sectors of culture, education, science, crediting and finance. Some workers fear losing their jobs because of close-downs and are ready to leave before it happens: these are chiefly women, the young and aged, who are the most vulnerable at the labour market and are the first to suffer from massive dismissals (Kuprijanowa, 1998b, p. 17).

We have already stated above that women surpass men in their education. Women's employment, however, has a pyramidal structure, and high level of education is not accompanied by an equally high social status. The statistics covering the first half of the 1990s show that the percentage of women-mangers (leading position) made 7.8 per cent, *versus* 10.0 per cent for men. Women professionals (specialists) made up 37.7 per cent *versus* 16.4 per cent for men (GOSCOMSTAT, 1996, p. 11). According to the averaged data obtained in industries with both a high degree for women segregation (as in low-paid budgetary sphere, education, etc.) and a decreasing number of comparatively high paid sectors, it can be found out that among managers, women are four times scarcer than men (Research

Center for Labour Market, 1995, p. 72). In the past, however, there was a general rule that women were the mangers of factories where the majority of employees were women. In female-managed enterprises, the share of women-employees made an average of 82.4 per cent, *versus* 46.1 per cent in male-managed entities (Research Center for Labour Market, 1995, p. 77).

This trend to decrease the ratio of women among managerial staff forms the idea of the so-called "glass ceiling" in women's professional careers.[7] Self-limitation as a response to objective barriers impeding social and professional mobility is also detrimental to other qualities of the female work-force in the labour market. In a sense, skills, education and position in the managerial hierarchy are indicators of an employee's performance, and low quality of any commodity in the market had its immediate effect on its price. Nevertheless, despite a high level of women's professional skills in Russia, male and female labour are not equally remunerated. This is the result of a lower administrative status of women, sectoral difference in payment, and concentration of women in low-remunerated industries. The economic restructuring only widened the growing gap between wages of "female", non-manufacturing sectors and average economic indices. According to the statistics, in the mid-1990s educators were 1.9 times smaller remuneration as compared to those in the fuel industry (ISEPN, 1997, p. 146). The ratio between wages of women and men made 2:3 for a lengthy period of time. In the new economic environment, the average wages of men are 1.5-1.6 times higher than those of women, and their income in general is 1.5-2 times higher (Rimashewskaja, 1997, pp. 35-40).

Among the factors that seriously disrupt the balance between wages and educational level are (in addition to sectoral differences) previous experiences and a form of property of the given enterprise. An analysis of family well-being, based upon many years of monitoring in Taganrog,[8] demonstrates the existence of regular differentiation of men's and women's payment through descriptions of social and physical burdens on a married woman with children (Rimashewskaja, 1997, p. 35). A woman's career interrupted by child bearing and additional unpaid household functions prevent women from participating in the production process on equal terms with men. The career interruption caused by child bearing or maternity leave creates the problem of so-called re-socialization, *i.e.* partial loss of working and communicating skills.

As to entrepreneurship or individual mini-business, these are also mainly male domains, and the difference in income here is even more striking. 45 per cent of entrepreneurs are women and 55 per cent are men, while in the sphere of private mini-business, 40 per cent are women and 55 per cent are men. At the top rank level, the difference is extreme, with 18 per cent women and 88 per cent men (ISPEN 1997, p. 148). The inflow of women into business intensified in 1991-92, when all input and production resources were practically distributed (Maljutina, 1997, p. 56). Gradually, women possessing a certain initial capital and occupational and administrative skills were entering new sectors of the market economy. They were chiefly recruited from the managerial staff of state-owned enterprises, which resulted in two-fold reduction of women—do rectors (from 11% in 1985 down to 5.6% in the 1990s).

According to the data from the Institute of Sociology of the Russian Academy of Science, 18 per cent of the first or the second leading positions in 200 Moscow private companies were filled by women; this twice exceeds the number of women-directors (Chirikova/Krithevskaja 1996, p. 13). According to the data collected by G.P. Sillaste, women accounted for one-fifth of enterprise or farms owners, as well as those engaged in business as an occupation (Sillaste, 1997). The different starting potential, however, of businessmen compared to business women-inertia—generally hampers rapid development of female entrepreneurship.

The nature of work motivation is an important factor when women choose to go into business. Here are some dominant motivations:

- to get an interesting job, promising new experience and new contacts.
- to see concrete and tangible fruit of her work.
- to obtain inner comfort and self-esteem.

The importance of "maternal" motivation for women is not so pronounced as for men: the fourth most important motivation for men, for women—the tenth (Chirikova, 1998, p. 252).

The data could be compared with the motivation of Russian employees in general, women included. Between 1990 and 1992,

Russia society survived a drastic change in motivation for work, reflected in the dynamic data series collected by the Institute of Public Opinion (Kuprijanova, 1998, p. 30). At the time, incomes of 95 per cent of the respondents started to lag behind price rises: 65 per cent of the lag was substantial. As a result, the so-called "instrumental" motivation was formed – that is, working only for money can be traced in nearly all social and demographic sections of respondents, with the exception of the military, law-enforcement officers, diploma holders and managers of all levels, who find their work interesting and important in itself. In 1997, men worked for money 1.2 times more often than women. Almost 2/3 of both men and women insist that their potential is underused as they have such feelings as "passivity, lack of initiative and healthy ambitions". The same majority of responders believe that an increase in payment (they consider payment to be an expression of a negative estimation of their performance) and working incentive does not usually depend on ones personal efforts, but is determined by external reasons only (Kuprijanova, 1998a, p. 32).

These trends, together with many other objective female labour market factors (*i.e.* unemployment, occupational segregation, unequal remuneration, hindrance of social and occupational mobility), testify of abnormal social relations at the labour market. It was not by chance that I. Korel produced a special term, "catastrophic adaptation" (Vershinina, 1998, p. 202), for describing processes of adaptation to new realities and relations at the labour market. The underlying meaning is that few employees can afford dismissal due to an economic necessity or an extreme job deficit. As a result, they have to adapt themselves to the new labour relations even at the cost of ruining their individual set of principles: neglecting law obedience, tax evasion, etc.

Multiple employment appeared to be an economic response to this threat to survival. Its structure often contains irregular and informal employment. More general interpretations of economic activity of a population include formal employment or pension schemes, informal employment (second job or dependence), and social employment (unpaid work or other informal exchange) (Menning, 1998, p. 78). According to the data of the Institute of Public Opinion, in 1997, 15 per cent of respondents (selected through representative sampling) had a second employment. In 1998, the analogous sampling brought in other results: 42 per cent of families with low incomes obtained informal extra earnings, 37 per cent with medium incomes, and 30 per cent with high earnings (Perova/ Khakhulina, 1998, p. 31). In other words, about 35 per cent-40 per cent of the population was moonlighting. And while employees have a higher degree of economic freedom, negative consequences are also evident: heavy load, lack of free time, lack of career development.

It is hard to estimate women's contribution to alternative incomes; it can be done only in an indirect way. N. Menning gives reference to the data that helps identify at least nine sources of additional income to the wages of the family head, normally a man. These are monetary incomes from a country house, pensions, salaries, irregular earnings, relatives' help, savings and rent from an apartment or a car (Menning, 1998, p. 86). Those women on holidays often enjoy additional incomes from harvesting their gardens, random earnings, pensions and relatives' help. All this, in turn, reduces the family's dependency on their main bread-winner and helps them to survive in a changed environment.

Besides economic adaptation, to new relations also poses a major challenge. The most important pre-conditions of the mentioned adaptation catastrophe are: the lack of employment guarantees and protective measure, high labour market intensity and dictatorship of the employer or the government. It also implies a rapid reduction of choices and switching from ideal working motivations to realistic ones (mentioned above-formation of an "instrumental" motivation). The analysis of oral interviews with employees revealed that social institutions fail to protect and defined the interests of deprived hired labour forces at the labour market. It also revealed a poor legal education of both employers and employees. The author believes that market interference into social and labour relations deformed the latter so much that they resemble semi-feudal relationships in combination with the market ones (Vershinina, 1998, p. 201). Nowadays, two thirds of applicants manage to find jobs only through personal connections (Statistics Edition, 1997, pp. 68-69). This is more typical of men than of women. Thus, the corporate and personal connections and some features of Orthodox Christian labour ethics make the emerging relations at the labour market largely archaic.

One of the contributing factors that aggravate discrimination of women are certain paternalistic principles embedded in the existing legal system and reflected in labour legislation. For decades, the Soviet employment policy rested upon various benefits, prohibitions and social regulations that stressed a special status of women. As an example, we can refer to Article 162 of the Labour Code of the Russian Federation that prohibits business trips, night shifts, extra working hours and work on holidays for women with children younger than three years of age. In fact, it is low-income women who get back to work without waiting till the end of their maternity leaves. This legal norm, however, make them a very inconvenient and costly work force for employers. This norm could be non-discriminatory if the prohibition were turned into a guarantee giving a working woman the right to choose whether to use the legislation or not.

We can provide example of the opposite nature: the legal guarantees themselves, without a due mechanism to implement them, reduce their effectiveness to almost zero. Article 16 of the Labour Code prohibits any ungrounded denial to provide employment and "any kind of direct or indirect limitation of rights or establishment of direct or indirect privileges when giving employment in respect of gender (...) as well as other circumstances having no connection to business qualities of workers" (INFRA-NORMA, 1997, The Russian Labour Legislation). Nonetheless, according to independent experts, about one-third of enterprise mangers would prefer to employ male workers (Samarina, 1998, 9.47). In the context of "feminization of poverty, many earlier prohibitions designed to protect women's health, such as the legislation on women's labour in hazardous or dangerous environments, deprive women of the chance to implement their rights in the labour market.

The term "mother and child", widely used in legislation, is also an obstacle to rational placement of labour and human resources, as it sets limitations on inter-family redistribution of functions. According to the standards of the more gender-oriented economy of the International Labour Office (ILO), we should prefer the more fitting terms, "parent" or "working men and women with family obligations," which can be, at least sometimes, correlated with situations where fathers take a "child-care" leave, where they are unemployed or low-paid in comparison to their spouses.

The lack of employment guarantees for women after maternity leaves presents the biggest problem. There are also no legal tools which offer an employee with family duties a flexible form of employment. And as experts stress-although the overwhelming majority of women would prefer to have partial or flexible employment (Samarina, 1998, p. 49), they cannot feel sure they would maintain their benefits and guarantees if they chose this option.

The methodology used to provide jobs descriptions in health-care, education, culture, academic science has proven to be ineffective and often underestimates the complexity of these jobs, thus bringing in elements of discrimination in compensation for women's labour. The high skills of women find no recognition, especially in women dominated sectors, because the existing tariff and qualification scheme do not take into account specific situations of working women. Many experts believe (Samarina, 1998, p. 49) that professional rights and choices of women could be significantly enhanced by applying progressive tariff indices, well calculated basic payment norms for women, qualification exams for women turning back to work after their maternity leaves, mandatory written refusal of employment, etc. It is high time the total legal system be revised with reference to women's employment, as current legal regulations very often come into conflict and support contradictory of egalitarianism and paternalism.

Conclusion

The above mentioned facts and trends related to women in the Russian labour market testify of the evident gender asymmetry. Macro-economic factors (decline in volume of production, default crisis, re-conversion processes), which go hand in hand with the rise of real unemployment, occupational segregation and payment distortions are pushing women out to the marginal positions in the labour market. Nor do the legislation relevant to women's market competitiveness. Women, indeed, have one advantage that is, a higher educational standard. Only a very limited category of managers and entrepreneurs, however, have implemented it to their advantage. The majority of women, traditionally bearing the burden of child and family care, are in an urgent need of social guarantees and legal protection at the labour market. At the risk of oversimplifying, I state that all this adds importance to the question of freedom of choice and guarantees, instead of benefits (which turned out quite numerous) while quitting paid employment. The centrifugal elbowing of women out of the market is taking place against the background of an underdeveloped institutional canvas of social intermediation/partnership at the labour market.

At the same time, governmental employment agencies which seek optimum balance between interests of male or female workers, employers, and the state are themselves suffering form financial problems, which undermine the effectiveness of ongoing programs. Their efficacy, however, could be improved by paying more attention to the phenomenon of long-term unemployment and focusing on prevention of unemployment, for both males and females.

NOTES

Bulletin for the Ministry of Family, Women and Children (1998): N. 2, Moscow.

Chirikova, A. and Krichevskaja, O. (1996): Social–Psychological Problems in Female Business, Moscow.

Chirikova, A. (1988): Women-Enterprise Leaders, Moscow.

GOSKOMSTAT (Ed.) 1996: Statistical Yearbook. Special Data on Women's Situation in Russian Federation, Moscow.

GOSKOMSTAT (Ed.) (1997): Men and Women in Russia. Brief Statistic Data Collection, Moscow.

Grigorjeva, V.(1998): Women at the Labour Market in Kuzbass. In: Man and Work, N. 2, pp. 38-39.

INFRA_NORMA (Ed.) (1997): The Russian Labour Legislation: Collection of New Acts. Vol. 2, Moscow.

ISPEN (Ed.) (1997): Social Consequences of the Market Reforms in Russia. Demography and Sociology Series. Vol. 17, Moscow.

Kuprijanova, Z. (1998a): The Work Motivation of Russia People. In: Public Opinion Monitoring. WZIOM (34), No. 2, pp. 30-34.

Kuprijanova, Z. (1998b): We Change the Work Place. The Labour Mobility in the Russian Federation. In: Public Opinion Monitoring. WZIOM (36), N. 4, pp. 15-20.

Maljutina, T. (1997): Women's Business: Problems, Perspectives. In: Business and Policy, N. 9, pp. 50-58.

Mening, N. (1998): Social Policy, Labour Markets, Unemployment and The Family in Russia. In Universe of Russia. No. 1-2, pp. 71-92.

Perova, J. and Khakhulina, L. (1998): The Evaluation of Income in Unregistered Employment. In Public Opinion Monitoring WZIOM (35), N. 3, pp. 29-31.

Prokopov, F. (1998): Unemployment in the Transforming Russian Economy. In: Man and Work, N. 1, pp. 37-46.

Research Center for Labour Market (1995): Women's Situation at the Reforming Economy. The Russian Experience, Moscow.

Rimashevskaja, N. (Ed.) (1997): Family's Welfare and Health. The Project

"Taganrog-3 ½." Vol. 1., Moscow.

Rimashevskaja, N. and Jakovlev, E. (Ed.) (1998): Russia-97. Social-Demographic Situation, Moscow.

Sammarian, O. (1998): To Make Equal Possibilities for Women and Men at the Labour Market, not only Equal Rights. In: Man and Work, N. 2, pp. 47-49.

Sillaste, G.P.(1997): Social-psychological Portrait of Russian Women. Abstract for the III International Gender Conference "Men and Women – Images and Roles in Change" (October 14th -16th 1997). Moscow . Unpublished.

Simagin, U.(1998): Indicators for the Unemployment in Labyrinth of Evaluation Methods. In: Man and Work, N. 4, pp. 73-75.

Smirnov, S. (1998): The Double Structure of the Employment. The Analysis of Change. In: Man and Work, N. 1, pp. 50-53.

Statistics Edition (Ed.) (1997): Man, Work, Employment. Novosibirsk.

Statistical Revue (1997), N. 3, Moscow.

Vershinina, T. (1998): The Adaptation to New Work Conditions at the Labour Market. In: Universe of Russian, N 1-2, pp. 193-200.

REFERENCES

1. For the statistical dates, which characterize the situation of women in the Russian Federation see GOSCOMSTAT 1996, p. 1. See as well as GOSCOMSTAT 1997, p. 5, where the number of the employed in the group of 25 to 49 years old is indicated as 85 per cent of women and 95 per cent of men.
2. Unemployment levels in Russia are assessed by two agencies: the Federal Employment Service (FES) and GOSCOMSTAT of the Russian Federation. The FES measures the level of so-called registered unemployment—that is, a ratio of citizens who addressed the government's employment agency and got a status of unemployed in accordance with the acting legislation , compared to the economically active methodology with the help if representative sampling (0.1% if the population) against the basis of census or micro-census data. A person is considered unemployed if he or she had no job at the time of testing and a weak afterwards, provided he or she was seeking one. So GOSCOMSTAT comes to 9.5 per cent. As experts note, the level of unemployment in Russia calculated with ILO methodology (Simagin, 1998, p. 73) is 3-6 times higher than the level of registered unemployment.
3. A law guaranties all children up to 16 years subvention from the state.
4. The official statistics for these data do not make more distinctions, *e.g.* between men and women or rural areas and towns.
5. Kemerovo, Kuzbas: important coal-mining areas with high social tension, which increase with each closed coal mine.

6. Ivanovo, Vladimir: areas near Moscow, which are characterized by textile industries with a very high level of female workers. The city Ivanovo is unofficially called "the city of brides."
7. The problems of women's promotion are especially evident in their representation in Administration, in 1997, women comprised ca. 15,000 or 56.2 per cent of the total amount of civil servants. Women's representation at the top rank level is ridiculously small: 1.3 per cent. The biggest share of women representation is found in the senior and junior groups—subordinate structural units, assistants, consultants and advisers. Female civil servants who support Chairpersons of the Federal Legislature make 32.8 per cent. The number of women deputies of the State Duma dropped from 13.6 per cent to 10 per cent. There is only one women among 178 members of the Federation Council. The analysis of employment of female civil servants in the Executive Federal bodies also demonstrates that, although women constitute 55.9 per cent in all officers, they make only 2.4 per cent of the "senior" group and 6.0 per cent of the "leading" group (Bulletin, 1998, pp. 26-29).
8. Taganrog is a typical middle-city in the province, representative of the social processes in Central-Russia, with all its social and economic problems.

7

Professionalization and Gender Hierarchy

ULRIKE TEUBNER, DARMSTADT

Concerning the Inequality of the Genders in the Workplace

When one examines the employment situation of women in industrial societies from a national and international viewpoint, one encounters forms of inequality between the genders, which have remained fixed despite wide-reaching changes. It would assume that the phenomenon of gender segregation in the workplace remains valid regardless of profession or differing social and cultural factors on which the different systems of work are based. For this reason, I begin my comments with a short overview.

A look at the historical dimension shows us that the segregation of men and women in employment can take different forms. Processes of desegregation and re-segregation can therefore be documented. A division of the genders seems to be dominant and remains intact over long periods of time. The forms and the extent of occupational segregation vary within and between different societies. The phenomenon exists, however, in all types of societies irrespective of the qualifications of the relative participation of women in the workforce, of the forms of work typically carried out by women or of the social and cultural provisions of the gender contract.[1]

Several reasons can be advanced for using gender segregation as the basis of an interdisciplinary programme of research in women's and gender studies.

To begin with, traditional efforts to explain gender segregation, such as the so-called theories of human capital or socialization (which are mostly concerned with the individual's possibilities of action in society) or theories based on structuralism, have shown themselves to be inadequate. As a result, it is women economists who repudiate a primarily statistical approach and demand an increased emphasis on research-based, interdisciplinary methods.

The institution "work" is of particular importance in this context. Occupations and professions cannot only be see as a collection of regulated tasks and necessary qualifications. They also represent one of the societalization institutions in which division of labour, social structure, job categories and gender norms come together.[2]

To summarize, the nucleus of gender segregation can described as follows: despite equal qualification, women and men hold different positions in all occupations and professions. In addition, they continue to be unequally represented in the different professions. One can therefore easily miss the characteristic role that gender separation and exclusion play in employment if one only looks at the area of so-called horizontal segregation. It remains true that equally qualified women doing the same job are paid less than male colleagues and that salaries in those professions dominated by women are lower than in those traditionally occupied by men.

It cannot be taken for granted that segregation based on gender is decreasing proportionally to the percentage of women gainfully employed, nor does it seem to be disappearing in response to a workforce of equally qualified men and women. In addition to already existing and continually emerging new gender-specific boundaries within and between profession, there is dimension of gender-based division of labour which has remained virtually unchanged despite women's new job orientation and life styles: almost without exception women have continued to be solely responsible for housework and shield-rearing.

It remains to be determined under what conditions boundaries between the genders continue to impose themselves and why these divisions are basically hierarchical in structure (Gottschall, 1995, Wettere, 1995; Teubner, 1992).

Researchers agree that present explanations of the function and stability of gender segregation have been proven inadequate. This is particularly true of so-called supply and demand oriented models, which are based on real differences between the genders, such as the qualifications they bring with or their occupational interests or career goals.

It will be necessary to expand the prevailing gensis of the discussion and to formulate the goals of the investigation in such a way that the multi-dimensionality of the phenomenon "segregation" is taken into account (cf. Hakim, 1996). In this context, a comparative model, despite the difficulties involved, would seem to be most promising, since it offers the chance to avoid over-emphasizing national configurations in the respective employment systems and differing social factors which influence forms of work. A whole series of questions to be investigated present themselves if one takes into account the fact that the simultaneous existence by the organization of employment, but also by the entirety socially influenced divisions of labour.

This should not be misunderstood as a new attempt to limit the work of women to the areas of home and family, which for a long time was characteristic of prevailing explanations. Along those lines, for instance, the prescribed responsibility of women for housework and family was made synonymous with a limited interest in a career. On this basis, it was not difficult to interpret the forms of segregation as an expression of women's supposedly different career wishes and work history. Citing in this manner a division of labour according to gender as an over-arching organizational principle in societies contributes to a consolidation of existing conditions. Both approaches are, accordingly, circular and ideologically motivated.[3]

Both models have long since been proven wrong in empirical studies. In view of the fact that young women in Europe, and in the last analysis, also in the Federal Republic of Germany (which is in last place in this regard), have succeeded in qualifying themselves, it is necessary to finally take leave of all those theories which attribute the inequality of the genders in the workplace to the assumption that they are "unequally endowed" with the necessary qualifications. At glance a altered patterns of behaviour, whether viewed from a national or a European perspective, shows us that the postulate of a uniform, female-lifetime work history has become untenable. It is women more than men who take control of their own lives and go beyond the standard biographies (which take on different forms in each country) of men and women.

Concerning some Challenges Offered Comparative International Studies

We find in the literature different suggestions about how the extent of gender segregation can and should be measured. It can be said against the dissimilarity index (already developed by Duncan and Duncan in 1955) and similarly constructed indices "that neither the DI nor the index of segregation nor any other single number index are appropriate for cross- national comparisons" (Hakim, 1996, p. 70).

The dissimilarity index measures the percentage of women or men who would have to change their occupation in order to achieve a proportionally equal distribution if the genders across the range of different professions. We generally speak of segregated occupations when their male or female practitioners constitute less than 20 per cent or (for the latter) 30 per cent of the work force. Particularly Catherine Hakim (1996) criticizes the misguided attempt to explain the extent of inequality present in a society by using a tool of measurement based on a single index, especially when the totality of the labour market is used to measure the extent of gender segregation. She suggests using instead "occupation" as a basis and classifies the different occupations as either male-typed, female-taped, or a so-called integrated occupations.

Even when "occupation" is taken as a basis, however, methodological problems cannot be avoided. The extent of identifiable segregation is obviously dependent on the choice of the items analyzed -- that is, on the way the occupations or professional activities are classified (cf. also Heintz *et al.* for example 1997, p. 16f.). A look at the International Standard Classification of Occupations (ISCO) show a clearly that the resulting variation is considerable, not to mention that the respective national classifications of occupations are often no more than rough estimations. When the extent of segregation can only be identified on the basis of the kind and number of categories of occupations and/or professional activities, the classification must adequately differentiate between occupations. The smaller the number of categories chosen, the greater the tendency to underestimate the extent of segregation.[4]

As a result, we can only recommend that professional activities be classified with as mush attention as possible to the elements which distinguish them from each other. In addition, the extent to which the respective systems of employment differ must always be kept in mind. Unfortunately, comparable data is not available for all countries (cf. Anker, 1998).

When Catherine Hakim (1996) suggests differentiating between segregated and integrated occupations in all future studies, it is because of the hopes in this way to prevent overlooking or systematically underestimating the extent of vertical segregation.

A look at only a few occupations with differing gender membership makes immediately clear to what extent gender itself, as an independent or as a causative factor, structures the differing access to gainful employment enjoyed by women and men is responsible for the amount of unequal opportunities within the different occupations (cf. Willms-Herget, 1985: Teubner, 1989; 1992; Wetterer, 1992; 1995; Cyba, 1993).

At the same time, it is impossible to overlook what kind of structures we are dealing with here. For the purpose of illustration, I cite here several studies, who completed their training at the same time, and who went to work full-time. The results show that at their entry into the labour market, women were already earning considerable less than men. In the course of time, the unequal income distribution tended to increase to the detriment of the women. This phenomenon was observed in all occupations, irrespective of where it was a question of a male, female, or so-called mixed occupation. The results reported by the author of a 1996 study of graduates, which included a random selection of 1, 780 men and women from different area of the natural sciences and engineering (Minks, 1996), show that the gross monthly income of the female graduates lay substantially under that of the male graduates. To the surprise of the author, this was also true of the women in the applied sciences, even when only those working full-time were included in the comparison (Minks, 1996).

Although the hierarchical importance of the category "gender" cannot be overlooked, there is a certain resistance to including gender as an independent structural category in employment. It has been some years since G. Engelbrech confirmed in his summary of the existing literature that there can be seen on all "levels of qualification and in all periods of life a considerable amount of gender-specific occupational segregation" (1991, p. 549). This can't be explained by recourse to human capital theories nor by arguments from research on socialization. He proceeds instead from the assumption that institutions and structural factors are responsible for differing professional opportunities for men and women. These are particularly worthy of note—for example, a study should be made of developing tendencies in occupational gender segregation, particularly in sub-groups with comparable qualifications at their entry into the workforce. The role of institutional and structural factors can only be examined in connection with the different stages of work histories at which the normative control factors, which regulate gender hierarchy, come into effect.

Before turning to these factors, I want to indicate a few points of reference concerning the phenomenon of gender segregation in employment.

The lines of demarcation between the genders can only at first be characterized as horizontal or vertical. A closer look shows that they must always be seen as hierarchical. The occupations and spheres of women's activities hold considerable less status and prestige than comparable male occupations. The ranks of the pre-requisites and level of qualification in a profession is not unconnected to the question of where men or women practice it. Accordingly, processes linking gender to work, which express a symbolic correlation between the two, are always processes of status distribution.

The latent or obvious contempt for jobs done by women makes no exception for professional careers which are clearly assigned to women and the activities practiced are gender coded, such as social work, health-care, education and similar professions.

The dividing lines between the genders in employment take on different forms. They exist between and within professions, and can even be found in those professions which are known as mixed. These professions are an illustration of the fact that even in cases where there is an approximate parity of men and women in a field, forms of segregation between the genders are present. Even in mixed occupations, the different activities assigned to men and women are subject to gender stereotyping, just as in male and female occupations. The term mixed occupation is in this regard misleading.

I would like to point out here an important different between men and women working I occupations not considered appropriate for their gender. Men in minority position in a female profession are no more hindered in their career advancement than in mixed or male profession. As a result, the relative placement of men in a female occupation is no different from the traditional hierarchical gender patterns within male or so-called mixed professions.[5]

Particularly interesting for an analysis of gender segregation are the processes that affect the gender composition of occupations and the resulting change of norms. Processes of de-and re-segregation occur under different constellations, as the following example suggests.

Once a previously male profession becomes a mixed and not a female occupation, the predominant pattern can be seen as one of integration through segmentation. Women and men in the profession work in different segments, whereby the assignment of segments is based on either formal, vertical hierarchy or on areas considered to have a different intrinsic worth. It follows that when both women and men work in a profession, we very often find that the kind of work the men and women do is differentiated by use of such labels as autonomous versus supervised, flexible *versus* prescribed or complete *versus* fragmented.

The boundaries are not always drawn according to these simple criteria, but in case, the different areas of work are given a corresponding symbolic value on an implied value system, which ranks men high and women below them. After each job segment has been coded male or female, the male segments are considered to covey more status and prestige and are more likely to lead to promotion then the female ones.

This does not necessarily mean that the proportion of highly paid jobs within a profession is larger in a male occupation. It is precisely in the numerically smaller group within mixed occupations that, according to C. Hakim (1996), a large proportion of highly paid occupations can be found. But, again, it is the men more than the women who profit, because these occupational segments show as unequivocal gender-based hierarchy.

The only requirement that defines gender-coded work is that men and women do not work in the same areas. There is only one factor that determines what type of separation of activities (and the gender-linked symbolization associated with them) is involved. This factor is that males and females work separately and are organized separately. If the segmentation is already more or less complete, or if it is a question of so-called female or male occupations, each profession and sector becomes symbolically tied to elements of traditional gender concepts and stereotypes. These signal the particular aptitude of men and women for the activities assigned to them.

In this context, it is fitting to present a series of intercultural comparisons. Even in societies with a comparable level of industrialization and living and working standards, professions can be associated with different gender stereotypes. I cite one current example: whereas in the various engineering and scientific fields in Germany, the study of architecture (including interior design) attracts a large percentage of women and has received the corresponding gender linked label, in the United States, it is considered to be an exclusively male profession, in which women can only find acceptance with difficulty. On the other hand, mining and metallurgy are considered in the USA to be more suitable subjects of study for women than architecture.[6]

This example is a good illustration of the fact that explanations for various forms of gender segregation cannot be found by looking solely at the job system and its internal structures nor solely at the system of gender norms. It promises to be rewarding, however, to study the function and the inter-relationship of structuring processes and differentiation in case of occupations which change their gender affiliation. Drawing boundaries between the genders in employment is complex. Each from of spatial or temporal division (gender-specific assignment of separate working hours) is symbolically coded according to the various forms given to the differences between the genders. Whatever, the symbolic content given to these differences (which also varies greatly and is therefore susceptible to adaptation), this process takes place within a two-gender system. It would be possible, in this context, to ask oneself which mechanisms are responsible for the harmony of form and content. Processes which link gender to work have also been studied as processes of a continuous re-thinking of the differences between the sexes.[7] As a result, processes of professionalization are always processes fronted with a dominance-difference system (Conrel, 1999), whose mechanisms will have to be studied in order to analyze the phenomenon of segregation.

When women and men remain to a large extent among themselves in the workplace, it often seems as if the reason for this is that the work in question were particularly appropriate for the one or the other gender. As soon as the genders are compared directly to each other, however, without first comparing their separate areas of work, the real extent of the inequality in career, income apparent (cf., for example, Engelbrech, 1991; Teubner, 1992; Wetterer, 1993, Willms-Herget, 1985; Heintz, 1997).

Social Inequality—The Social Structuring of Work

It follows that it should be the main task of a study of segregation to give a theoretical framework to the relationship between gender as a structural category and as a symbolic category, and from this starting point to develop questions for further study. Despite all possible temptation to do so, the status-assigning function of the category "gender" should not be reduced to differences (actual or objective present) within the demands and patterns of job activities. These have to be seen in perspective. As examples of approaches which do not do this sufficiently, I could mention those theories (Whatever basis they give their arguments), which postulate the total incompatibility of a normal female personal biography with qualified work, as well as all approaches which expect women to have a particularly well-developed critical view *vis-à-vis* supposedly male oriented career paths.

A recent example of this kind of view point is represented by those who put their hope in the new forms of organizing and structuring work, which are being discussed particularly in connection with new information and communications technologies. To the extent, so the theory goes, that work structures which are adapted to the normal male worker fade away, the objective reasons for excluding women from areas of qualified work also change. In this way, the argument continues, the objective reasons for women's limited ability to compete for qualified positions no longer apply. There are those who go even farther and claim women will have advantages over men with the advent of more flexible forms of work and working hours, since women, due to their extensive experience of combining housework and career, have particular talents, whose true value will then be recognized.

I would like to suggest that these approaches also be studied empirically on an international level, and that they be concentrated with an approach which focuses on the normative expectations for women and men, which, up to now, have always been based on a socially constructed binary constellation. Gender separation is then one social practice, which sets up and maintains gender differences (Lorber, 1998).

Because gender is a factor of social and symbolic structures in all areas of society, as well as in all work institutions, it is important to analyze the relationship between the forms of gender structuring, positioning and symbolizing of work. It is also necessary to verify the conclusions reached with the aid of empirical studies (Lorber 1994; Wetterer, 1995; Heintz, for example 1997; Anker, 1998; Gosttschal, 1995; Beckmann/Engelbrech, 1994).

Concerning the Relationship between Hierarchy and Difference

One objection to the theory of dominance, according to which the relationship between the genders has a hierarchical structure and the category "gender" accentuates this hierarchy between the genders, is that is lacks theoretical complexity.[8] The principal criticism is that this theory under-handedly introduces a collective subject—women and men—which can (no longer) be found in the real world of men and women. In my opinion, this theory overlooks the fact that the hierarchical distance between the genders can take on many different forms, and that social gender has a complex inner structure. Consequently, the theory would be quite capable of registering fine distinctions in the male group and the group of women.

The question to what extent the dualistic differentiation of the genders provides the basic controlling mechanism for the creation and reproduction of gender hierarchy in employment can only be answered against the background of different forms taken by the lives and working lives of women. Expressed more paradoxically: it is only since women have been seen to step out of the framework of normal female life histories that the real extent of statistically unequal treatment has become visible. Similarly, an explanation must be found for the co-existence of equality and inequality of treatment.

It follows form the above that the gender-coding of work has an intrinsically variable and flexible nature and that it takes place in a highly selective way, that it screens out and distorts elements of social reality. As a result, it is no longer necessary to take into account those explanations that attempt to relate gender segregation to social forms of a division of labour by recourse to intrinsic similarities between housework and women's work outside the home. Instead, I will discuss mechanisms of differentiation in their role as providers of symbolic meaning for hierarchies. "The genders must first be separated, set apart from each other in their cultural differences, before their relationship can take shape in the sense of of above/ below, higher/lower, etc." (Tyrell, 1989, p. 67).

The symbolic differences between the genders must be seen as pre-condition for their placement in a hierarchical relationship to each other. In order to explain the inter-relationship hierarchy and difference, it is necessary to take a look at the nature of the difference involved. It takes the form of dichotomy and has, therefore, a disqualifying effect. "Maleness" and "femaleness" as symbolic constructions are mutually exclusive, are exact opposites of each other. Because of the construction method, the distinction becomes a qualitative difference (Luhmann, 1988; Wetterer, 1993), and this difference, conversely, ensures that any and all hierarchical structures can be used for the purpose of exclusion.

It is of particular importance for the study of segregation to refer to the mechanism responsible for the construction of gender differences. Processes which link gender to work take place, as has been discussed above, on two different interrelated levels. On the one hand, it is a question of the hierarchical position of men and male jobs in relation to women and women's jobs that creates a division, and, on the other hand, it is the definition of the differences between the genders for each specific occupation (cf. especially Gildemeister/ Wetterer, 1993; Wetterer, 1993; Teubner, 1995). It would seem that in times of upheaval and change in the world of work of new form of segregation between the genders can always be found.

Evidence for the fact that it isn't the substance of gender differences that is responsible for the forms of gender segregation is furnished by the already mentioned example of occupations which change their gender designation. This phenomenon is a perfect illustration of how inner corelations between job activities and gender membership is symbolically postulated.

Not all occupations which seem to us today to be typically female have behind them a similar history. On the contrary, some of them began as typically male occupations and remained so far a certain period of time. This is true, for example, for the professions of teacher, hairdresser, secretary and book-keeper.

A more recent example of an occupation which has experienced a change in gender assignment in the USA is that of real estate broker. Here, a well-known pattern led to the opening up of a profession previously practiced by men and stereotyped as male.

After men moved into other areas which promised to be more profitable, vacuum was created, which was then filled by women. As women moved into the profession, a process of rationalization set in, which seemed to have the goal of emphasizing the particular aptitude of women for that kind of salesmanship, provided that percentage of men versus women stays flexible. Both genders take part in this process in that both see in themselves in and in the opposite gender the appropriate aptitudes. The way gender is viewed on a day-to-day basis by those involved runs approximately as follows: since women have entered the profession and practiced it successfully, then it must be because they are particularly knowledgeable in the areas of home and family, and because they are capable they are capable of tuning into the real needs of their clients in finding just the right thing for them. As a male profession, the job of realtor was always thought to require a certain amount of aggressiveness. The emphasis was put, especially by men, on the competition inherent in the job. Even the act of selling called up comparisons to battle for instance, when one talked of bringing the client to the point where a deal could be closed, would be worth one's while etc. (cf. Leinder, 1991; Lorber, 1994).

It is clear that not only the interlocking of career and gender behaviour is almost exclusively imaginary, but also that so-called boundary work plays a role, especially in the more open areas of work, areas in which new cards are being dealt to the genders. Arlie R. Hochschild (1983) has studied the professional behaviour strategies of female and male flight attendants in this context. She found that both, through doing the same job, are forced in the performance of this job to express their gender membership as dissimilarity.

An example of the opposite tendency—the increasingly male image of an occupation and its increased exclusivity as such-can be seen in the field of computer science during the last fifty years.

The extreme shown in the gender stereotyping of these jobs is not only true for the examples given and does not apply only to gender-linking in job activities performed. Thus, the norms for work done by women are seen in connection with women's responsibility for housework and child-rearing and made synonymous with regular working hours or the opportunities offered by part-time employment. This stereotype completely ignores the fact that in large sectors of women's work, it is neither a question of regular working hours, as, for example, in the area of nursing and health care, nor of work schedules that encourage the combining of career and family, as in sales jobs.

The annals of newly emerging jobs and professions, which reflect traditional gender hierarchy and existing gender stereotypes in their job descriptions, are very revealing in connection with this issue. Here, I will briefly discuss the history of computer science.

Even though, in the beginnings of computer science over fifty years ago, it was a large number of qualified women, mostly mathematicians, who had to perform the task of programming the then new machine "computer", it is difficult today to find a trace of them in the history of computer science. With increasing professionalization, the job of programming has become gender-linked. Today, it is to large extent coded male, even to the point that the image of the male hacker is considered to be synonymous with esoteric rites practiced in many computer science departments.

Of course, the programming done today is different from that done by the women mathematicians of fifty years ago. It's just that this difference cannot be equated with the difference between a monotonous, subordinate activity and a creative, analytical or intellectual one (which is an often encountered stereotype of female work in comparison to male work). After programming concepts and invented programming languages (cf. Hoffmann, 1987; Becker-Schmidt, 1992; Oechtering, 1995).

The example offered by the beginnings of computer science also shows that we cannot assume that linear processes are responsible for the breaking up of gender barriers in employment. Even when there is a minority group of qualified and innovative women working in a field, this doesn't mean they can consolidate their position. Female pioneers can only to a limited extent find successors. Conversely, an increase in the number of women in a field not previously occupied by them is in no way a guarantee of social integration. This seems to be mainly dependent on the way in which the entire professional system and the hierarchy among professions as a whole develop. If more men crowd, into these professions, well-known processes set in-processes of banishment, exclusion of women, and a cutting off of the genders from each other.

In my opinion, one approach that promises to provide an explanation for forms of gender segregation has been developed by

Barbara F. Reskin and Patricia Roos (1990) (cf., for example, Reskin, 1994). Their approach has the advantage of being compatible with a constructivist view point, and in that way allows institutional and interactive parameters to be seen in relationship to each other. B.F. Reskin and P. Roos see women's possibility of access to occupations and jobs as an interaction of two queues, each in which members of the workforce are interested and for which they can offer the necessary qualifications. On the other hand, there is a rank of applicants whose relative placement is dependent on normative factors set by the employers.

The inter-relationship of these two queues shows us a whole series of conditions or circumstances which are responsible for processes of increased exclusion and segregation or conversely of desegregation and re-segregation. In general, this approach provides a systematic framework for the documentation of over-representation of men in promising occupations as well as changes in the relative strength of the genders within occupations.

Taking as a starting point the fact that employers in new, expanding fields tend initially to look for male workers, it follows that women will only have chance in these fields when there is not a sufficiently large number of male applicants for the positions available. That this window of opportunity only remains open for a certain amount of time has been shown by a number of studies.

It has been some years since A. Willms-Herget (1985) came to the conclusion that the opening up of a male occupation is more likely in fields that are on the wane, that in expanding fields, the tendency is to close the doors to women rather than to let them in according to B. Reskin (1994), the ranking within the labour queue is particularly based on gender. The accepted gender stereotypes and normative gender roles of the employers influence the structuring of the ranking. Furthermore, loyalty to male employees on the part of male employers determines the ranking of waiting applicants. Sufficient examples can be found which illustrate both these phenomena.

Again according to B. Reskin, a productive disruption of the functioning of these two interrelated ranking systems will occur when, for example, employers are required to demonstrate their lack of gender prejudice in the filling of capacities. All in all, the approach seems to be promising as the basis for intercultural case studies, which in their turn could deal with a whole series of further factors such as national forms of the gender contract and the socio-political conditions which affect female work.

Angelika Wetterer (1992, 1995) has examined in depth the difficulties connected with the basic structure of a hierarchical gender difference and its roles as a more or less integral part of segregation in the workplace. She not only comes to the conclusion "that in processes of professionalization, processes of status distribution based on gender hierarchy are always included " (Wetterer, 1995, p. 19), but also states that similarly motivated segregation processes play a role in lending support to the supposedly pre-ordained nature of the bi-polar gender classification. They not only serve to lend a certain plausibility, but in addition, they bestow acceptance and legitimacy. Whether forms of segregation are also an expression of women's men's pursuits and plans or not is accordingly dependent solely on the dual construction of each difference between the genders.

Symbolism of Gender Difference–Reality of Gender Difference: not without the Participation of those Concerned

If we take a look at gender segregation, it would seem to be the case that the saying "when two people do the same thing it isn't, after all, necessarily the same," hits the nail on the head.

Taking the self-perpetuating nature of gender hierarchy as a reference point, one could turn one's attention to the question of the tenacity of this continually self-renewing simultaneity of hierarchy and difference, whereby the hierarchy serves as the structural constant and the differences between the genders, and in gender-coded work, appear an aspect of modernity (Hagemann-White, 1984; 1993).

In this context, one could turn one's attention to the question of whether social change could lead to break-up of the relationship and changes of the mutual inter-dependence of gender separation, gender hierarchy and gender differentiation.

Although in general it can be assumed that both men and women contribute to the transmission of hierarchy and difference, research shows us that the contributions of the groups concerned must be weighted differently.

It has been shown in several studies that it is men more than women who want to make sure that the dividing lines between the genders in employment remain in place (cf. Tyrell, 1989; Wetterer 1993; Teubner, 1995; Knapp, 1995; Heintz, 1997).

In a recent study of the employment fields nursing, administrative assistance and computer science, Bettina Heintz (1997) has come to the conclusion that in each of these three fields, the drawing of a double boundary line usually originates with the male practitioners. "Male boundary work takes place especially in areas where men have to fortify their position: where men are in a minority or where women have achieved access to new occupational fields or positions" (Heintz, 1997, p. 244).

One can, however, do without this tool for setting up barriers in cases where career paths are clearly structured, for instance when we come up against the phenomenon of the glass ceiling.

G. Axeli Knapp (1995) also clearly demonstrated that the genders react differently to their difference. And several years previously, H. Tyrell (1989) had already attributed the stronger need of men to set themselves apart of desire to preserve gender hierarchy. It follows that it is related to hierarchical ambitions and is based on a need to prove one's superiority (Tyrell, 1989, p. 68)

When as in the system of gender segregation -visible differences is linked to status, then it stands to reason, reports Angelika Wetterer (1993), that the dominant gender is given the role of emphasizing the difference or takes this role on itself.

Above, all the unequal sharing of housework takes on the function of symbolizing the difference between the genders beyond all women's acquired job qualifications, career plans and all recent rhetoric on the subject of partnerships. The repeated call for gender segregation researchers to provide a theoretical examination of the total system of division of labour could be followed by considering this aspect. As long as the proof of masculinity is synonymous with the incapability of doing housework, the failure and incompetence in this area of work is nothing more than a self-staged exclusion from the domain of women's work (Hirshcauer, 1993). Presumably, it is not just chance that the birth of a child contributes to the strengthening of the traditionally unequal patterns of division of labour in the family, a phenomenon which has been observed even in Scandinavian societies, which are committed to an egalitarian gender contract. At he same time, it is an example of the way the supposed normality of the difference between the genders can be socially staged.

There is a further group of studies which describes different consequences and forms of the symbolic demarcation of the boundaries between the genders. Women in male professions are confronted with the fact that male colleagues strongly emphasize the differences between them and their female colleagues, whereby, potential parity in the quality of their work disappears form view.

For women in male professions it would seem to be the case that they are required to visibly and unmistakably act like women. The make-up regulations for women in the armed forces belong illustrate this. In general, nothing seems to threaten the interconnected system of hierarchy and difference more than the visible equality of the genders conveyed when an equal value is put on their job activities.

Years ago, G. Rubin (1975) already characterized the comprehensive guiding principle governing the different position of the genders in employment as the sameness taboo. In my opinion, it could also be understood as a competition prohibition. This competition prohibition makes itself felt at the different so-called thresholds on the way to highly qualified occupations. It means that the genders are not allowed to use the same means to compete for the same things. As if by magic, enforces of order do their best, often starting in the preliminary stages, to limit or even completely avoid potential situations of competition between the gender in employment.

It should be possible to examine, by means of intra-cultural research models, the extent to which occupations are segregated according to gender, to what extent housework and the care of family are considered to be women's work, what gender stereotypes for the symbolizing of work are called into play etc. All conceptions of gender difference should not only be analyzed in connection with their content, but also in connection with their historical and structural aspects.

Perspectives for the Future

We can observe, in few words, that is not primarily the factors of qualification and organization of work that determine the different patterns of gender segregation in employment. It is, rather, factors based on the organization of the relations between the genders, on the gender contract and on gender hierarchy.

There emerges, accordingly, a whole series of subjects for study, which could illuminate the different aspects and attitudes of the phenomenon of segregation. In this context, the goal could be to investigate the relationship between division, hierarchy and differentiation in connection with not only various systems of work, labour markets and social systems, but also in connection with the organizing principles behind the relationship between the genders or the gender contract, and in this way to also cover the importance of gender norms and stereotypes. This presupposes a multi-dimensional research model-offers the advantage, however, of insights which would transcend prevailing limitations. Bringing into play the difference between the genders—so runs thesis being presented here-legitimizes over and over again the division of the genders, the question remains of where and how women can take the formation of these processes into their own hands, thereby benefiting their own career interests and positions. A point of depature could be experience made dealing with institutionalized barriers, whether in connection with family and job or with access to management positions, among other things.

REFERENCES

1. The term "gender contract" was coined by Scandinavian researchers to describe the gender-segregated division of labour. It includes several levels—a structural component, a workplace and a family component (Gunnarsson, 1998). It is similar to the concept of gender relationship, which expresses the gendered social order in a given society.
2. Here I leave the confines of traditional sociology of occupations. Looking at the institution "employment" from the perspective of a system of labour division based on gender and the forms of gender symbolism opens up an approach to the analysis of gender as a structural category in employment, which promises increased insights.
3. The ideological nature of previous explanations is a result of how the prescribed role of women as workers in the private sphere is translated into individual and collective attitudes and actions of women. I am not going to discuss here the bi-polar system of gender as a hierarchical system or the dual system of gender as a social category resting on a supposedly natural basis (cf., among others, Hagemann-White, 1984, 1993; Lorber, 1994).
4. I agree here with Anker (1998) that, especially in comparative studies, the occupational classification with the highest degree of

differentiation should serve as a basis for the study—that is, no one-digit classification should be used.

5. This is further point that argues against the distinction between horizontal and vertical segregation and consequently, also against the theory that gender-linked income differences are the result of horizontal segregation and that the structural effects for gender refer to the context of the work done by the women and that done by men.
6. In this context, it is question for identifying, with concrete examples, the deciding factors for women's access to each occupational and profession. Based on the above remarks, it follows that several aspects will pay a role here. In this way, the fixed framework of opposition which applies to the work done by men and that done by women will be broken up on all levels. The example is taken form Schwartz-Cowan 1987.
7. When in this article the term sex is used it connotes a physiological and biological category which is socially constructed as gender is too. (Lorber 1994: IX)
8. This is especially the criticism of B. Heintz *et. al* (1997), whose research results, however, support the theory rather than disprove it. The advantage of the dominance theory, in my opinion, lies in the fact that differentiation in the male group as well as in the female group can be described without denying the resulting inequality. This is made, however, quite clear in the title "Inequality among Equals."

LITERATURE

Anker, Richard (1998), Gender and jobs, Genf (ILO).

Becker-Schmidt, Regina (1992), Verdrangung, Rationalizierung, Ideologie, in: G.A. Knapp/A. Wetterer (Hg), Traditionen–Bruche, Freiburg.

Backer–Schmidt, Regina (1998), Relationalitat zwischen den Geschlechtern–Konnexionen im Geschlechterverhaltnis, in: Zeitschrift fur Frauenforshung, 3/98.

Becker–Schmidt, Regina/Knapp, Gudrun–Axeli (Hg) (1995), Das Geschlechterverhaltnis als Nurnberg.

Beckmann, Petra/Engelbrech, Gerhard (Hg) (1994), Arbeitsmarkt fur Frauen 2000–ein schritt vor order ein Schritt zuruck? Beitr AB 179, Nurnberg.

Cockburn, Cynthia (1998), Die Herrschaftsmaschine, Hamburg.

Connell, Robert W. (1999), Der gemachte Mann, Opladen.

Cyba, Eva (1993), Uberlegungen zu einer Theorie geschlechtsspezifischer Ungeliechheiten, in: P. Frerichs/M.Steinrucke (Hg), Soziale Ungleichhiet and Geschlechterverhaltnisse, Opladen.

Engelbrech, Gerhard (1991), Berufsausbildung, Berufseinstieg and Berufsverlauf von Frauen, in: MittAB 3/1991.

Fagan, Collette/Rubery Jill (1996), The Dynamics of Occupational Segregation in Comparative Context, in: Beckmann, Petra (Ed.) (1996), a.a.O.

Gildemeister, Regine/Wetterer, Angelika (1992), Wie Geschlechter gemacht warden, in: Knapp, G.A./Wetterer, A. (Hg), Tradiionen - Bruche, Freiburg.

Gunnarasson, Ewa (1998), Telearbeit in Schweden aus geschlechtssepzifischer Sicht, in: EU-Konferenz: Arbeit 2002-Zukunft der Frauen, hrsg.v. Bundeskanzleramt Wien.

Hagemann - White, Carol (1984), Sozialisation: Weiblich - mannlich? Opladen

Haremann - White, Carol (1993), Die Konstrukteure des Geschlechts auf frischer Tat ertappen? In:Feministische Studien, 2/1993.

Hakim, Catherine (1996), Theoretical and Measurement Issues in the Analysis of Occupational Segregation, in: Beckmann, p. (Ed.) (1996), a.a.O.

Heintz, Bettina, u.a., Ungleich unter Gleichen, Frankfurt 1997.

Hirschauer, Stefan (1994), Die soziale Fortpflanzug der Zweigeschlechtilichkiet, in:Kolner seitschrift fur Siziologie and Soziaplsycholgie, 4/1994.

Hochschild, Arlie R. (1983), The Managers Heart: Commercialization of Human Fellings, Berkeley (Ca).

Hoffimann, Ute (1987), Computerfrauen, Munchen 1987.

Knapp, Gudrun-Axeli (1995), Unterschiede machen: zur Sozialpsychologie der Hierarchisierung im Geschlechterverhaltnis, in:Becker-Schmidt, R./ Knapp, G.A. (Hg.) (1995), a.a.O.

Leidner, Raobin (1991), Serving Hamburgers and Selling Insurances, in: Gender & Society, 2/1991.

Lorber, Judith (1994), Gender Paradoxes, New Haven.

Lorber, Judith (1998), Gender Inequality, Feminist Theories and Politics, Los Angeles.

Luhmann, Niklas (1988), Frauen, Manner und George Spencer Brown, in: Zeitschrift fir Soziologie, 1/1988.

Minks, Karl-Heinz (1996), Frauen aus technisch-naturwissenschaftlichen Studienfangen, Hanoover (HIS).

Oechtering, Veronika (1995), Grace Murray Hopper-Die Pionierin der Computerprogamierung, in: Pilz, P.u.a (Hg.) (1995), Forschende Frauen, Mossingen-Tahlheim.

Reskin, Barbara F./Roos, Patricia (1990), Job Queues, Philadephia.

Reskin, Barbara F. (1994), Sex Segregation: Explaining Stability and Change in the Sex Composition of Work, in: Beckmann, P./Engelbrech G. (Hg.) (1994), a.a.O.

Robak, Brigitee (1992), Schriftsetzerinnen und Machinenifuhrungsstrategien im 19. Jahrhundert, in: Wetterer Angelika (Hg) (1992), Profession und Geschlecht, Frankfurt.

Rubin, Gayle (1975), The Traffic in Women, in: Reiter, R.R. (Ed.) (1975). Toward and Anthropology of Women, London, New York.

Schwartz-Cowan, Ruth (1987), The Industrial Revolution in the Home: Household Technology and Social Change in the 20th Century, in: Technology and Culture, 17/1987.

Teubner, Ulrike (1989), Neue Berufe fur Frauen, Modeller zur Uberwindung der Geschlechterhierarchie im Erwbersbereich, Frankfurt.

Teubner, Ulrike (1992), Geschlecht und Hierachie, in: Wetterer, Angelika (H.g.) (1995), a.a.O.

Teubner, Ulrike (1995), Das Fiktionale der Geschlechterdifferenz, in: Wetterer, Angelika (H.g) (1995), a.a.O.

Tyrell, Hartmann (1989), Uberlegungen zur Universalitat geschlechtlicher Differenzierung, in: Martin, J./Zoepfel, R.(H.g) (1989), Aufgaben, Rolle and Raume von Frau und Mann, Freiburg.

Wetterer, Angelika (H.g) (1992), Profession and Geschlecht, Frankfurt.

Wetterer, Angelika (1995), Dekinstruktion und Alltagshandeln, in: wetterer, Angelika (H.g) (1995), Die soziale Konstruktion von Geschlecht in Professionalisirungsprozessen, Frankfurt.

Willims-Herget, Angelika (1985), Frauenarbeit, Frankfurt.

8
Shaping the Future of Work

GISELA NOTZ, BONN

When we talk about labor, what kinds of work do we have in mind? If we want to organize the ensemble of activities that produce and reproduce social life, we must be able to answer this question. And another one, too: For whom do we wish to alter working conditions and on what ideas do we base fantasies about the "future"?

The Private Sphere is Political

On September 15, 1968 during the delegates' conference of the SDS (Socialist German Student Association) in Frankfurt on the Main, a tomato was thrown that was to become legendary: this tomato is considered to have triggered off the beginning of the new women's movement in West Germany. It was thrown out of protest: The male-dominated executive board of the SDS took no notice of a speech given by Helke Sanders in which she accused her comrades of ignoring the exploitation of women through domestic work in families and other living arrangements. Discrimination against women had remained a taboo in the socio-critical analyses of the New Left. Helke Sanders defended herself against the ignorance of the men who took for granted that the female gender had sole responsibility for domestic work and the rearing of small children. And thus the fact that these kinds of responsibilities in the private sphere of reproduction hindered women from engaging in political work on equal footing with men was ignored was well. This was when the maxim "the private sphere is political" originated, which meant that the private sphere is also political and not only political, as it was often later mistakenly interpreted to mean.

The demands made by the "new" women's movement have not been met to this very day. Male scientist and politicians still exclude work performed in the so-called private from their analyses, and their own participation in this work continues to be absent from their dreams and ideas about "the good life."

What is the Future?

And what is the future? Statistically speaking, there are more than four million people without gainful employment in the Federal Republic of Germany. According to the report on young people published in 1997 by the "Jugendwerk der Deustchen Shell" (pp. 15f.), nearly two-thirds of unemployed youths and half of all young people in Germany are anxious about the future. Almost 50 per cent of those interviewed identified unemployment as the "main problem of young people today", a response that became more frequent the older the young people were–regardless of whether they were women or men. Ninety per cent of those interviewed consider the increasing numbers of unemployed a large or very large problem for our society, and more than 88 per cent see this trend as a "problem that strongly impairs my own future." These young people lack a sense of trust in democracy. If it continues to be economized in this way, any remaining perspective they have for their future will be destroyed.

Many of those in responsible positions in economics and politics view unemployment amongst women to be much less of a problem than that amongst men. During their "choice of a career", women are already called on to consider that they have an "alternative role" in the family and that here is where they should primarily seek meaning in their lives.

For most young women, however, being a housewife and rearing children are not real alternative to qualified job training or to gainful employment that secures a livelihood. Today, women in the old German states—the pre-unification FRG—still find themselves in the process of learning that gainful employment in an area of work they can take for granted. Women in the new German states—the former GDR—are steadfast in their desire to be able to secure their own livelihood through paid work. And yet they are being confronted with ideologies aimed at convincing them that the family will lend meaning to their lives. It is therefore no wonder that according to the "Shell Study", women in eastern Germany assess their personal future more pessimistically than their western German peers (p. 22).

And they do so despite the fact throughout history, their have never been so many well-educated and self-confident women in a position to articulate their own interest as there are today.

In the following, I would first of all like to pursue the question of whether occupational society is really running out of work, a claim that continues to be made over and over. I will subsequently ask what work is actually comprised of what problem -solving models are available for overcoming the "crisis" that is so often cited. Finally, I would like to present considerations on what is desirable from the vantage point of women's policy.

Is Occupational Society Running out of Work?

"What lies ahead of us is the prospect of a society that has run out of work, that is: the only activity it is expert at. What could be more disastrous?" Hannah Arendt wrote these words in 1958 (Arendt, pp. 11f.). Certainly she was referring to paid labor that secured a livelihood and was oriented towards specifically male life patterns and moral concepts. After all, labor and occupational society are not currently undergoing a "crisis" because there is not enough to do, but rather because work is primarily understood to mean industrial labor, which serves the manufacture and production of commodities, and because distribution of this labor and influence on the structuring of labor relations remains essentially limited to the male gender.

The decisive question is therefore not whether there is enough gainful employment to allow all human beings to secure their own livelihood, but rather how it is distributed and what value is placed on it.

Furthermore, the rapid cutback in jobs that secure a livelihood is not a "crisis" in the conventional sense. This is because "crisis" suggests that it is a temporary situation that could be remedied with this or that measure, or that—in other words—will eventually settle down into normality. What we are dealing with today is an epoch- making situation of radical change which is perhaps comparable to the situation at the beginning of industrialization. It is not rare that the epoch we are presently living in is referred to as the second Industrial Revolution.

Unemployment is the Most Urgent Problem of Our Time

"There is no social problem more obtrusive than unemployment." This quote does not stem from a current newspaper article, but from one appearing in the "Fliegende Blatter des Rauhen Hauses" from 1897 (Oldenburg, p. 3). Although it will not be examined in detail here, the article cited makes reference to the usefulness of unemployment for the continued existence of the prevailing economic system. What appears important for our purpose is the author's reference to unemployment as a disciplining force for employees. At that time, the unemployment has always stood at 7 per cent. Under no circumstances should it serve as a comfort that unemployment has always been a problem. The economic, technical and cultural progress made since the appearance of the article in the "Fliegende Blatter" more than a hundred years ago has certainly been enormous. Our complaint is that "economic progress" does not benefit all people in the same way: the level of economic activity is by no means automatically accompanied by positive social developments. White its serious consequences for society, unemployment, both then and now, increases the division of society into job-holders and the unemployed, the poor and the rich, the disadvantaged and the better off. The merciless competition for the scarce resource of "gainful employment" leads to the young being played off against the old, women against men, Germans against immigrants, etc. Entire segments of the population are branded as social problem groups. And because employees are made responsible for their own destiny—because they are poorly or wrongly qualified, not flexible enough and apparently not prepared to adapt to changing market conditions—the overall problem is individualized.

What is Work Actually?

The major portion of socially necessary labor still manifests as non-labor; unpaid work in the family and in other private living arrangement; child-rearing; care of old people, the disabled and those in need; work in neighbourhood help schemes, honorary posts, in self-help projects and civil commitment; and subsistence work. Society will certainly never run out of this kind of work, for which women are primarily deemed responsible and which they actually perform, even if this is not taken so much for granted today as it once was. The unequal distribution and evaluation of gainful employment and the one-sided assignment of domestic work and care work to women are central problems in today's society. It is the different value placed on work that leads to women throughout Europe earning 30 per cent less than men. On a worldwide level, women work many more hours than men but have less significantly income at their disposal.

A Career (also) has Priority for Women

The reconstruction of the "normal biography" — *e.g.* uninterrupted full employment from training or higher education until retirement for both genders — requires that men participate in domestic and care work. "Full employment" and a "standard employment relationship", which was designed with men in mind and which assigned them a housewife or "second wage-earner", require a new definition. From the vantage point of women's policy, traditional forms of full employment are therefore no longer even desirable.

"A career has priority for women": This is the result of a recent study carried out by the Zentrum fur Umfragen, Methoden and Analysen (Centre for Surveys, Methods and Analyses) in Mannheim (cf. Statistisches Bundesamt, 1997). This applies for women in both eastern and western Germany. The "provider marriage" model has completely lost its attraction. Under no circumstances will they be content with the role of "full-time housewife", and many men, primarily in eastern Germany, share this attitude. And so now it is women who are made responsible for unemployment. The unbroken (east) and the rising (west) tendency of women to join the labor force is looked upon as a fatal (east) or contagious (west) disease. If this tendency could be turned back to the levels of the sixties and seventies (west), overall unemployment would be less explosive (cf. *e.g.* Miegel 1996, p. 20). However, the wheel of time cannot be turned back. Like (most) men, (most) women strive for an independent livelihood and economic autonomy, and for both genders — with the exception of a few wealthy people — this is only possible through access to the paid job market. Despite the frequently cited "change of values", participation in socially organized labor has more aspects than merely earning money. Work gives life meaning, structures a person's day and expands the human horizon. It provides people with possibility of exercising their rights of codetermination and — if often only in a limited way — participating in decision-making processes at the workplace. Work conveys important social experiences: It is the background for formulation of collective goals; it creates a common ground and in doing so constitutes forms of a person's identity at the same time. Work assigns social status to people, thus is has the function of influencing positions in society (Jahoda, 1983, p. 136).

What "Problem-Solving Models" are Available?

Globalization and location factors are used as argument to justify and kind of deregulation and the reduction of jobs and training measures. And they appear to be welcome diversionary tactics in order to alter our society in a neo-liberal sense and dissolve social consensus.

Part-time Work

The expansion of part-time work is located at the top of the long list of employment policy options. Part-time work does not imply a precarious employment relation per se: High-wage-bracket jobs are unfortunately the least of those "parted", i.e. shared. When propagating part-time employment for the creation of new jobs we may not overlook the fact that this form of employment represents a reduction in working hours without compensatory wage increases (almost exclusively) for women. In the Federal Republic of Germany, approx. 36 per cent of all employed women currently work part-time as opposed to 4 per cent of employed men. Even in the employment wonderland of the Netherlands, 62.2 per cent of all employed women work less than the collectively agreed on working hours—mostly at the expense of an independent livelihood—whereas only 116.7 per cent of the men do so. The situation is similar in Great Britain, where 43.7 per cent of all employed women and 5.5 per cent of the men work part-time. Many women who have small children or persons in need of care at home express the desire to work shorter hours. Due to the lack of a sufficient social infrastructure and in view of women's private obligations, part-time employment is often the only possibility of being employed at all. The lack of an independent livelihood and the reduced level of a person's pension, circumstances associated with low-wage jobs, are disadvantages that cannot be ignored. Of course, this is particularly the case for so-called "marginal" part-time work. A satisfactory solution has still not been found for the conflict surrounding the rearrangement of labor relations not covered by the social security system.

The "Third Sector"

In his book Das Ende der Arbeit und ihre Zukunft (1995), Jeremy Rifkin, a journalist from the United States, warns his readers of impoverishment and lawlessness, which he fears will occur if we do not give the unemployed something meaningful to do. He challenges us to give up our fixation on the market and the state. He place hope in a "third sector" for victims of the second Industrial Revolution that will absorb those workers who have "no value" on the free-market. These people will work in non-profit organizations, community projects, relief organizations and do volunteer work for shadow wages. These are all areas in which women already perform work which is necessary for the reproduction of society, but which is assigned only minor value or none at all.

When Rifkin talks about meaningfully employing the "hosts of unemployed" in third sector", providing them with pocket money in the form of shadow wages and thus preventing them from becoming rebels" driven by fear and rage" (p. 216), the structural problems of the job market are played down to difficulties in adapting: one either belongs to the new elite and is absorbed by the newly created "sector of knowledge", or one is replaced by machines and is no longer needed in the economic cycle.

There is currently no research taking place to examine the reasons why certain technologies, forms of labor organization and business hierarchies lead to a further division between the well and the poorly paid, to the creation of new lower classes, and to the formation of groups that are discriminated against. Thus, these phenomena are absent from public discussion.

Rifkin's model of the "third sector" is only one of many similar models for the future. Because they opt for divided society, almost all of them are based on the continued existence or establishment of social and gender-specific inequalities. This also applies for the concept of "citizen's work."

Citizen's Work

Ulrich Beck (1997, pp. 6 ff) recommends "citizen's work" as a counter-ferment to decreasing gainful employment, for "mothers following maternity leave, for older people in transition from full-time employment to retirement", and also for the unemployed and "young people prior to formal job training" (Kommission fur Zukunftsfragen der Freistaaten Sachsen und Bayern, 1997). Honorary work for people in need could be made economically visible and remunerated through a form of compensation approximately corresponding to welfare. According to this model, this allowance would be paid to those who already qualify for welfare. The unemployed would be required to decide between the remaining unemployed and receiving welfare in the long-term or performing public work in the volunteer sector. In view of the discrimination the unemployed and welfare recipients are subjects to, some of them will have no other choice.

Civil commitment is certainly suitable for reviving an (apparently) lost sense of community. However, this cannot be done at the expense of women's jobs or at the expense of the poor and those on the periphery of society. Without the contribution of honorary unpaid work, 80 per cent of which is currently performed by women, our entire health-care system would collapse.

In this concept it is expressly emphasized that the work is voluntary and that no one will be obligated to perform citizen's work. The "new volunteers" obviously need not anticipate sanctions in the form of a reduction of their benefits if they prefer to define themselves as welfare recipients even after the introduction of citizen's work.

In contrast, other concepts such as *e.g.* the "multi-layer model of work" as developed for the Club of Rome (Girarini, Liedtke, 1998, pp. 231 ff.) speak openly about compulsory work, which is intended for the so-called "first layer". Persons working there perform "productive work" in the range of approx. 20 hours per week and receive state benefits. In the "second year", however, paid work can be performed in the private sector. There are no restrictions on who may work there (provided they are granted access to this sector) or how long. The "third layer" comprises work for one's personal needs and non-paid honorary "volunteer work."

Concepts on the "future" of work stemming from political parties, labor unions or church circles can hardly by viewed as real ideas for reform; rather they are merely vague ideas that seem unsuitable for rescuing the "one world" from social and ecological collapse. All of these models sufferer form the fact that what economies have in mind is solely the production of subsistence goods never the reproduction of life. That would imply asking what we need in order to exist and not what is superfluous or what causes illness and is destructive. And none of the concepts cited here appears suitable for driving forward the abolishment of social and gender-specific inequality (cf. Notz, 1998).

We Need Alternatives

It is high time to counter the dismal progresses that depict a two-thirds or four-fifths society, a shadow economy or a three-class economy with alternatives. The fact is: Gainful employment that secures a livelihood is declining in all of the highly industrialized countries while unpaid work is increasing to the same extent that paid work is being reduced. For this reason it has become urgently necessary to think about concepts beyond the traditional "standard working day" and to find a new definition for the standard employment relationship."

Purely economic or ecological recipes are not sufficient to achieve a fundamental restructuring of society for the better. Above all, we require social concepts counter to the existing ones, namely for the restructuring of all institutions in which work is embedded: business enterprises, administrations, the community, and all forms of private living arrangements. It is certainly becoming more urgent to think about possibilities for activities honoured by society beyond heteronomous wage labour. The people of the future are going to spend and less and less time at their workplace and have more and more "free time" at their disposal. It remains an unsolved political problem whether free time will be compulsory due to involuntary part-time work, unprotected labor relations, domestic work or unemployment, or whether it will result from the redistribution of production growth and be accompanied by shorter working hours in the area of market-mediated activities. The solution will also be dependent on how people defend themselves. After all, they are not only victims of the circumstances, they are active subjects as well.

We Need a New Training Campaign

Responsible citizens are required to be able to develop alternatives and then to act accordingly. For this reason we need a new training campaign that is suitable for qualifying women and men to articulate their interests together and to develop their potential for contradiction and resistance. It is an issue of the formation and support of critical social authority that puts people in a position of critically analyze industrial, societal and economic reality and the distribution of resources and goods, and to assume "social responsibility" (Lempert, 1993, p. 178). And this implies the "ability for self-determination" (Ulrich).

However, collective strategies for action only develop if people formulate common political goals, if they, in words—learn to take a political stance. Learning concepts that aid in achieving this would have to emphasize that caring for other people as well as being a parent are important tasks for both women and men, but that the meaning of life can also be found outside of family tasks for both women and men, but that meaning of life can also be found outside family relationships. This multi-dimensional orientation presupposes certain abilities: *e.g.* the examination of traditional gendered role patterns and normative assignments of priorities. These kinds of qualifications are still not conveyed by general education, vocational training, or by political education. We need them in order to deal with ourselves, our environment and other people without losing out upright carriage or sticking our head in the sand. They must be acquired in a lifelong process of learning, and they can be learned-but also forgotten-just like reading, writing and arithmetic.

A Holistic of Work

For the future it will be necessary to give up restricting our understanding of labour and economy to paid labour. This means directing out view towards work as whole. Simply extending the notion of work to include domestic and care work will not be enough. People form large and small factories, from administration, the "new self-employed", people from shadow, alternative and local economies as well as from the domestic economy and honorary posts must be included in concept developments and strategies for action. And the concepts for action will not only have to be direct towards employment-creation measures and working hours, but also towards the humanization and democratization of work, its structuring with regard to content and organization, and towards the usefulness of products and services. For the future the issue is socially necessary and meaningful work in all areas of production, service and private reproduction. This means that we cannot simply redistribute the existing stale cake, rather we will have to bake a new one. We will probably have to shake up the whole bakery. We have to rethink with whom, for whom and under what working conditions and with what resources and to energy we want to bake, even a cake a made entirely of organically-grown ingredients can be baked under inhumane working conditions that cause emotional and physical illness. A small factory designed according to the criteria of humane working conditions can become an apparatus of destruction if it produces weapons of war.

We will also have to think about alternative ways of arranging domestic work so that the emancipatory efforts of women with higher salaries does not occur at the expense of women who are compelled to work in precarious employment relationships under conditions of personal dependency as cleaning women or servants (cf. Notz, 1997). The division of work according to gender hierarchy will not be resolved by means of such a "redistribution"; on the contrary, new low-income substrata and hierarchies will emerge (also amongst women).

Reevaluation and Redistribution of Work

Concepts on the future of work from the vantage point of women's policy require that the quality of work necessary for the reproduction of society be reestablished and its quantity redistributed. Redistribution is necessary in several directions: we need an increase in ecological investments as well as in investments for the more humane organization and structuring of work, equal distribution of paid and unpaid work to both genders, a redistribution and of societal wealth, and social transfers into the poor regions of the world. The following also belongs to a different and better way of economizing: Women may not be forced to have to choose between the family and a career because work outside the home would mean that children are not sufficiently looked after or the care of family members in need is not guaranteed. Talk of women as "second wage-earners" must also be rejected as conservative and misogynous discourse.

Work in all areas should be reactivated as a place where communication and cooperation, social participation and opportunities for acting in solidarity are fostered. Even citizen's work and work for one's personal needs do not correspond per se to these conditions. Without differentiating wage levels, it seems questionable to discuss the reduction of working hours solely in connection with wage concession. Because they are primarily employed in the lower wage brackets, women would be forced even further below the subsistence level and be subject to poverty in retirement. What does a hair stylist or a supermarket shelf packer have left if they concerned their wages? As it is, they do not net more than approx. DM1, 200 a month working full time. For this reason, what must be discussed is a wage policy based on the idea of solidarity (as in Sweden). Within the scope of such a policy, employees in the higher wage brackets (primarily men) could accept certain restrictions in favour of improving the financial position of those currently employed in the lower wage brackets.

The pre-condition required for the redistribution of work and responsibility to both genders is a radical reduction of working hours in the area of full-time employment (six-hour day). However, a reduction of working hours alone will not be enough as it could leaf to men producing more domestic work in their free time while compelling women to perform more. On the other hand, if it is accompanied by a redistribution of unpaid work it would mean that a women's working day is shortened. That this could mean the extension of a man's working day can hardly be avoided. We must not lose sight of the duel-objective: On the other hand, it is necessary to guarantee all people work that is both meaningful and secures a livelihood and which they can accept. On the other hand, everyone, independent of gender, class or ethnic membership—should be able to develop a multitude of social skills: skills in the household, in the areas of care work, culture, art and politics, and in the community. In any case, an economic system can only earn the label "social" if it creates conditions that enable the dismantling of the hierarchical division of labor, above all between the genders, and the weakening and dissolution of social inequality.

Different community-oriented industries at regional levels, alternative business projects, or communal living arrangements in which people join together to improve their lives and strengthen their possibilities all point the way ahead.

It is necessary to develop concrete utopias for the much cited "good life" and to fight for their realization. Finally, it is a question of the opportunity for women and men to participate in all facets of life. This cannot be achieved without criticizing the organization and control of the societal work process and the distribution of what has been obtained. The mere promise of reducing unemployment by half by the year 2000 is worthless. "The only solution for approaching the unpredictable is to make promises and simply keep them" (Hannah Arendt, pp. 11f.). Concrete utopias for another way of economizing cannot remain issues that are postponed again and again. If life on this planet-also for our children—is be guaranteed, then the time has come to make an immediate beginning.

LITERATURE

Arendt, Hannah (1958), The Human Conditions, Chicago, quoted in vita active (1994), Vomtatigen Leben, 8th edition, Munich, pp. 11f.

Beck, Ulrich (1977), Was its Globalizening?, Frankfurt am Main.

Giarini, Orio & Liedtke, Patrick M. (1998), Wie wir arbeiten warden: Der neue Bericht an den Club of Rome, Hamburg.

Jahoda, Marie (1983), Wieviel Arbeit braucht der Mensch? Weinheim.

Jugendwerk der Deutschen Shell (1997), Jugend 97, Opladen.

Kommission fur Zukunftsfragen der Freistaaten Bayern and Sachsen (1997), Erwerbstatigkeit and Arbeitslosigker in Deutschland. Entwicklungen, Ursachen and Mabnahmen, Parts I, II & III, Bonn.

Lempert, Wolfgang (1983), Moralisches Denken, Handeln and Lernen in der betrieblichen Berufsarbeit, in: Buttler, F., Czycholl, R. & Putz, H. (eds.), Modernisierung beruflicher Bildung vor den Anspruchen von Vereinheitlichung and Differenzierung. Beitrage zur Arbeitsmarkt - and Berufsforschung, Nurnberg, pp. 178–200.

Miegel, Meinhard (1996), DEr ausgefranste Arbeitsmarkt, in: Die Zeit, 9.2.1996, p. 20.

Notz, Gisela (1991), Du bist als Frau um einiges mehr gebunden als der Mann. Die Auswirkungen der Geburt des ersten Kindes auf die Lebens - and Arbeitsplanung von Muttern and Vatern, Bonn.

Dies (1997), Wi(e) der die Ruckkehr der Dienstbotinnen - gesellschaft, in: spw (97), pp. 18-24.

Dies (1998), Die neuen Freiwilligen. Das Ehrenamt - Eine Antwort auf die Krise?, Neu-Ulm Oldenberg, K. (1897), Arbeistlosigkeit, in: Fliegende Blatter des Rauhen Hauses, Hamburg, April/May.

Rifkin, Jeremy (1995), Das Ende der Arbeit and ihre Zukunft, Frankfurt am Main/New York.

Statistisches Bundesamt (ed.) (1997), Datenreport 1997, Bundeszentrale fur politische Bildung, Schriftenreihe, vol. 340, Bonn.

9

Work and Gender: A European Perspective

DR. B. RATNA KUMARI, INDIA

The European Union recognizes equal opportunities for men and women to be at the heart of the reformation of the labour market. Member states have committed themselves to equality for the sexes at the workplace. This should be accompanied by the adoption of a gender mainstreaming approach to improve employability and encourage adaptability of businesses and employees, to reduce the disadvantaged status of women at the workplace.

Gender discrimination and gender inequities, embedded in the psyche of populations across the globe, and has started attracting serious attention from policy-makers in several countries. The term gender is closely linked to the pattern of women's employment/work and to their disadvantaged position in the labour market. However, the percentage of women in the labour force in developing countries is rising, although still smaller than that of women in industrialized market economies, at 31 per cent versus 60 per cent in OECD countries in 1990. In the European Union, women have achieved equality in social development indictors like literacy and health. However, it is an established fact that gender equality has not yet been achieved in the labour market even in the European Union.

This paper reviews four studies by research teams on work, time, pay and gender in a European perspective and observes that the results of the studies on time and work, both paid and unpaid, waged, greater employment flexibility and the reorganization of working time gave a largely pessimistic picture of current trends, although some advances have been made. The study also discusses the Vienna summit, which reinforces the approach to equal opportunities based on bench-marking and gender mainstreaming.

According to the report of the Commission on Equal Opportunities [EU 1999], the unemployment rate of women is higher than that of men in all member states (except in Sweden and the UK). In the Union as a whole, the pool of inactive women aged 25 and over is larger than that of women in employment (72 million against 63 million). Important barriers remain for women who want to integrate into the labour market, which remains largely segregated by sex. Sixty per cent of all employed women work in six of the 60 NACE (2-digit) classification sectors and over 40 per cent in just three (health and social services, education and retailing). Almost all part-time workers are women.

Recent data collected by Eurostat (statistical office of the European Commission) on the earnings of women and men show that the gender pay gap remains wide in all member states. The hourly pay of women employed full-time is on average (except in Ireland, Austria and Portugal) 27.5 per cent lower than that of men. The gender gap ranges from 12 per cent in the new German land (the former East Germany) and 17 per cent in Sweden, to 31 per cent in the Netherlands, 32 per cent in Greece and 34 per cent in the UK. In the other EU countries, except Belgium (18%) and Luxembourg, the gap is between 22 per cent and 29 per cent (*Ibid.*, p. 2). On the whole the available data indicate that the EU is no exception to gender bias at the workplace.

Flexible Working and Reconciliation

During the past decade, job flexibility has been put forward as one of the cures for the EU's employment and economic ills and as one way of achieving the Union's objective of equal opportunities for women and men both in their private and professional lives. According to Diana Persons (1997) job flexibility has been expanded to all member states of EU, and women are overrepresented. Women form 83 per cent of all part-time workers, 70 per cent of family workers and 50 per cent of temporary workers. The report says that though there were *"potentially positive and progressive features associated with this form of working, it cannot be assured to contribute towards equal opportunities except in the rudimentary way of increasing the entry of women into paid work."*

Research done is Spain, Greece, the UK, Germany, France and Sweden on the retail sector shows that job flexibility is often characterized by part-time work, split shifts at both ends of the working day, rolling contracts requiring both full-and part-time employees to work some evenings and at weekends, permanent *'flex-contracts'* with a variable weekly focus of work and temporary contracts with intermittent periods of unemployment.

Though the study believes that flexible working was essentially a response to the drive towards long-term competitiveness and improved market efficiency, it also undermines equal-opportunity objectives. The study also found that four factors limit promotion opportunities for women who work part-time or in flexible jobs.

Managerial and supervisory jobs were reserved for employees willing to work full-time, and these people often worked excessively long hours. There was also a limited range of job opportunities. Qualified employees were few, training offered was limited and there were differential gender expectations that played a role in practice despite the existence of equal opportunities legislation.

Low pay and job insecurity were another EU-wide characteristic of this sector, leading to uncertainty or economic dependence on the partner or the state.

In terms of child care for workers in this sector, two major problems were identified: because of the general low pay, retail workers had difficulties meeting the costs of child care, even when it was subsidized and the costs are income related; child care services were often not available in the evenings or weekends when workers in this sector needed them most.

The author concluded that, based on evidence from the case studies, *"flexible working has opened up some employment opportunities but in a way that leaves the gender division of labour within the home largely but not completely unchanged."* The author said this remained a key obstacle to the realization of equal opportunities for women and men in paid work.

Another research team, coordinated by Maria Angels Duran, has investigated the *'Future of Work in Europe (Gendered Patterns of Time Distribution)'*. The study examines the concept and culture of both paid and unpaid work in modern European societies. It looks at the structural conditions of access to paid employment and the role played by social security benefits and taxes in the redistribution of time and money among women and men. The study covered Denmark, the Scandinavian countries, Spain, France, Portugal, the UK, Ireland, Greece and Belgium.

The researchers say that women's share of the paid and unpaid workload is generally much higher than that of men. The authors argued for a new concept of work, which is not restricted to the idea of salary or payment, as is the case now. Here the work refers to a process of a combination of all social activities like child care, paid work, unpaid work and voluntary care. The current situation was *'unacceptable'*, they said, because it discriminated against those excluded from *'non-active'*, *'dependent'* or *'non-productive'*. This was irrespective of their real unpaid working hours or how necessary such work was for other people.

According to the report, unpaid work in the EU remained *'overwhelmingly'* invisible and unrecognized. The EU also ignored unpaid work in the non-profit sector, voluntary work, work in the black economy (estimated to involve 7-19% of Europe's labour force) or work done for leisure, social or personal usefulness.

The authors commented that although women had *"massively"* taken on paid work during the past three decades, men had not assumed, to the same degree, domestic and care duties.

Men devoted less time to voluntary and care work, leaving them free to opt for work in the public sphere, including politics and trade unions, or to pursue more leisure activities. This resulted in a much higher total workload on women than on men throughout their lives.

Again this unequal workload between women and men had a direct effect on the distribution of economic resources by gender. Women were disadvantaged in terms of labour market access, career opportunities and occupational and earning status.

In addition, in times of economic hardship in the family, women are *'more readily'* prepared to work in *'informal jobs'* and working in such jobs often turned into a permanent activity offering women no health or retirement guarantees. The result was that many women ended up being dependent on the family after a lifetime of informal work.

According to the study, the complex system of tax, social security and benefits in different EU member states also had their consequences on women's access to employment and on their incomes. It said the tax and benefit policies were *'obsolete'* because they failed to take account of social and demographic changes. For example, tax exemptions and social benefits currently target children and not the elderly, who also require care. Also, where taxes were levied on families, rather than on individuals, the women's salary was often considered to be at tax levels. This acted as a disincentive for women to find a job, the study warned.

The study also said that social security systems were found to be heavily gender-biased both in their paying conditions (who has to pay, why and how much) and when paying out (who receives benefit, why and how much); most benefits paid out by these systems were related to involvement in the formal labour market while excluding or penalizing many women.

Finally, they commented that paid work remained the only type of work taken into consideration in the National Accounting System (NAS). But they also wanted the EU to take account of unpaid work done by women. They called for action in this field if efforts were to go beyond *"words and mere formal agreements."*

Equal Opportunities and Job Creation

Time means different things to working women and men, and the question of reorganizing or reducing working time to boost employment, and its impact on workplace equality, has been the subject of other researchers. Annie Junter and Nicole Maples (1997) coordinated such a study. Due to their dual workload both in the public and private spheres, women's employment more structured and more fragmented than that of men. The social risks of the duality can be high as women often sacrifice their own personal time to carry out family or care duties or opt for working arrangements like flexible, annualized or reduced working hours, which often have negative effects on their career.

The study selected 14 public and private sector companies in seven EU member states (Germany, Spain, Finland, France, Italy, the Netherlands and the UK) to examine how equal-opportunity policies in these companies affected their policies to reorganize or reduce working time for essentially economic reasons but using social innovative methods.

Two were big multinational companies and nine of the companies had at some stage in their histories put in place equal opportunities provisions for their staff in the framework of local national or EU-wide initiatives in the field.

This experience also had a positive impact on how decisions were taken on working time with women playing a much more active role in negotiations.

The study had allowed the debate on the issue of working hours to be opened up in these companies and made employers much more aware of the benefits of reconciling different time needs. The study resulted in introducing a culture that was much more favourable to reorganizing working time and the development of more structured and better supported forms of work flexibility; the study was instrumental in the development and implementation of measures to reorganize or reduce working time, which took women's time needs into account.

The authors concluded that companies that combined equal-opportunity measures with those to reduce or reorganize working time and job creation had, in fact, participated with different degrees of success to *"the definitions of a new gender-based contract both within and outside work."*

This study based its findings on the structure of earnings survey (SES) carried out by Eurostat in 1995. The study used the data from the survey to identify the extent of the wage gap between men and women and to see if it could be explained or influenced by factors such as age, education attainment levels or job experience. In addition, many women employed in this sector have high levels of education and were therefore more likely to be better paid. The study was limited to fulltime workers and covered only nine EU member states.

The study reveals that the average hourly rate of pay for women in full-time employment is 27.5 per cent lower than for men. Although these gaps narrowed when account was taken of age, occupational and sectoral differences for women and men, education attainment levels, average length of service and the size of the employing company, the study said more of these factors either taken alone or combination, were capable of explaining why pay differential existed.

The findings of the study reveal that the wage gap remained within the age groups and occupations and for people with the same educational attainment level and length of service in virtually all the nine countries, through its size differed significantly between people of different ages, in different jobs. The gap was much higher for older than for younger workers and for managers than for office workers or unskilled manual workers and for those with high education levels than for those with lower ones; the gap between women and men's earnings was much wider at the top end of the earnings scale, among the employees earning the highest wages than at the bottom among the lowest paid workers.

They concluded that *"the hourly pay of the bottom 10 per cent of women in terms of wages received was about 15 per cent lower than that of the bottom 10 per cent of men, the pay of the top 10 per cent of women was some 35 per cent lower"* than that of men.

The findings suggested that women were proportionately less well represented at the top of their professions. This could be due to the fact that more women than men take career breaks to look after children or other family members but the authors were doubtful.

The four studies reveal that *"it appears simply to be the case that women advance far less than men in their career, or even if they do advance as far, are less well paid for their efforts for no obvious reasons."*

Therefore, different indicators on the gender gap in the labour market demand strategic and reinforced action at both community and national level. The Amsterdam Treaty of 1998 gives the basis for this. This new strategy has proved successful in reinforcing member states' action on equality. It was maintained and strengthened in 1999 with the new guidelines for employment agreed at the Vienna European Council, 1998.

It is recognized that equality of opportunity is at the heart of the process of reforming labour markets in the EU. Member states have committed themselves to mainstream equality in acting on employment policies. This should be accompanied by the adoption of a gender mainstreaming approach in implementing all principles such as improving employability, develop entrepreneurship and encourage adaptability of businesses and their employees and strengthening equal opportunity policies for women and men.

The Vienna summit recommended that the European Social Fund, which is under reform, should be used to better support the employment strategy. The information and communication technologies sector is a leading sector in employment growth in the EU, accounting for one in every four new jobs. The report estimated at 5,00,000 the number of unfilled job vacancies in this sector because of skill shortages. The employment potential of the sector was believed to be enormous with the European audio-visual market alone expected to grow by some 70 per cent between now and 2005, meaning 3,00,000 new jobs.

To meet the challenge, the Commission called for action in three priority areas, namely, developing an enterprise culture, modernizing the organization of work and boosting skills and technical literacy levels through *"revitalized and advanced"* education and training system. In order to produce concrete results, member states of the EU are urged to support the process of defining and collecting comparable data in order to implement its ideas of equalities of opportunity.

NOTES

Annie, Junter and Nicole Maples (1997): Working Time, Equal Opportunities and Job Creation Engender asbl, Brussels.

Diana, Persons (1997): 'Flexible Working and the Reconciliation of Work and Family Life', London School of Economics, London.

EU (1999): Equal Opportunities (1996-2000), Vol. 7, European Commission.

This Report is published in Economic Political Weekly, September 22-28, 2001, Vol. XXXVI, No. 38.

Director, Dr. Durgabai Deshmukh Centre for Women's Studies, Andhra University, Visakhapatnam, Andhra Pradesh, India.

10

Globalization and Its Impact on Women Workers in Visakha Special Economic Zones

DR. B. RATNA KUMARI, INDIA

Introduction

Special economic zones are global phenomenon, where goods are produced mainly for exports or world market. In order to keep the price of goods competitive the zone authorities give certain concession to the exporters. India has 7 such zones.

The first export processing zone of modern era was set up in 1959 at Shannon, in Ireland. In 1962, the concept was adopted by Puerto Rico with the establishment of an EPZ in Island. The concept soon spread to Asia. India was the first country to establish SEZ, at Kandla, in the Asia pacific region in 1996. Sixteen years later here was merely 175 spread across fifty countries. Since then exporting zones have been created in nearly half the world's countries mainly in the third world. According to the latest ILO figures there are, at present, some 850 export processing zones world wide, employing almost 27 million people. As per ILO, the main objective behind setting SEZ is to attract investment that would otherwise not materialize. Developed countries have created Special Economic Zones (SEZ) mainly for the purpose of promoting development of export oriented manufacturing industries.

In our country EPZs (Export Processing Zones) have been changed into SEZs (Special Economical Zones) since 4 decades. First the NDA Government introduced EPZs system. In India, the SEZs are constituted as departmental undertakings under Ministry of Commerce, Government of India. Each zone is headed by a development commissioner, a civil servant, appointed by Central Government. In the year 1994 Visakha Special Economic Zone

(VSEZ) has been initiated in the city of destiny. There are several processing units existing in this VSEZ. Diamond cutting and polishing, fruit processing and juice making are some of the major units which required the women force. As women are known for their patience and diligence these units opened gates for women workers. In VSEZ there are nearly 700-800 hundred women a worker who works on the basis of permanent and temporary and on contract basis. The concerned unit authorities have given necessary short-term skill training for women workers. The VSEZ has created more employment opportunities for women. With this back drop the Dr. Durgabhai Deshmukh Centre for women studies, Andhra University has taken up a study to examine the impact of globalization process on the lives of women workers in VSEZ.

Review of Literature

Rajan Ray (2003) in his article explained about globalization, the last three decades of the 20th century have seen a significant integration of markets in community, services, finance and technology between countries. Goods produced in one country increasingly find their way to markets in other countries. Capital and not just labour is increasingly mobile between countries.

The recent and rapid growth of information technology has aided the integration of markets world wide by making communications easier and in many cases, instantaneous. These developments have been broadly referred to as a global village largely unhindered by geographical distances, time zones or other physical barriers to movement between countries. The world wide move towards globalization and free trade coincided with the process of structural reforms and economic liberalization that began in India in July 1991. Under the stewardship of Man Mohan Singh as Finance Minister.

Susmita Rakshit (2003) looks at the implications of the structural reforms agenda in India for currency convertibility. She provides a detailed analysis of this issue and argues against the convertibility of the rupee on the capital account. She could have enhanced the value of her analysis by tracing the history or experience of countries which have adopted full current. In the context of a concerted assault on US affirmative action policies that began more then 10 years ago, and the current dominance of the right–wing in political discourse and action in the US this Supreme Court stance is certainly surprising. The explanation lies in recognizing that affirmative action won the day not as a policy serving the goals of social justice and greater economic equality for America's disadvantaged and stigmatized ethnic minorities. Rather affirmative action prevailed because it serves the interests of wide- ranging coalition of. Elites in the efficient management of America are major in an age of globalization. Significantly, globalization puts a high premium on the capacity to speak fluent and articulate English, which is hard to India without the benefit of attending English–language schools and option available mainly to upper class urban families. So, globalization has thus weakened support for reservations policies among India's power – that is. Yet precisely convertibility in recent years.

Rohini Hensman (2004) explained in her article about Globalization, Globalization included in 3 dimensions those are:

1. Capitalist globalization, these system based on the exploitation of workers and production for profit.
2. Imperialist globalization, means the political, economic and military domination over some stats by others.
3. Neo-liberal globalization means the policy of allowing the market to determine everything, including wage levels, health care, education etc.

The other main objective would be concrete action to shape the global order in accordance with women's agenda for justice and equity as well as caring and nurturing. The author asked women employers why employment is important? Whether women would prefer it if their fathers or husbands earned enough to keep them at home and answer has invariably no;' so that employment is important for women. Globalization has come to be researched so much that any volume aimed at studying the phenomena has to justify and highlight the unique task undertaken by it.

S. Uma Devi (2004) mainly concentrated on identity politics and social conflict in the process of globalization one aim of the project was to examine the manner in which the issues of identify politics and globalization may intersect. Global and the national media are the texts and the discourse they focus on is social conflict. The effect of economic globalization on cultural identity and social conflict and points out that culture has become an economic good being identified with things, which can be traced. The main objective of this paper, impact of globalization and domestic economic reforms on small industry. So, small industry is one of the major planks of India's economic development strategy since independence. Today small industry occupies a position of strategic importance in the Indian economic structure due to its significant contribution in terms of out put, exports and employment. Rohini Hensman explained about globalization, that the industrial revolution was the great transformation, the great transformation is globalization. •The process of globalization is based on the proliferation of wage labourers. Hers object is how female work force grows rapidly.

The global proletariat doubled between 1975 and 1995 to reach 2.5 billion workers with the bulk of this growth in the third world: in 1995 the World Bank projected that fully 99 per cent of the workers who would join the labour force in the next three decades would be from the low-and middle–income countries. The female work force also grew rapidly by the mid-1980s, more than half the world's working–age women were in paid employment. The Breton Wood's agreement of 1994 linked the dollar to gold; the IMF was set up and established. Parties between major currencies US MNCs explained phenomenally in the 1950s and 1960s and were joined thereafter by European and Japanese MNCs The author feels that while the social clause has been the most divisive issue facing the trade union movement it is also the strategy best placed to unify the world's workers.

N.S. Siddharthan (2004) had given an overview on globalization, productivity, efficiency and growth. In his words, India liberalizing its economy in particular, its manufacture sector over a decade ago. One of the objectives of liberalization has been to make Indian industries more efficient and globally competitive. Towards this end, the Government of India has been pursuing three sets of reforms. Disbanding the complex network of Industrial controls, Industrial licensing and currency transactions and, instituting several measures to facilitate foreign direct investment inflows.

After a decade of experience, we now have enough data to test the impact of the globalization and liberalization policies on Indian industry. During an era of liberalization, new firms with more advanced technology are likely to enter an industry and the existing firms are expected to develop a strategy. However after 1996, there has been an improvement in the average efficiency through it has not reached the 1991 levels. And the growth accounting approach depends on the existence of an aggregate production function and the validity of the marginal productivity theory of pricing. Finally, he has summarized, some firms have gained by the liberalization and globalization policies while others have lost. The main gainers have been Multi-national enterprises MNE and their affiliates which have better access to technology and other intangible assets to survive and succeed in the global regime and to compete against the MNEs, some of the domestic firms have adopted a strategy of entering into non-equity strategic alliance with foreign and domestic firms resulting in technology impacts against royalty payments.

According to the Aashutosh Kumar (2002) world became a village. The new village reflects the universal acceptance of the western arrangements of governments and management of social problems in a post-communist world. It also increasingly shares a world culture dominated by the affluent west. In the author's view the political and social changes taking place in India as a result of market liberalization and integration into the world economy, rather than seeking explanation through referring to the past and traditions, concentrates on the modernizing forces at work in India through an analysis of major themes: caste, class, religion and gender. While analyzing the effects of globalization on nearly all corners of Indian life the contemporary issues confronting an increasingly globalize, liberalized and privatized India, like environmental problems emigration and the anti-nuclear peace movements and integrates this discussion into an examination of the new structures emerging from an increasing dependence on global markets. The author argues that the new economic policy was not merely an inevitable result of the economic crisis but was brought upon by the forces with the support of the affluent urbanites belonging to the middle mass. The elderly people of all classes, on the other hand, feel threatened by the changes around them, not just the technological and fashion changes which perplex ageing people everywhere, but deep structural and value changes about people and relationships. As most of these views are critical nature our well meaning author also ends up looking at the problems of a new India experiencing transition. The author Thomas E. Weisskoph gave a brief article about globalization and affirmative action. In his view affirmative action stated unambiguously that the nation has a compelling interest in promoting diversity in higher education, and it approved the use of "race" as a plus factor in determining who should be admitted to selective colleges and university. Yet precisely because globalization brings India more closely into the US orbit, the US Supreme Court judgment in favour of preferential policies will no doubt reverberate throughout India.

Arjunsen Gupta (2004) gave an article about globalization that managing globalization can be properly addressed without bringing out clearly the nations of accountability in terms of the rights and aspirations of the people. Globalization is supposed to achieve certain outcomes, which for a state, particularly it is a democracy, must be those, which give the state its legitimacy. So, management of globalization must be assessed in terms of its ability to produce these outcomes. Globalization a process associated with increasing economic openness, growing economic inter-dependence and deepening economic integration between countries in the world economy. And if globalization has to be assessed in terms of its instrumentality it is important to set out at very beginning, what are goals and objectives of which globalization is supposed to achieve in any country. However, there are two additional reasons why the goals of globalization should be appropriate viewed as the fulfillment of rights of the people. (1) The first point is associated with the nation of globalization it self which relates to an acceleration of process of interaction between nation states. A point which has been discussed managing globalization would imply in that context how these states can effectively fulfill their obligations. Women's studies have been a critical actor in the journey. Learning about women came from two sources: the collective voice of those working in communities and those challenging the academy. Knowledge was created and disseminated through a multiple set of sources. One was research that documented grassroots success stories; another was research that provided a more sophisticated analysis of women's location in the world. This is very difference from men. In the era of thought/in knowing, that has inhibited the adoption, accommodation of women's views into the policy spaces, but also inhibited women from participating in those spaces.

However, this very characteristic of difference between men and women in what is thought and what is knowledge, truth, and disagreement with the idea of the final word, has generated a self-created alienation from the big world of MIND what seems to suggest itself then is think how to use the knowledge and self-strength, and that has been garnered by feminist reasoning to really move forward to affirm its power.

Need for the Study

The project was executed in the VSEZ of Visakhapatnam. This is the only zone which has located in Visakhapatnam district of Andhra Pradesh. It has several sub-zones like food proceeding industry and diamond cutting which has created employment opportunities for many unskilled, semi-skilled and skilled resources. The zone has opened gates for women in their industries for their quailing work patience diligence and commitment. Many women were given short time training by the industry as per their skill requirement since its inception. Present study has been conducted at VSEZ to understand the impact of globalization process in the lives of women workers in VSEZ.

Profile of Andhra Pradesh and Visakhapatnam

Located in the southern part of India, Andhra Pradesh is the fifth largest state in the country in terms of both area and population as per 2001 census. It was the first state in independent India that came into existence on purely linguistic basis with Hyderabad as its capital city in the year 1956. The state is divided into 23 districts distributed in three regions: costal Andhra Pradesh, Telangana and Rayalaseema. From being a predominantly agriculture based economy, the state has been making rapid economic progress in the past one decade primarily by developing information technology.

Table-1
A Brief Profile of Andhra Pradesh

		1991	*2001*
1.	Geographical are (thousand sq. km.)	275	275
2.	Population (in thousands)	6,65,08	7,57,28
3.	Males	3,37,25	3,82,87
4.	Females	3,27,83	3,74,41
5.	Rural population	4,86,21	5,52,24
6.	Urban population	1,78,87	2,05,04
7.	Density (per sq. km)	242	275
8.	Literacy Rate (%)	44.1	61.1

Contd...

		1991	2001
9.	Sex ratio (Females per thousand of males)	972	978
10.	Percentage of urban population	26.9	27.08
11.	Per capita income (base: 1990-91) (Rs.)	4,531	NA
12.	No. of Zilla Parishad	22	23
13.	Gram Panchayats	19,492	NA
14.	Gram Panchayat Samitis/ Mandal Praja Parishads	1,092	NA

Source: www.apaonegov.in

Andhra Pradesh is the largest maritime state in India with a coastline of 970 km. Visakhapatnam, the second largest city in the state of Andhra Pradesh and an important port city on the south-eastern coast of India is witnessing rapid growth as well as socio-economic and demographic changes in the past few decades. As per 2001 census, the total population of Visakhapatnam city was 9,82,904 in which 50,106 are males and 4,81,498 are females. Out of the total population 69.42 per cent are literate (39.01% males and 30.49% females). The city has 44 health centers including 7 general hospitals, 37 primary health centers, nursing homes and dispensaries (Visakhapatnam urban development authority, 2003). The local language is Telugu, but most educated people also know English and Hindi.

Methodology

Objectives

Following are the objectives of the present study:

To analyze the socio- economic profile of the working women in VSEZ.

- To examine the distribution of work schedule between men and women in VSEZ company.
- To study the details of economic activities of the workers in VSEZ
- To observe the time schedule of domestic work and economic activity of the working women in VSEZ company.
- To examines the facilities for working women in the VSEZ company.
- To know how the women struggling to survive in the company and at home with role conflict.

- To analyze the constraints faced by the workers in VSEZ company.

Research Setting

The selection of the data mainly based on the primary source (field work) in Visakha Special economical zones in Visakhapatnam. The present study identifies the work force of the women in the industry and at home and the facilities of the women workers in the zone. All women workers are working in manufacturing sectors (worldwide diamond manufacturing, LID, and fruit juice company).

Sample

The study was conducted in the VSEZ of Visakhapatnam during Oct-Dec 2006. 100 women workers were selected as sample for the present study. 20 men workers were also selected for the study as sample to make comparisons.

Data Collection

The tools for collecting socio-economic and demographic data job profile data included the following:

(*a*) Personal data sheet consisted of details of the respondents such as information on the age education, occupation, family type and family size, amenities at home and marital status.

(*b*) Information on job profile like period working hours, leave and medical facilities, crèche facility, canteen facility and recreation facilities and wages.

(*c*) Information on dual role, child care practices, children educational status and acquired fixed assets and expenditure patterns.

Tools

To collect the above necessary information a well structured schedule has been prepared and administered on 120 women who were drawn as sample for the study.

Analysis

The collected data has been analyzed with appropriative statistical measures:

Table–2
Socio Demographic Profile of Respondent Women

S. No.		*Frequency*	*Per cent*
Employment			
1.	1-3 years	39	32
2.	4-6 years	20	17
3.	7-9 years	61	51
	Total	120	100
Occupation			
4.	Yes	9	8
5.	No	111	92
	Total	120	100
Nature of Employment			
6.	8-10 hours	93	77.5
7.	6-8 hours	27	22.5
	Total	120	100
Family Expenditure per Month			
8.	1500-3000	35	29.17
9.	3001-5000	77	64.17
10.	5001-9000	8	6.66
	Total	120	100
Time Spent on Domestic Chores			
11.	1 hr	19	16
12.	2 hrs	32	27
13.	3 hrs	49	41
14.	4 hrs	18	15
15.	5 hrs	2	2
	Total	120	100
Family Members Help for Domestic Chores			
16.	Yes	103	86
17.	No	17	14
	Total	120	100
Child-Care			
18.	Parents	65	54
19.	Family	55	46
	Total	120	100

Time Spent on Children Education			
20.	1 hr	52	43
21.	2 hrs	56	47
22.	3 hrs	12	10
	Total	120	100
Nature of Employment			
23.	Contract basis and Daily-wages	99	82.5
24.	Temporary	11	8.3
25.	Permanent	10	9.1
	Total	120	100
Skill Training			
26.	Diamond	35	29.5
27.	Training-based on unit	85	70.8
	Total	120	100
Mode of Transport/Travel			
28.	Bus	93	77.5
29.	Train	2	1.7
30.	Auto	15	12.5
31.	Other	10	8.3
	Total	120	100
Constraints in Travel			
32.	Yes	1	0.8
33.	No	119	99.2
	Total	120	100
Anxiety in Attending Job on Right Time			
34.	Yes	75	62.5
35.	No	45	37.5
	Total	120	100
Medical Aid			
36.	Yes	119	99.2
37.	No	1	0.8
	Total	120	100
Medical Check Ups			
38.	Yes	7	5.8
39.	No	113	94.2
	Total	120	100

Ailments Due to Work			
40.	Yes	14	11.7
41.	No	106	88.3
	Total	120	100
Benefit by Medical Dispensary			
42.	Yes	119	99.2
43.	No	1	0.8
	Total	120	100
Weekly Holiday			
44.	Yes	85	70.8
45.	No	35	29.2
	Total	120	100
Time Spent for Entertainment			
46.	1 hour	772	60
47.	2 hours	30	25
48.	No time	18	15
	Total	120	100
Participation in Voluntary Organization			
49.	Yes	38	31.7
50.	No	82	68.3
	Total	120	100

Source: Field Study.

Findings

The findings of the study are provided in this chapter under 3 major sections:

1. Socio-demographic characteristics of the respondents and of their spouses.
2. Job profile of respondents.
3. Family relationships.

Section–I

SOCIO-DEMOGRAPHIC CHARACTERISTICS OF THE RESPONDENT AND THEIR SPOUSES

This section focuses on the socio-demographics background characteristics of the respondents. Similar information about their husbands was also taken in order to examine differences, if any their socio-economic backgrounds.

Age of the Respondents

The mean age of the sample of women workers (VSEZ) was found to be tears the age range of the sample varied from 20-30 years and above.

Fig. 1 indicates that 9.2 per cent of the respondents were below 20 years of age and 83.3 per cent of were 21-30 years of age and 7.5 per cent were above 30 years of age.

Fig. 1: Percentage Distribution of Respondents by their Current Age

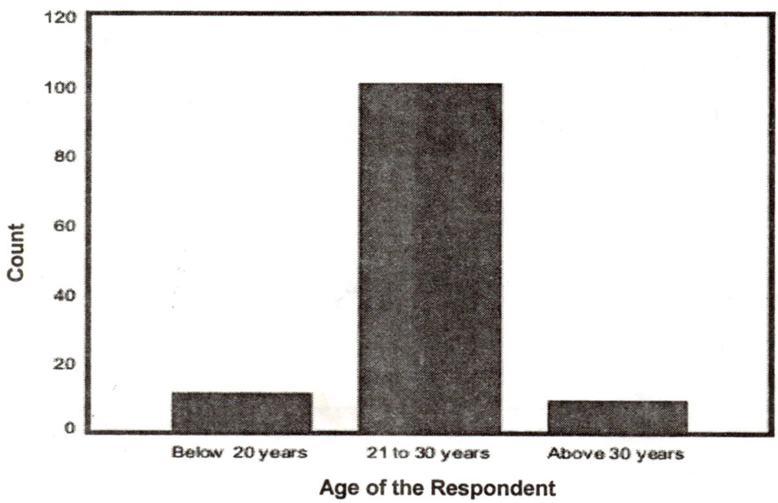

Source: Field Study.

Education

As mentioned in the introduction the educational status of women is positively associated with knowledge, health communication with outside world, control over resources and above all autonomy (Jejeebhoy 1998). Figure 1 presented the educational status of respondents in the present sample. 45 per cent of that have attained secondary level education, 35 per cent of them have intermediate level, 18.3 per cent of them have completed graduation. Very little *i.e.,* 0.8 per cent has primary level of education. The most significant finding in this category is all the women workers are literates. 0.8 per cent of the have post graduation level of education.

Table-3
Percentage Distribution of Respondents by their Education Attainment

Education of the Respondent	*Frequency*	*Per cent*
Primary education	1	.8
Secondary education	54	45.0
Intermediate	42	35.0
Degree	22	18.3
P.G.	1	.8
Total	120	100

Source: Field Study.

Martial Status

Table 4 reveals the information about martial status of respondent women workers. 65 per cent of the were married, 27.5 per cent of the were unmarried. 2.5 per cent of them were remarried. 1.7 per cent each was widows divorces and separated. It has been observed that, majority of the women workers were married.

Table-4
Percentage Distribution of Respondents by their Martial Status

Marital Status of the Respondent	*Frequency*	*Per cent*
Married	78	65.0
Widow	2	1.7
Divorced	2	1.7
Separated	2	1.7
Remarried	3	2.5
Unmarried	33	27.5
Total	120	100

Source: Field Study.

Family Monthly Income

Table 5 reveals about the respondent women workers family monthly income. It is understood that, women workers are also earning on far with their husbands. 34.2 per cent of women are earning Rs. 2001-3000. 31.7 per cent of they were earning Rs. 3001-4000. 25.8 per cent of them were earning below Rs. 2000 6.7 per cent of them were earning Rs. 4001-5000. Very little *i.e.,* per cent of them were earning Rs. 5000 and above.

Table–5
Percentage Distribution of Monthly Income of Respondent Women Workers

Income of the Respondent	*Frequency*	*Per cent*
Below 2000	31	25.8
2001–3000	41	34.2
3001–4000	38	31.7
4001–5000	8	6.7
5001 Above	2	1.7
Total	120	100

Source: Field Study.

Table 6 reveals the information about respondent women workers husbands' family monthly income. 42.00 per cent of them were earning below Rs. 2000. 12.00 per cent of them were earning Rs. 2001-3000. 26.00 per cent of them were earning Rs. 3001-4000. 5.00 per cent of them were earning Rs. 4000-5000. 15.00 per cent of them were earning Rs. 5000 and above. It is evident than, women are earning equally with men to supplement the family income.

Table–6
Percentage Distribution of Monthly Income of Respondent Women Workers Husbands

Monthly Income of Respondent Husband	*Frequency*	*Percentage*
Below 2000	34	42.00
2001–3000	10	12.34
3001–4000	21	26.00
4001–5000	4	5.00
Above 5000	12	15.00
Total	81	100

Source: Field Study.

Known Languages

Table 7 Indicates the information about the know languages of respondents 41.7 per cent of them were knows only Telugu,

22.5 per cent of the knows Telugu and Hindi 35.8 per cent of the knows Telugu, Hindi and English.

Table-7
Percentage Distribution of Respondent Women by Known Languages

Languages Known by the Respondent	*Frequency*	*Per cent*
Telugu	50	41.7
Telugu, Hindi	27	22.5
Telugu, Hindi and English	43	35.8
Total	120	100

Source: Field Study.

Type of House

Table 8 Indicates the respondent's house type. 1.7 per cent of them were staying in Kucha house. 25.0 per cent of them were residing in Semi Pucca house. 73.3 per cent of them were staying in Pucca house.

Table-8
Percentage Distribution of Respondent Women by their Type of House

Type of the House	*Frequency*	*Per cent*
Kucha	2	1.7
S. Pucca	30	25.0
Pucca	88	73.3
Total	120	100

Source: Field Study.

Electrification

Table 9 reveals the information about respondent's house electrification. 99.2 per cent of respondent houses were electrified. Only 0.8 per cent of respondent houses were not electrified.

Source of Water

Table 10 gives the information about the source of water for respondent's domestic use. 40.00 per cent of them fetch the water from public tap. 17.00 per cent of them had tap at their houses. 28 per cent of them had well at their house premises. 11 per cent of them fetch water from neighbours well. 2 per cent of them fetch from tankers, public well and from other sources.

Table–9
Percentage Distribution of Respondent Women by Electrification of their Houses

Electrification at Respondent Household	*Frequency*	*Per cent*
Yes	119	99.2
No	1	0.8
Total	120	100

Source: Field Study.

Table–10
Percentage Distribution of Respondent Women by Source of their Houses

Source of Water	*Frequency*	*Per cent*
Piped water (public tap)	48	40.0
Piped water (own tap)	20	16.7
Public well	1	0.8
Own well	34	28.3
Neighbour tap	13	10.8
Neighbour well	2	1.7
Tanker	1	0.8
Others (specify)	1	0.8
Total	120	100

Source: Field Study.

Toilet Facility

Table 11 reveals the information about the toilet facility at the respondent's house. 1.7 per cent of them had no toilet at their house. 2.5 per cent of them had flush type toilet at their house. 80.00 per cent of them have pit type toilet at their house. 15.8 per cent of them had shared pit toilet facility at their houses.

Separate Kitchen

Table 12 reveals the information about the separate kitchen facility at respondent's house. 77 per cent of them had separate kitchen and 23 per cent of them had no separate kitchen.

Family Size

Table 13 indicates about the respondent's family size. 31 per cent of them had 2 members family. 31 per cent of them had two members family. 45 per cent of them herd 3 members family, 14 per cent of them had 4 members family, and 7.5 per cent had 5 members family. 2 per cent had 6 members family, 8 per cent of the respondent family size is 11 members.

Table-11

Percentage Distributions of Respondent Women by Toilet Facility are their Houses

Available Toilet Facility	*Frequency*	*Per cent*
No toilet	3	2.5
Own flush toilet	2	1.7
Own pit toilet	96	80.0
Shared pit toilet	19	15.8
Total	120	100

Source: Field Study.

Table-12

Percentage Distribution of Respondent Women House by Separate Kitchen

Do You Have Separate Room for Kitchen	*Frequency*	*Per cent*
Yes	92	76.7
No	28	23.3
Total	120	100

Source: Field Study.

Table-13

Percentage Distribution of Respondent Women by their Family Size

Size of the Family	*Frequency*	*Per cent*
2	37	30.8
3	54	45.0
4	17	14.2
5	9	7.5
6	2	1.7
11	1	0.8
Total	120	100

Source: Field Study.

Fixed Assets

Table 14 indicates the information about the fixed assets possessed by the respondents. 18.3 per cent of respondents have own houses. 3.3 per cent of them have house plots. 17.5 per cent have agricultural lands, 2 per cent of them have bank balances deposits. 2 per cent them have share in various companies 19 per cent of them have own vehicles (two wheelers). 38 per cent of them do not have any fixed assets.

Table–14
Percentage Distribution of Respondent Women by Fixed Assets Possessed by them

Fixed Assets	*Frequency*	*Percentage*
House	22	18.3
House sites	4	3.3
Agricultural	21	17.5
Bank deposits	2	2
Shares	2	2
Vehicles	23	19
None	46	38
Total	120	100

Source: Field Study.

Nativity

Table 15 indicates the information about respondent women nativity status. 70 per cent of respondents were native of Visakhapatnam and 30 per cent of them were migrants of other districts (or) places.

Table–15
Percentage Distribution of Respondent Women by their Nativity Status

Are You Native or Migrant?	*Frequency*	*Per cent*
Native	84	70.0
Migrant	36	30.0
Total	120	100

Source: Field Study.

Period of Stay

Table: 16 indicates about the respondent's period of stay at the present location (place). 7 per cent of the respondent was staying since 1-5 years. 93 per cent of them were staying since 5-10 years.

Table-16
Percentage Distribution of Respondent Women by their Stay at Present Place

No. of Years Stay	*Frequency*	*Per cent*
1-5 years	8	7
5-10 years	112	93
Total	120	100

Source: Field Study.

Section-II

INFORMATION ABOUT RESPONDENT EMPLOYMENT

Duration of Employment

Table 17 reveals the information about respondent women's duration of employment. 32 per cent of them were working since 1-3 years. 17 per cent if they were working since 4-6 years and 51 per cent of them were working since 7-9 years.

Table-17
Percentage Distribution of Respondent Women by their Duration of Employment

Duration (in Years)	*Frequency*	*Per cent*
1-3 years	39	32
4-6 years	20	17
7-9 years	61	51
Total	120	100

Source: Field Study.

Respondents Previous Occupation

Table 18 reveals the information about respondent women's previous occupation. 92 per cent of them do not have any previous occupational experience. 8 per cent of them had previous experience.

Table-18
Percentage Distribution of Respondent Women by their Previous Occupation

Previous Occupation (Yes/No)	*Frequency*	*Per cent*
Yes	9	8
No	111	92
Total	120	100

Source: Field Study.

Nature of Employment (Working Hours)

Table 19 indicates about respondent women working hours per day at work place. 77.5 per cent of the respondent women work at (VSEZ) for 8-10 hours/day 22.5 per cent of them work for 6-8 hours/day.

Table-19
Percentage Distribution of Respondent Women by their Working Hours at Work Place

No. of Hours	*Frequency*	*Per cent*
8-10 hours	93	77.5
6-8 hours	27	22.5
Total	120	100

Source: Field Study.

Section–III

Family Expenditure Pattern

Table 20 explains about respondent women family expenditure pattern. 29.17 per cent of the respondent women family expenditure was Rs. 1500-3000 per month. 64.17 per cent of their expenditure was Rs. 3001-5000 and 6.66 per cent respondent women's family expenditure was Rs. 5001-9000.

Table-20
Percentage Distribution of Respondent Women Family Expenditure

Expenditure per Month	*Frequency*	*Per cent*
1500-3000	35	29.17
3001-5000	77	64.17
5001-9000	8	6.66
Total	120	100

Source: Field Study.

Time Spent on Domestic Chores

Table 21 reveals the information about time spent on domestic chores by the respondent women. 16 per cent of the respondent women work at home for domestic chores for 1 hour daily. 28 per cent of them workers for 2 hours, 41 per cent of the works for 3 hours, 15 per cent of them work for 4 hours and 2 per cent of them works for 5 hours.

Table–21
Percentage Distribution of Respondent Women by their Time Spent on Domestic Chores

Time on (Hr.) Domestic Chores	*Frequency*	*Per cent*
1 hr	19	16
2 hrs	32	27
3 hrs	49	41
4 hrs	18	15
5 hrs	2	2
Total	120	100

Source: Field Study.

Family Members Help for Domestic Chores

Table 22 gives the information about respondent women family members help for domestic chores. 86 per cent of respondent women get help from their family members for the domestic chores, 14 per cent of them do not get any help from their family members.

Table–22
Percentage Distribution of Respondent Women by their Family Members Help for Domestic Chores

Family Members Help (Yes/No)	*Frequency*	*Per cent*
Yes	103	86
No	17	14
Total	120	100

Source: Field Study.

Child-Care

Table 23 reveals the information about respondent women's child-care takers when they were at work place. 54 per cent of them had reported that their parents will look after their children during their absence. For 46 per cent respondents family members will look after their children.

Table–23
Percentage Distribution of Respondent Women by their Child-Care Gives

Child-Care Gives	*Frequency*	*Per cent*
Parents	65	54
Family	55	46
Total	120	100

Source: Field Study.

Time Spent on Children Education

Table 24 reveals the information about respondent women time spent on children education. 43 per cent of respondent women spend 1 hour per day for their children education. 47 per cent of them spend 2 hours and 10 per cent of them spend 3 hours per day for their children education.

Table–24
Percentage Distribution of Respondent Women by their Time Spent for Children Education

Time (Hr.)	*Frequency*	*Per cent*
1 hr	52	43
2 hrs	56	47
3 hrs	12	10
Total	120	100

Source: Field Study.

Nature of Employment

Table 25 indicates about nature of employment in the VSEZ. 82.5 per cent of them are working on contract basis. 9.16 per cent are working on temporary basis. 8.3 per cent are working on permanent basis. This indicates very less per cent of respondent women have job security.

Skill Training

Table 26 indicates about skill training received by respondent women to upgrade their skills. 29.2 per cent of the respondent women

Table-25
Percentage Distribution of Respondent Women by their Nature of Employment

Nature of Employment	*Frequency*	*Per cent*
Contract basis and Daily wages	99	82.5
Temporary	11	8.3
Permanent	10	9.1
Total	120	100

Source: Field Study.

received diamond polishing training. 70.8 per cent of them received training for various unit (industry) training provided by the organization (VSEZ).

Table-26
Percentage Distribution of Respondent Women by their Skill Training

Skill Training	*Frequency*	*Per cent*
Diamond	35	29.5
Training based on unit	85	70.8
Total	120	100

Source: Field Study.

Mode of Transport/Travel

Table 27 reveals the information about the travel facility to the respondent women. 77.5 per cent of the respondent women travel by bus. 2 per cent of them travel by train 12.5 per cent of them travel by auto and 8.3 per cent of the them will travel by other modes of transport and reach to the work place.

Table-27
Percentage Distribution of Respondent Women by their Mode of Travel to Work Place

Mode of Travel	*Frequency*	*Per cent*
Bus	93	77.5
Train	2	1.7
Auto	15	12.5
Other	10	8.3
Total	120	100

Source: Field Study.

Constraints in Travel

Table 28 explains about the constraints faced by the respondent women because of their mode of travel. 99 per cent of them do not have any problem about their travelling mode. Only 1 per cent of them have some problem in travelling.

Table–28
Percentage Distribution of Respondent Women by their Problem in Travel

Problem in Travel	*Frequency*	*Per cent*
Yes	1	0.8
No	119	99.2
Total	120	100

Source: Field Study.

Anxiety in Attending Job on Right Time

Table 29 indicates about anxiety faced by the respondent women in attending the job on right time. 62.5 per cent of them face problem and anxiety in attending the job on right time. 37.5 per cent of them face no problem and anxiety in attending the job on time.

Table–29
Percentage Distribution of Respondent Women by their Anxiety in Attending the Job on Time

Anxiety	*Frequency*	*Per cent*
Yes	75	62.5
No	45	37.5
Total	120	100

Source: Field Study.

Medical Aid

Table 30 explains about medical facilities available at the work place. 99 per cent of them have respondent positively. (*i.e.,* they reported that the industry provide medical aid). 1 per cent of them reported that they do not have any medical facility at the work place.

Medical Check Ups

Table 31 indicates the information about the periodical medical check ups conducted by the industry. 5.8 per cent of them have reported that the industry authorities will organize to conduct

Table-30
Percentage Distribution of Respondent Women by Awareness on Medical Aid in the Industry

Medical Aid	*Frequency*	*Per cent*
Yes	119	99.2
No	1	0.8
Total	120	100

Source: Field Study.

medical check ups periodically. 94.2 per cent of them have reported that authorities of the industry do not organize any medical check up camps.

Table-31
Percentage Distribution of Respondent Women by their Awareness on Medical Check Up Camps

Awareness on Medical Check Ups	*Frequency*	*Per cent*
Yes	7	5.8
No	113	94.2
Total	120	100

Source: Field Study.

Ailments Due to Work

Table 32 indicates about the ailments suffered by the respondent women due to work. 12 per cent of them have some work related ailments. 88 per cent of them have not any work related ailments.

Table-32
Percentage Distribution of Respondent Women by their Ailments Due to Work

Work Related Ailments	*Frequency*	*Per cent*
Yes	14	11.7
No	106	88.3
Total	120	100

Source: Field Study.

Benefit by Medical Dispensary

Table 33 explains about respondent women opinion about benefits by medical dispensary in VSEZ. 99 per cent of them have opined that they have benefited by the medical dispensary of VSEZ. 1 per cent of them have opined that the medical dispensary in the VSEZ has no use (or) benefit for them.

Table–33
Percentage Distribution of Respondent Women by their Opinion about Medical Dispensary

Medical Dispensary Benefit	*Frequency*	*Per cent*
Yes	119	99.2
No	1	0.8
Total	120	100

Source: Field Study.

Weekly Holiday

Table 34 indicates about the weekly holiday *i.e.,* Sunday. 71 per cent of them have weekly holiday. 29 per cent of them do no have weekly holiday.

Table–34
Percentage Distribution of Respondent Women by their Weekly Holiday

Awareness on Medical Check Ups	*Frequency*	*Per cent*
Yes	85	70.8
No	35	29.2
Total	120	100

Source: Field Study.

Entertainment

Table 35 explains about respondent for entertainment. 60 per cent of them spend 1 hour and 25 per cent of them spend for 2 hours for entertainment. 14.2 per cent of them do not find time for entertainment.

Table–35
Percentage Distribution of Respondent Women by their Time Spent on Entertainment

Time Spent for Entertainment	*Frequency*	*Per cent*
1 hour	772	60
2 hours	30	25
No time	18	15
Total	120	100

Source: Field Study.

Participation in Voluntary Organization

Table 36 reveals the information about respondent women participation in voluntary organization. 32 per cent of them participate and have association with voluntary organizations. 68 per cent of them have no association with any voluntary organization.

Table-36
Percentage Distribution of Respondent Women by their Association with Voluntary Organizations

Association in Voluntary Organization	*Frequency*	*Per cent*
Yes	38	31.7
No	82	68.3
Total	120	100

Source: Field Study.

Findings in Brief

- Majority (83.3%) of respondents belongs to the group of 21- 30 years.
- Monthly income of more respondents (34.2%) is Rs. 200-3000.
- Husband's monthly income is around below Rs. 2000 only.
- Majority (41.7%) of the respondents known Telugu language only.
- 25 per cent of the respondents staying in Semi-Pucca houses.
- 99.2 per cent of the respondents have power supply (electricity at their houses).
- Majority of the respondents (40%) depend on public tap.
- 80 per cent of the respondents have own pit toilet facility.
- 76.7 per cent of the respondents have separate kitchen.
- 45 per cent of the respondents family size is three members.
- 18 per cent of respondents have own house and 17.5 per cent respondents have agricultural landing.
- 70 per cent of the respondents are native people.
- 93 per cent of the respondents are staying here from 5-10 years.

Employment Status of Women's Respondents

- Majority (51%) of respondents are working for the last 7-9 years.
- Majority (92%) of respondents do not have professional experience.

- Majority (77.5%) of respondents are working for 8-10 hours per a day.
- Majority (64.17%) of the respondents expenditure per month was Rs. 3000-5000.
- 41 per cent of the respondents spent three hours per a day on domestic chores.
- Majority (86%) of respondents have help from their family members in attending domestic chores.
- 54 per cent of respondents depend on their parents for child care.
- 47 per cent of the respondents spend two hours per a day on their children's education as main thing.
- Majority (82.5%) of respondents are working on contract basis and on daily-wages.
- Majority (100%) of the respondents have received skill training from their respective companies.
- Majority (77.5%) of the respondents travel by bus and not finding any constraints.
- Majority (62.5%) women facing austerity in attending the job.
- Majority (99.2%) respondents have availed medical aid from the industry.
- Majority (94.2%) of respondents reported that the SEZ do not organize medical check up camps.
- 12 per cent have some work related ailments.
- Majority (99%) of them have opined that they have benefited by the medical dispensary of VSEZ.
- 71 per cent have weekly holiday (Sunday).
- 60 per cent of the respondents spent one hour per day on entertainment.
- 68 per cent of the respondents have no association with voluntary organizations.

Key Issues

- Monthly income is below than Rs. 3000-4000. So there is a need to enhance the wage rate per a day.
- Because of depending on public tap for water supply the women workers do not find proper mental rest. Need to supply municipal water in their colonies.
- In our observation, the workers are not free to express their views as they were interviewed before the authorities of the company. Need to give freedom to express their views.

- No child care at VSZS. Provide crèches at the work place.
- Majority of the respondents have not find time to concentrate on their children's education.
- Majority of them are working on contract basis and on daily wage. So, they have to attend work due to insecurity in the job.
- Majority of them have work related ailments *e.g.* Diamond industry loosing eye sight, infection...etc.
- Workers are not having any associations with workers trade unions or civil societies.

Strategies to Empower Women

While the SEZs have significant role in now-a-days land problems especially in Kolkatta, Andhra Pradesh, Uttar Pradesh. We need to address some policy issues such as contract labour, job insecurity and job recognition, upgradation of skills. It enabled courses, communication skills and medical aid for work related ailments. We need to encourage trade unions to boost up their skills under multi-national corporate culture.

REFERENCES

Albrechat Douglas and Adrian Ziderman (2000). Financing Universities in Developing Countries, The World Bank.

Arora, Guljit (2002). Globalization, Federalism and Decentralization, Implications for India: Bookwell.

Azad, J.L. (1971). Report of the Study of the Patterns, Procedures and Policies of Financing of Higher Education in India, Planning Commission (mimeo).

________ (1975). Financing of Higher Education in India, Sterling.

________ (1986). Government Support for Higher Education and Research, Concept.

________ (1989). State Grants: Patterns, Procedures and Policies in Higher Education, The Institutional Context, published in Amrik Singh *et. al.* (ed.), Konark.

________ (1993). Higher Education in India: The Deepening Financial Crisis, Radiant.

________ (2003). Financing of Secondary School Education, Aravalli Publications.

Five Year Plans: New Delhi, Planning Commission, Government of India. Mid-Term Reviews, Planning Commission.

Hallak, Jacques (1999). Globalization, Human Rights and Education, UNESCO, IIEP. Paris.

Higher Education in Developing Countries (2000). Peril and Praomise, Report of the Task Force; The World Bank.

Human Development in South Asia (2000). Oxford.

Human Development Reports, (1999, 2000, 2002 & 2003) UNDP, Oxford.

International Association of Universities (2001). Issues in Higher Education, the OECD, Globalization and Educational Policy, Pergamon.

John, Ryle ed. (2002). Globalization, Universities and Issues of Sustainable Development; Edgar and Edgar Publishers Ltd.

Kaul J.N. (1975). (ed): Higher Education: Social, Change National Development, Indian Institute of Advanced Study, Shimla.

Learning: The Treasure Within (1996). International Commission on Education for the Twenty-First Century, UNESCO.

Martin Carnoy (2000). Globalization and Educational Reforms in Globalization and Education, ed. By Nelly P. Stromquist, Rowman and Littlefield Publishers.

National Policy on Education; Government of India, Ministry of MHRD, 1986, 1992.

Nigvekar Arun (2001). GATS and Higher Education, University Grants Commission, (mimeo).

Panchamukhi, P.R. (2002). Social Sector Development and Economic Reforms. A Focus on Education Sector in Reform and Employment, IAMR.

Parikh, Kirit S. (Ed.) 2002. India Development Report; Indira Gandhi Institute of Development Research (Oxford).

Report of the Education Commission 1964-66, Ministry of Education, 1966.

Sanyal Bikas C. (1995). Innovations in University Management; UNESCO, IIEP, Paris.

Sharma, G.D. (2001). Internationalization of Higher Education; Status and Policy Suggestions, NIEPA (mimeo).

Sharma, G.D. (2001) Trade in Education Service: An Indian Response, NIEPA, New Delhi, (mimeo).

Stromquist, Nelly P. *et. al.* (ed.) (2000). Globalization and Educational Reforms, *op. cit.*

UNESCO (2000). Statistical Year Book, various years.

Wells Amy Stuart, *et. al.* (1998). Globalization and Educational Changes in Andy Hergreaves (ed.) International Hand Book of Educational Change, Vol. 5, Kluwer Academic Publishers, London.

World Bank (2002). Higher Education in Developing Countries, Peril and Promise, the Report of the Task Force on Education and Society, Washington.

World Bank Country Study (1999). India, Reducing Poverty, Accelerating Development, Oxford.

11

Globalization and Its Impact on Women Students in Higher Education

DR. B. RATNA KUMARI, INDIA

Introduction

The women's emancipation movement in the western world started in the nineteenth century with an attack against the exclusion of women from higher education. After considerable struggle and determined efforts by leaders of the movement, the universities in the west gave grudging consent to women's entry to the formal establishment of higher education. The University of London opened its gates to women in 1878. The traditional universities of Oxford and Cambridge, being more conservative, delayed admitting women to their degrees till after the First World War, though they were permitted to appear at the examinations from 1872 in Cambridge and from 1884 in Oxford. American and European Universities were equally if not more grudging in welcoming women into their fraternity. The appointment of women on the faculties of the universities met with even stronger resistance, and with a few exceptions, really happened only after the Second World War. It may come as new to many in India that women were not appointed as full professors in American Universities till very recently, and their scales of pay were also lower than men.

Objectives

Present paper focus attention on the *Role of UGC in Women's Development and Women Empowerment* in terms of Women's Higher education and empowerment in general in India.

The impact of globalization processes on women's higher education in Andhra Pradesh, especially in Andhra University which has achieved NAAC highest rank in Andhra Pradesh.

In 2000-01, out of total enrolment in higher education, 33,06,410 were women *i.e.* contributing to 39.4 per cent. In the year 2001-02, total enrolment (provisional) of women student in higher education was 35,14,000 *i.e.* 39.84 per cent as against the total enrolment of 40,000 in 1950-51. Further against 100 enrolled, only 14 women were pursuing higher education during 1950-51, which has now increased, to 66 in 2001-02.

The technological course at undergraduate level for women in women university were introduced to provide opportunities for women in important technological areas and also to reduce gender imbalance in the sphere of Engineering and Technology. In this connection the present study made an attempt to study the impact of globalization processes on weaker sections.

India embarked upon the process of deregulation and liberalization of its economy from 1980s. The process received a big boost from early nineties, when significant changes were introduced by abolishing licensing for domestic manufacturing for all but a few industries and private sector was allowed to enter areas hitherto reserved for the public sector. Further, import tariffs were drastically reduced (Parikh *et al.,* 2002). Considered in international terms, globalization as the on-going process of economic, technological, social and political integration of the world is reported to have started after the Second World War. Globalization is impacting the institutional framework in both developing and industrial countries. It is changing the way in which governments perceive their role in the society. It has also far reaching implications for socio-economic development and educational systems of countries all over the world.

The Role of UGC in Women's Development and Women Empowerment

Provision of educational opportunities for girls and women has been a part of the national endeavour since independence. The Constitutional of India is clearly committed to the cause of education and unequivocally endorses state intervention to redress an adverse educational scenario. The Supreme Court has given the right to education, the status of a fundamental right.

The Constitution directs the state to provide free and compulsory education to all children up to the age of 14. The Supreme Court has held that the right to education of children up to the age of 14 years is a fundamental right.

The National Policy on Education (NPE) reformulated in 1992, is committed to a well conceived edge in favour of women. "The NPE recognizes that the empowerment of women is possibly the most critical precondition of the participation of girls and women in the education process. The consequent programme of Action which includes Education for Women's Equality, looks at the role of education as an instrument to bring about change in the status of women. Departing form the First National Education Policy of 1986 which was committed to the provision of equal education opportunity, the NPE brought the fundamental issue of women's equality centre-stage 1.

Seventh Five Year Plan has rightly pinpointed the linkage between Education and development. To quote the Plan, "Human resources, development has necessarily to be assigned a key role in any development strategy, particularly in a country with a large population. Trained and educated on sound lined, a large population can itself become an asset in accelerating economic growth and in ensuring social change in desired directions. Education develops basic skills and abilities an fosters a value system conducive to, and is support of national development goals, both long-term and immediate. In a world where knowledge is increasing at an exponential rate, the task of education in the diffusion of new knowledge and at the same time in the preservation and promotion of what is basic to India's culture and ethos, is both complex and challenging."

Dr. K.L. Shrimali, the then Minister of Education while addressing the First Conference of Vice-Chancellors held from 30th July to 1st August, 1957 at New Delhi, remarked, "A state, which does not finance higher education liberally undermines the very basis of civilization. Whether we look from the point of view of the cultural growth of the individual of practical necessities of social life, higher education is vital for society."

"Higher education, a sub-system of the larger societal system, aims at contributing to national development by way of dissemination of knowledge, skills and attitudes; excellence of standards of achievement; providing opportunities to reflect upon the social, political, economic and moral issues facing the country; and its key role in generating leader ship and manpower resource" (Gakhar, 1993).

Role of UGC in Promoting Women Higher Education and Empowerment

Growth in Enrolment of Women in Higher Education

There has been a phenomenal growth in the number of women students enrolled in higher education, since independence. Women enrolment was less than 10 per cent of the total enrolment on the eve of Independence and it rose to 39.84 per cent in 2001-02.

The pace of growth has been particularly faster in the last two decades. As the data in Table: 1 show that the number of women enrolled per hundred manes registered a fivefold increase during the period 1950-51 to 2001-02.

Table–1
Women's Student per Hundred Men Students (Gender Gap)

Year	*Total Women Enrolment*	*Enrolment per Hundred Men*
1950-51	40	14
2001-02	3,514	66

Distribution of Women Enrolment by State, Stage and Faculty

State-wise Distribute of Women Enrolment

Distribute of Women Enrolment by state shows that there has been a marginal increase of 2.19 per cent in the enrolment of women as a percentage of total enrolment in all the states during 2001-02 over the preceding year. Among the states, Kerala with 60 per cent topped in terms of women enrolment as a percentage of total enrolment in 2001-02, followed by Goa (58.6%), Punjab (52.9%) etc. there were 18 states which had higher enrolment of women than the national percentage of 39.84 per cent. In the rest of the states, the percentage of women enrolled was less than the national level, with Bihar recording the lowest women enrolment of 23.0 per cent only.

Distribution of Women Enrolment by Stage of Education

During the decennial period 1992-93 to 2001-02, the enrolment of women as a percentage of total enrolment has been consistently going up at all stages of education—Graduate, Postgraduate, etc.

Distribution of Women Enrolment by Faculty

The faculty-wise distribution of women enrolment during 2001-02 is as given in table.

Table–2
Distribution of Women Enrolment by Stage of Education

Year/ Stage	*Graduate*	*Postgraduate*	*Research*	*Diploma/Certificate*
1992-93	33.0	34.9	37.4	26.0
2001-02*	40.9	42.2	38.9	35.8

*Provisional: A noteworthy of women enrolment is that their incidence is the highest at the Postgraduate level as compared to other levels.

Source: Annual Report of UGC, 2001-02, p. 98.

Table–3
Women Enrolment by Faculty: 2001-02

S. No.	*Faculty*	*Enrolment**	*Percentage*
1.	Art	18,20,134	51.79
2.	Science	6,99,379	19.90
3.	Commerce/Management	5,81,993	46.56
4.	Education	59,394	1.69
5.	Engineering/Technology	1,31,792	3.75
6.	Medicine	1,23,006	3.50
7.	Agriculture	9,137	0.26
8.	Veterinary Science	3,163	0.09
9.	Law	56,934	1.62
10.	Others	29,521	0.84
	Total	35,14,450	100.00

Source: Ibid.

Table shows that women enrolment in the faculty of Arts has been 51.79 per cent of total women enrolment, followed by the faculty of Science (19.90%), the faculty of Commerce (16.56%) etc. there was no much change in the percentage of women enrolled in any faculty in 2001-02 as compared to 2000-01.

Women Colleges

The number of women colleges, as shown in Table 4 shows that there has been a substantial increase during the last decade i.e. 1992-93—2001-02 and thus resulting in increase of women enrolment as a whole.

Table–4
Number of Women Colleges During
1992-93 to 2001-02

Year	*Number of Women Colleges*
1992-93	994
1993-94	1033
1994-95	1107
1995-96	1146
1996-97	1195
1997-98	1260
1998-99	1359
1999-2000	1503
2000-01	1578
2001-02	1600*

Source: Ibid., p. 299.

*Provisional: A noteworthy of women enrolment is that their incidence is the highest at the Postgraduate level as compared to other levels.

Cells to Combat Sexual Harassment

In addition to the above, the UGC has issued two circulars dated 30.5.2001 and 2.5.2002 to all the Indian Universities to set up a permanent cell in each University for combating sexual harassment to women in the University campus as per the directives of the Supreme Court of India. Only 20 universities have so far informed the UGC that they have constituted a permanent cell in the University and rest of the universities have been reminded to set up such a cell to combat on the issues of violence and sexual harassment against women in the University campuses.

Part-time Research Associateships for Women

The scheme of part-time Research Associateship for Women is intended to provide opportunities to the women, who are employed or unemployed, to take up research work in Humanities including Languages, Social Sciences, Sciences, and Engineering and Technology independently and on project basis. The duration of the Associateship is five years with no further extension.

The part-time Research Associateship for Women existed in Eighth Plan. The scheme was revised in the Ninth Plan with certain modification. Earlier, the scheme was meant only for unemployed women. The revised scheme is opened to unemployed as well as employed women. Under the revised scheme, selections were made in the year 1999. The scheme is suspended for the time being.

No physical target was set for this scheme a well. During the first selection in the year 1999, 165 candidates were selected and 162 are working at present. During 2001-02, an amount of Rs. 135.32 lakh was released from the allocated budget of Rs. 150.00 lakh.

The year-wise position of release of grants to Part-time Women Research Associates during the Ninth Plan period is as shown below.

Year Grants	*Released*
1997-98	160.39
1998-99	190.62
1999-2000	129.26
2000-01	137.50
2001-02	135.32
Total	753.09

Day-Care Centers in Universities

Under the scheme, day-care facilities are provided at the campuses for children of three months to six years age group, whose parents (University employees/Students/Researcher) are away from home for the day. During the year 2001-02, grants amounting to Rs. 12.00 lakh were released to six State Universities and Rs. 6.00 lakh to three deemed to be universities.

Tenth Plan has Beautifully Proposed that

The bold decision to declare 'Education as the Fundamental Right' reflects the Government's concern and commitment to ensure that everyone born in this country is literate/educated an thus fulfil the constitutional commitment of 'Education for All' by 2007. Through the specially targeted programme of Sarva Shiksha Abhiyan (SSA), launched in 2000, efforts will be made to reach the unreached women and the girl child. Thus, all out efforts will be made during the Tenth Plan to ensure that the SSA achieves its commitment within the time targets set.

The Tenth Plan will further endeavour to consolidate the progress made under female education and carry it forward for achieving the set goal of 'Education for Women's Equality' as advocated by the National Policy on Education, 1986 (revised in 1992) by reducing the gender gaps at the secondary and higher levels. Also, special attention will be paid to the already identified low female literacy pockets and to the women and girl children socially disadvantaged groups viz. Scheduled Castes (SCs), Scheduled Tribes (STs), Other Backward Classes (OBCs), Minorities, Disabled etc. as they still lag behind the rest of the population with female literacy rates as low as 5 to 10 per cent, while the national average of female literacy stands at 54.16 per cent in 2001.

Recognizing the fact that the application of science and technology is vital for the advancement of women and technology is vital for the advancement of women, the Tenth Plan will encourage women to participate in science and technology activities, especially in rural areas as it reduces the drudgery of household chores and provides a better quality of life. These will include measures to motive girls to take up subjects of science and technology in higher education and ensure that development projects with scientific and technical inputs involve women fully. Efforts to develop a scientific temper and awareness will also be stepped up. Special measures will be taken to train women in areas where they have special skills like communication and information technology. Efforts to develop appropriate technologies suited to women's needs as well as to reduce their drudgery will be made through the on-going programme of 'Science and Technology Project for Women'. Also, special efforts/ provisions will be made to cover the existing gap in disseminating and reaching the technologies to rural women for whose benefit these were designed.

Further, to encourage more girls to enter into the mainstream of higher education, the Tenth Plan endeavours to put into action the governmental commitment of providing free education for girls up to the college level, including professional courses, so as to quicken the process of empowerment of women. All these efforts will continue during the Tenth Plan with the strength and support of the National Policy on Education, as it extends the most positive interventionist role in empowering women.

We may not be pessimistic. We should hope that the present momentum of women study centers built-up since by UGC would continue. The Central and State Governments, the mass media and educational institutions, teacher, students, youth, voluntary agencies, social activist groups, and employers, who must reinforce their commitment to literacy campaigns, awareness among about the socio-economic reality and the possibility to change. We should not hesitate to bring about innovative changes to make the programme realistic. We cannot afford to allow the programme to go slow as the programme is a source of strength to all other schemes of socio-economic development, whatever may be their immediate goal.

The Concept and Ramifications of Globalization

Globalization is a newly emerging phenomenon. It has been defined as "a set of processes by which the world is rapidly being integrated into one economic space via increased international trade, the internationalization of production and financial markets; the internationalization of a commodity culture promoted by an increasingly networked global telecommunication system" (Graham, 1996).

Globalization transcends socio-economic and political barriers that the countries of the world are prone to build around themselves. It is not only a process "integrating just economy, but culture, technology and governance. It is giving rise to new markets, foreign exchange and capital markets linked globally, new tools, internet links, cellular phones, media network, new actors; the World Trade Organization with authority over national governments, the multi-national cooperation with more economic power than many states, new rules, multi-national agreements and intellectual property, multi-lateral agreements on trade" (Human Development Report, 1999).

Globalization is expected to have a positive influence on the volume, quality and spread of knowledge through increased interaction among the various states. In a globalized world, as technology becomes its main motor, knowledge assumes a powerful role in production, making its possession essential for nations, if they are successfully to pursue economic growth and competitiveness (Stromquist, 2000). Education, being the most potent instrument of creation, assimilation and transmission of knowledge, assumes a central role in the process.

In a market oriented competitive world, unleashed by the forces of globalization, education has to assume a somewhat different role. It cannot afford to be conventional, rigid and impervious to change.

It has to keep abreast of the latest developments in various fields and be capable of creating, absorbing and transacting neo-technology and information systems that are sweeping across the countries of the world. There has also to be a paradigm shift in the contents of education with substantial emphasis on the productivity aspect of the curriculum. It would also call for adequate emphasis on Research and Development (R&D).

It is, however, necessary to guard against being swept off our feet by the new 'cult of technology', and consequently, 'the diminution of respect for spiritual and cultural values' (Maugey, cited in Namer, 1999). An unfettered and ruthless pursuit of economic goals, without regard to considerations of moral and social values is bound to be disastrous for the people, particularly in developing countries.

Not an Unmixed Blessing

In spite of the cataclysmic changes brought about in most countries, it would be wrong to consider globalization as a panacea for all economic and social ills. As stated by the Planning Commission: "the accelerated process of liberalization and globalization in the world has increased the opportunities for growth and development, but it has also added new complexities and risks in the management of global interdependence" (Tenth Five Year Plan, Vol. I, p. 97). Some of the complexities identified at the international level are:

Globalization is forging greater interdependence, yet the world seems more fragmented—between the rich and the poor, between the powerful and the powerless.

Economically, politically and technologically, the world has never seemed more free or more unjust.

If the present global progress continues at such a snails' pace, it will take more than 130 years to rid the world of hunger (The Human Development Report, UNDP, 2002).

Globalization is a "tricky term for some, it connotes free flow of ideas, capital, people and goods around the world. For others, it implies the hegemony of the capitalist system, the domination of rich nations and corporations and the loss of national identity" (Madeline Green *et al.*, 2002).

The Humane Face of Globalization

It would thus appear that globalization is not an unmixed blessing. It may promote "growth through increased technology and knowledge transfers in developing countries but it could also be sometime a source of instability...." (The Human Development Report in South Asia, UNDP, 1999). It should, therefore, not be construed purely as a faceless economic mechanism but be based on:

Ethics: Ensuring less violation of human rights;

Equity: Resulting in reducing disparities within and between nations;

Inclusion: Less marginalization of people and countries;

Human Security: Less instability of societies and less vulnerability of people;

Sustainability: Less destruction of environment; and

Development: Less poverty and deprivation.

Globalization Processes and Education

Education, as a service industry, is part of globalization process under the umbrella of General Agreement on Trade in Services (GATS). There is, however, distinct possibility that this might "force countries with quite different academic needs and resources to conform to structures inevitably designed to service the interest of the most powerful academic systems and corporate educational providers... breeding inequality and dependence" (Altbach, 2002). Further, "Globalization... can lead to unregulated and poor quality higher education, with the worldwide marketing of fraudulent degrees or other so-called higher education credentials..." (World Bank's Task Force, 2000). India, is likely to turn into "an increasingly attractive market for foreign universities and hence other nations are going to use GATS provisions to their advantage" (Arun Nigvekar, 2002). While these are obvious problems, globalization can also have advantages, particularly for India, which has a large educational system and infrastructure and diverse human capabilities.

Given the array of theoretical and epistemological perspective presented in the general social science literature on 'globalization', it is difficult to assess not only the nature and dimensions of globalization, but also what it might mean to the field of education. Very few educational researchers or theorists have attempted to make connections between the economic, political and cultural dimensions of globalization and the policies and practices of education

It appears as though the phenomenon of globalization will mean many different things for education. Most certainly, in the near future, "it will mean a more competitive and deregulated educational system modelled after free market but with more pressure on it to assure that the next generation of workers are prepared for some amorphous 'job market of 21st century'. It will also mean... "that educational system will increasingly provide the sites of struggle over the meaning and power of national identity and a national culture. And finally, schools will no doubt also be the sites of various counter-hegemonic movements and pedagogies" (Wells, *et. al.,* 1998).

Globalization as a Reality

We have discussed the main features of globalization and its likely impact on socio-economic development. At this stage, it must be emphasized that globalization, though a recent phenomenon, is a reality, which cannot be wished away. It is, however, difficult to measure its long-term effect on the course of socio-economic development in various countries. In fact, because of the large disparities in the economic position of the countries inhabiting the globe, it would be imprudent to arrive at any standardized formula of assessing the effects. Each country is an entity in itself and requires to be studied differently. It is however necessary to stress that a thoughtless and unimaginative entry into the globalised market would not be in the best interests of the countries, particularly those, which are striving to grapple with the problems of slow economic and social development.

Impact of Globalization

Globalization has a wide ranging potential to influence all sectors of development. Besides its impact on the pace and pattern of economic development, it also casts its shadow on the system of education. It would, therefore, be pertinent to analyze its impact on the process and progress of education. The impact of globalization on education and the manner in which the system should respond to the needs of globalization would require to be studied basically under two broad heads.

The needed reforms within the educational system like content, equity and excellence etc. and the fall out of globalization, which will entail determining strategies relating to the impending internationalization of education; finance related issues and privatization of secondary and higher education.

Needed Reforms within the Educational System

Content of Education

Curriculum Upgradation

The modern advances in information technology have revolutionized, among others, the content of knowledge and the processes of educational transaction. The ever-growing use of electronic media has brought education to the doorsteps of the common man. Information processing technologies provide an efficient framework for the storage, management, analysis and application of information. In the process, popular culture and education alike have adopted what may be called 'computational paradigm', the use of computer metaphors, to understand how human beings cognize themselves and the world.

The operative part of the introduction of the information technology is the need for a continuous upgradation of the curriculum in order to introduce the latest developments relating to various disciplines in the curriculum. Alongside, pruning of the existing curriculum would be a necessary condition in order to remove the obsolete and irrelevant details.

It also needs to be stressed that education should help to engender a new "humanism that contains an essential ethical component and sets considerable store by knowledge of, and respect for, the culture and spiritual values of different civilizations, as a much needed counter weight to a globalization that would otherwise be seen only in economical or technological terms. The sense of shared values as a common destiny is in fact the basis on which any scheme of international cooperation must be founded" (Delors Commission, 1996).

The fast developing stock of knowledge and the need for its continuous updating has also initiated an era of lifelong learning. No longer is education confined to a particular period of life. It is a continuum with no artificial time barriers restricting the process.

Productivity Orientation

The basic objective of globalization is to enhance productivity and to make the educational system an instrument of preparing students, who can compete in the world markets as productive members of the society. This would necessitate making skill training as an integral part of the curriculum besides making attitudinal changes so that the students do not consider it infra-dig to work with hands.

Unfortunately our experience of introducing an element of skill training has not been adequately successful. The schemes of vocationalization, both at the school and college stages, have been languishing for want of enthusiasm on the part of students (and teachers). It has also not received the required social recognition. It may be recalled that the scheme of vocational education at the secondary stage was launched in 1988 as a centrally sponsored programme. Against a target of diverting 10 per cent of students to vocational stream by 1995 and 25 per cent by 2000, only 11 per cent of students have been covered at the plus two stage. At the college stage also, scheme of vocationalisation has been in operation since 1994. Till date, it has hardly covered twenty thousand students out of a total university enrolment of more than eight million.

The reasons for the slow progress of these programmes are many, but the most significant is lack of acceptance – by the parents, teachers and students – of introducing an element of skill training as a part of the general curriculum. Education is still considered as an academic discipline in which the intrusion of vocational training is considered unacceptable. Further, the craze for degrees is also an important retarding factor. There is also lack of parity of status between students and teachers of vocational and general streams leading to the former hesitating to join vocational courses.

Value Education

In order to ward off the evils of untrammeled competitiveness and use of unethical practices to go up in the socio-economic ladder, it is necessary that education should lay stress on value education, which emphasizes cooperation rather than competition; sharing of experience rather than personal aggrandizement and learning to live together rather than living in mutually hostile camps.

Research

Indian professionals, particularly in Information Technology, have successfully competed in the world markets especially in software development and data analysis. This, however, cannot continue for a long time to come especially because competition from the developing countries is likely to be very intense in times to come. This underscores the need for emphasizing Research and

Development (R&D) particularly in the newly emerging areas in our university institutions. As suggested by Iyengar (2000): "Our human resource development in the future should be planned such that there are identified areas in which India could compete effectively, and be innovators rather than just followers. These could include areas such as biotechnology, new power sources, education etc. The Government should focus on these areas, and offer incentives to researchers for innovative research in these fields."

Equity, Excellence Syndrome

At this stage, I would like to draw your attention to the seemingly contradictory situation, inherent in our race towards globalization. For want of better phrase, I have termed it as 'Equity-Excellence Syndrome'. It is explained thus:

An important component of globalization in relation of education is the need for producing higher quality manpower that can successfully face competition in the world markets. This would imply selecting the best possible human material and giving them education of the highest quality. This would naturally be relevant to secondary and higher education, because education at the primary level has been considered as the fundamental right of every child in the relevant age group. It would also be necessary to grant financial and other incentives to the meritorious students so that want of resources is not an impediment in their ascent towards the highest forms of education.

It can be argued that nurturing of excellence will be inequitable in that it may deny opportunities to a very large segment of student population, who are not so intellectually endowed, to get into institutions of higher education. It is also feared that the present day techniques of students' assessment are not very reliable tools for measuring the potentiality of students, particularly from rural areas and those belonging to the deprived sections of the society.

It is difficult to deny the force of these arguments. The remedy, however, lies not in denigrating the need for nurturing excellence but in creating opportunities for expanding the field of excellence, so as to enable more and more promising students to join institutions of higher learning. This would necessitate qualitative upgradation of the academic and physical infrastructure, reforming teacher education and improving the system of student assessment so that no student with potentiality for benefiting from education is denied that opportunity. It may also require special coaching facilities for the students belonging to the traditionally deprived sections of the society.

The Fallout of Globalization

Internationalization of Education

Implicit in the system of Globalization is the inevitability of internationalization of the educational system, particularly at the higher education stage. This is not peculiar to India but has become a worldwide phenomenon. The entry of the World Trade Organization (WTO) and the inclusion of educational services under the General Agreement on Trade in Services (GATS) has given a boost to the internationalization of higher education.

Merits of Internationalization

The merits of internationalization of education are:

- Education will improve if it is internationalized and healthy competition takes place;
- It will provide global opportunities and promote international good will; and
- It will encourage exchange of scholars. This can be done by involvement of reputed scholars in the respective countries in curriculum designing and transaction of knowledge.

Notwithstanding the merits of internationalization of education, it will be harmful for our country to allow an unregulated entry of foreign institutions in India. Quite a few of these institutions are of dubious quality—some of them not even been recognized in their own countries. In a Study "Partnership of Private Sector in Financing and Management of Higher Education" (2002). In consultation with academics, educational planners and representatives of the industry, the following guidelines were suggested about the entry of foreign institutions in India:

While the foreign institutions may be allowed to set up their campuses in India, they should function under the control of the government or specialized bodies like the National Assessment and Accreditation Council (NAAC) set up by the Government for the purpose. The universities which want to function in India should have been accredited in their own countries. The foreign institutions should be subjected to pre-entry academic audit and accreditation norms devised by the designated government agencies. They should sign Memoranda of Understanding (MOU) with the government or a body designated by it. The Memorandum should give details of the courses of studies, infrastructural facilities, both academic and non-academic and the amount of expected cost recoveries from Indian students.

The entry of foreign institutions should be allowed on the basis of reciprocity. The countries exporting education to India should also permit the opening of Indian university campuses in their countries. There should be provision for exchange of faculty among the various countries participating in the programme; and in the entire process of the entry of foreign institutions the paramountcy of national interests should be the crucial guiding factor.

Finance Related Issues

In order to be a part of the global configuration, the requirements of funds for social services including education will increase manifold. For this purpose, it will be necessary to augment government funding for these sectors. Unfortunately, the reverse process has been set in motion. According to Panchamukhi (2002), the impact of reforms has not been quite favourable for Social Services including Education. Before reforms period, social services constituted 39.4 per cent of total government expenditure. The percentage declined to 36 during 1991-92 to 1996-97. In the case of education, the decline was from 21 per cent to less than 20 per cent during the same period.

Down Sizing Secondary and Higher Education

Indian higher education has attracted special attention by the 'Reformists', particularly by the international organizations. Based on the 'Rate of Return' studies, the World Bank came to the conclusion that its lending strategy should emphasize primary education relegating higher education to a relatively minor place in its development agenda. The plea has been repeated by Carnoy (1999). According to him "Higher education is a high cost level of schooling and basic education is relatively low cost. In addition, in many countries, public university education costs are heavily weighted toward non-teaching and non-research expenditures such as student subsidies and administrative costs". The shift of emphasis, it is argued, would enhance opportunities for larger number of primary students at the expense of subsidizing a relatively elite group of families that could bear the cost of university education."

That the Government of India succumbed to these specious arguments would be evident from the fact that in 1997, the Ministry of Finance circulated a note on 'Subsidies', in which, among other things, higher education was described as a 'non-merit' good, unworthy of government subventions.

A deeper consideration of this suggestion will bring out its utter shortsightedness. In the first instance, it is wrong to presume that at the higher education stage, costs are heavily weighted towards non-teaching and non-research expenditure. Moreover, it is academically preposterous to segment the education, whose different stages are complementary rather than competitive. For example, if university education is starved of funds, it will be impossible to provide good and competent teachers for the school stage. As emphasized by Panchamukhi (2002); "At any point of time, weakening of higher education sector would weaken the forces of competitiveness and efficiency in the functioning of different sectors of economy..."

The implementation of this too simplistic suggestion will also impede the progress of basic research, which is the essential responsibility of the universities. Further, any scaling down of the financial inputs for higher education would result in the qualitative deterioration of the highly trained scientific and technical manpower, which is the mainstay of our economic and social development.

It is heartening to note that a recent Task Force of the World Bank (2000), while fully supporting the continuation of larger investment in primary and secondary education rebutted the traditional economic argument, which is based on "limited understanding of what higher education institutions contribute". The Task Force challenged the notion that public investment in higher education is socially inequitable. It said: "Rate-of-Return Studies treat educated people as valuable only through their higher earnings and the greater tax revenues extracted by society. But educated people clearly have many other effects on society: educated people are well - positioned to be economic and social entrepreneurs, having far reaching impact on the economic and social well-being of their communities. Rates of return analysis entirely misses the impact of university based research on the economy—a far reaching social benefit that is at the heart of the argument for developing strong higher education system." (emphasis added)

It may be stressed that education is a continuum in which the various stages are complement arrant earthen competitive. Any attempt at compartmentalizing education in order to deny the requisite funding to a particular sector would be retrogressive and retard the progress of education.

Privatization of Secondary and Higher Education

As a corollary to the suggestions about reducing public investment in secondary and higher education, a plea has been made to hand over these sectors to private bodies. It has also been suggested that institutions beyond primary basic education should increasingly depend upon tuition fees, the philanthropy of the general public and the industrial and commercial organizations, which should be allowed to set up, manage and finance institutions of post elementary education.

In the preceding section, it has been argued that it would be counter-productive for the government to withdraw from secondary and higher education in view of their close relationship with the production of highly trained technical and professional manpower. Furthermore some of the disciplines, which have no apparent market value, will go by default resulting into a skewed development of the educational system. There is also strong apprehension that privatization would lead to commercialization of education. As pointed out by Altbach (2000), "The motivation for establishing (Private) institutions is always to make money. British and Australian institutions have been active internationally as a way of making up for budget cuts at home". The emergence of capitation fee charging and self-financing institutions in India, with predominantly commercial motives, is an eloquent testimony to the abject surrender of education to commercial forces.

In view of the above considerations; while the participation of private bodies in investment and management of education should be encouraged, complete privatization of these sectors of education should be ruled out. Further, market needs should be kept in view while developing the curriculum. The element of productivity orientation should guide the formulation of curriculum framework. It is also necessary that while deciding about the fee structure and other student levies, the tendency towards commercialization of education should be guarded against.

Methodology

In the light of globalization process Education system has taken several modifications. Women education in general and higher education of women in particular has opened several channels for women.

The present study examines the growth and empowerment of women students in higher education in Andhra University Visakhapatnam at micro level and examines whether the globalization processes has promoted women students in Andhra University.

Objectives

Following are the major objectives specified for the present study:

- To analyze the socio-economic profile of weaker sections women in higher Education
- To asses the study expenditure levels of weaker sections women student in higher education in the context of globalization process
- To study aspirations of the weaker sections women students with relevance to empowerment and economic security
- To suggest some policy options for weaker sections women empowerment through higher education in Andhra Pradesh.

Sample and Data Collection

To collect the data, well structural questionnaires were administered on 378 women students of Andhra University, Visakhapatnam.

Analysis

To analyze the data, appropriate statistical tools were used.

Findings

Socio-Demographic Profile of Sample Women Students

Table-5

Distribution of Respondent Women by their Age

Age of Respondent	*Frequency*	*Per cent*
15-20	49	13.0
21-25	321	84.9
26-30	6	1.6
31-35	2	0.5
Total	378	100

The Table 5 explains that the distribution of the age of the respondent women. Out of the total respondents 84.9 per cent of respondent are in 21-25 years age group 13 per cent of the respondents are in 15-20 years age group. 1.6 per cent of the respondents are in 26-30 years of age group. A small percentage (5) respondents are in 31-35 years and above age group.

Table-6

Distribution of Respondent Women by their Religion

Religion	*Frequency*	*Per cent*
Christian	20	5.3
Hindu	355	93.9
Islam	3	0.8
Total	378	100

The Table 6 explains that the distribution religion of the respondents. The table indicates out of the total 93 per cent of them are Hindus and 5.3 per cent of them are Christians and 0.8 per cent of the respondents are Muslims.

Table-7

Distribution of Respondent Women by their Caste

Caste	*Frequency*	*Per cent*
SC	81	21.4
ST	19	5.0
OC	103	27.2
BC	175	46.3
Total	378	100

The Table 7 explains that the distribution of respondent women by their caste. Out of the total respondents 46.3 per cent belong to BC, 27.2 per cent of the respondent belongs to OC, 21.4 per cent of the respondent belongs to the SC and a small (5) per cent of them are STs.

Table-8

Distribution of Respondent Women by their Martial Status

Martial Status	*Frequency*	*Per cent*
Married	14	3.7
Unmarried	364	96.3
Total	378	100

The Table 8 explains about respondent women martial status. 96.3 per cent respondents were unmarried and 3.7 per cent of respondents were married.

Table-9
Distribution of Respondent Women by their Languages Known

Languages You Known	*Frequency*	*Per cent*
Telugu	62	16.4
English	14	3.7
Telugu-English	254	67.2
Hindi-Telugu-English	47	12.4
Others	1	0.3
Total	378	100

The Table 9 indicates about the languages known by the respondents. Out of the total respondents 67.2 per cent knows Telugu and English, 16.4 per cent knows Telugu only, 12.4 per cent knows Telugu, English and Hindi and a small (3) per cent knows other languages.

Table-10
Distribution of the Respondent Women by their Parent's Occupation

Occupation of the Parent	*Father*	*Mother*	*Husband*	*Total (%)*
Agricultural Labours	72	3	2	77 (20.37)
Farmer	107	–	–	107 (28.37)
Private Employee	27	1	–	28 (7.41)
Govt. Service	88	3	–	11 (24.07)
Self-Employee	35	1	1	37 (9.80)
Others	35	3	–	38 (10.05)
Total	364	11	3	378 (100)

Table 10 indicates the respondent women parental occupational status. 20.37 per cent parents are agricultural labourers. 28.37 per cent of them are farmers. 7.41 per cent of parents are private employees. 24.07 per cent are in government service. 9.80 per cent of parents are involved in self-employment. 10.05 per cent of parents are involved in other activities.

Table-11
Distribution of Respondent Women by their Course Duration

Duration of Course	*Frequency*	*Per cent*
Two years course	313	82.8
Three years course	41	10.8
Four years course	2	0.5
One year course	19	5.0
Five years course	3	0.8
Total	378	100

The Table 11 explains the respondent women course duration in the university. It reveals that, 82.8 per cent respondents are studying 2 years course, 10.8 per cent are in three years course, 5.0 per cent of them are doing one year course 0.8 and 0.5 per cent of respondent are doing five years and four years course respectively.

Table-12
Distribution of Respondent Women by their Medium of Study

Medium	*Frequency*	*Per cent*
Telugu	121	32.0
English	255	67.5
Hindi	2	0.5
Total	378	100

The Table 12 explains that the number of respondents women by their medium of study. Out of the total respondents, from 67.5 per cent are studying in English medium, 32.0 per cent are studying in Telugu medium only and a small (0.5) per cent in Hindi medium.

Table-13
Distributions of Respondent Women by their Purpose for Join this Course

Why Did You Join this Course?	*Frequency*	*Per cent*
To get employment	250	66.1
No alternative	8	2.1
Seat allotted	12	3.2
Self-motivation	108	28.6
Total	378	100

Table 13 explains that the distributions of respondent women by their purpose for join this course. Out of the total, 66.1 respondents are answered to get employment, 28.6 per cent respondents are by self-motivation, 3.2 per cent respondents joined as the seat was allotted and a small (2.1) per cent are reported as they have no other alternative to do.

Table-14

Distribution of Respondent Women by their Opinion on Expenditure on Education

Do You Feel Expenditure on Education is High?	*Frequency*	*Per cent*
Yes	285	75.4
No	93	24.6
Total	378	100

Table 14 explains that, 75.4 per cent of respondent women felt that expenditure on education is high. 24.6 per cent of respondent women opinion about expenditure on education is not high.

Table-15

If Yes-What are the Reasons?

If Yes-What are the Reasons?	*Frequency*	*Per cent*
Private institutions entry in to	103	27.2
Globalization processes	67	17.7
To read in English medium	20	5.3
Less grants from Central Government	96	25.4
None	92	24.3
Total	378	100

Out of 378 respondents, 285 (75.4) per cent of women opined that, the expenditure on education is high. The reasons they have mentioned are 27.2 per cent of them felt that, the entry of private institutes, 17.7 per cent of them opined that, because of globalization process, 25.4 per cent of them felt that, insufficient grants from Central Government for education also makes the expenditure on education as high. 5.3 per cent of them opined that, medium of instruction as English also one of the reason for high expenditure on education. 24.3 per cent of them did not mention any specific reason.

Table-16
Distribution of Respondent Women by their Source of Expenses

How Did You Meet Your Expenses?	*Frequency*	*Per cent*
Father/mothers income	307	81.2
Relatives help	34	9.0
Private lenders	12	3.2
Banks loans	25	6.6
Total	378	100

The Table 16 reveals that, respondent women source of expenses for their higher studies. 81.2 per cent of respondents meet their expenses from father/mother income, 9.0 per cent seek help from relatives and 3.2 per cent take loans from private lenders. 6.6 per cent of them take loans from banks.

Table-17
Distribution of Respondent Women by Amount Paid for their Studies (2/3 Years Courses; Rs.)

How Much Amount You Paid for Your Studies?	*Frequency*	*Per cent*
1,000-10,000	157	41.5
11,000-20,000	58	15.3
21,000-30,000	34	9.0
31,000-40,000	39	10.3
41,000-50,000	51	13.5
51,000-above	39	10.3
Total	378	100

Table 17 reveals that, the amount paid by the respondent women for their studies (course). 41.5 per cent reported that they have spent Rs. 1,000-10,000 for their course. 15.3 per cent have reported that, the incurred expenditure on their course was Rs. 11,000-20,000. 9.0 per cent reported that they have spent Rs. 21,000-30,000 for their course. 10.3 per cent reported that, they have spent Rs. 31,000-40,000 for their course. 13.5 per cent have reported that, they have spent Rs. 41,000-50,000 and 10.3 per cent of them have spent more than 50 thousand.

Table–18
Distribution of Respondent Women by Kind of Preference for Course

What Kind of Courses you Like to Prefer?	*Frequency*	*Per cent*
Income oriented	53	14.0
Knowledge oriented	110	29.1
Skill oriented	94	24.9
Training oriented	15	4.0
Employment oriented	106	28.0
Total	378	100

Table 18 explains that, the respondent women's preference of the course. 14.0 per cent preferred to study income oriented course. 29.1 per cent preferred knowledge oriented courses. 24.9 per cent preferred skill oriented courses, 4.0 per cent wants training oriented courses and 28.0 per cent of them preferred employment oriented courses.

Table–19
Distribution of Respondent Women by their Order of Generation in Attaining Higher Education

Are You First Generation in the Family to Attain Higher Education?	*Frequency*	*Per cent*
Yes	238	63.0
No	140	37.0
Total	378	100

Table 19 reveals that, 63.0 per cent of respondent women are first generation in their family to pursue higher education. 37.0 per cent of them are not the first generation who pursues higher education.

Table 20 explains about respondent women opinion about higher education for girls. 40.2 per cent have expressed that, the higher education gives self-motivation for their lives. 44.2 per cent felt that by doing higher studies they may get good job, 13.2 per cent felt that, higher studies increase their knowledge. Very little per cent 1.1 each felt that by doing higher studies they may get martial alliance and other reasons.

Table–20
Distribution of Respondent Women Opinion about Higher Education for Girls

Why there is More Entry of Girls in Higher Education?	*Frequency*	*Per cent*
Self-motivation	152	40.2
To get good job	168	44.4
To get knowledge	50	13.2
Better martial alliance	4	1.1
Others	4	1.1
Total	378	100

Table–21
Distribution of Respondent Women by their Opinion about Gender Bias in Education System

Do you Feel Gender Bias in the Present Education System?	*Frequency*	*Per cent*
Yes	134	35.4
No	244	64.6
Total	378	100

Table 21 explains about respondent women opinion on gender bias in education system 35.4 per cent reported that, there is gender bias in education system. 64.6 per cent felt that there is no gender bias.

Table–22
Distributions of Respondent Women by their Awareness on Globalization

What is Globalization?	*Frequency*	*Per cent*
Boarder less economy	95	25.1
networking with markets /institutions	110	29.1
Trade without barriers	76	20.1
Opened economy	97	25.7
Total	378	100

Table 22 explains about respondent women's awareness on globalization. 29.1 per cent felt that globalization is networking with markets/institutions. 20.1 per cent felt that, it's a trade without barriers. 25.7 felt that it is an open economy.

Table–23

Distributions of Respondent Women by their Awareness on Globalization and its Impact on Expenses on Higher Education

Do You Feel Globalization Processes has Increased the Expenses on the HE?	*Frequency*	*Per cent*
Yes	297	78.6
No	81	21.4
Total	378	100

Table 23 reveals that, 78.6 per cent of respondent women felt that, the globalization process has increased expenses on Higher Education. 21.4 per cent felt that, the process of globalization has not increased the Higher Education expenses.

Summary and Conclusions

The Women students' empowerment has positive correlation with higher education.

- Out of the total respondent 84.9 per cent of respondents are in 21-25 years age group 13 per cent of the respondents are in 15-20 years age group. 1.6 per cent of the respondents are in 26-30 years of age group. Small percentage (5) respondents are in 31-35 years and above age group.
- 93 per cent of them are Hindus and 5.3 per cent of the respondents are Christians and 8 per cent of the respondents are Muslims.
- Out of the total respondents 46.3 per cent belong to BC, 27.2 per cent of the respondent belongs to OC, 21.4 per cent of the respondent belongs to the SC and a small 5 per cent of them are STs.
- Out of the total respondents 96.3 per cent respondent were unmarried and 3.7 per cent of respondents were married.
- Out of the total respondents 67.2 per cent knows Telugu and English, 16.4 per cent knows Telugu only, 12.4 per cent knows Telugu, English and Hindi and a small 3 per cent knows other languages.
- 20.37 per cent parents are agricultural labourers. 28.37 per cent of them are farmers. 7.41 per cent of parents are private employees. 24.07 per cent are in government service. 9.80

per cent of parents are involved in self-employment. 10.05 per cent of parents are involved in other activities.

- Data reveals that, 82.8 per cent respondents are studying 2 years course, 10.8 per cent are in three years course, 5.0 per cent of them are doing one year course 0.8 and 0.5 per cent of respondent are doing five years and four years course respectively.
- Out of the total respondents 67.5 per cent are studying in English medium, 32.0 per cent are studying in Telugu medium only and a small (0.5) per cent are in Hindi medium.
- Out of the total respondents 66.1 per cent joined the curse to get a job, 28.6 per cent joined by self-motivation, 3.2 per cent joined as they have obtained/secured a seat in the course, a small 2.1 per cent have joined as they do not have any other alternative to do.
- 81.2 per cent of respondent meet their expenses from father/mother income, 9.0 per cent seek help from relatives and 3.2 per cent take loans from private lenders. 6.6 per cent of them take loans from banks.
- 41.5 per cent reported that they have spent Rs. 1,000-10,000 for their course. 15.3 per cent have reported that, the incurred expenditure on their course was Rs. 11,000-20,000. 9.0 per cent reported that they have spent Rs. 21,000-30,000 for their course. 10.3 per cent reported that, they have spent Rs. 31,000-40,000 for their course.
- 14.0 per cent preferred to study income oriented course. 29.1 per cent preferred knowledge oriented courses. 24.9 per cent preferred skill oriented courses, 4.0 per cent wants training oriented courses and 28.0 per cent of them preferred employment oriented courses.
- Respondent women students' opinion about higher education for girls. 40.2 per cent have expressed that, the higher education gives self-motivation for their lives. 44.2 per cent felt that by doing higher studies they may get good job, 13.2 per cent felt that, higher studies increase their knowledge. Very little per cent 1.1 each felt that by doing higher studies they may get martial alliance and some other reasons.
- Respondent women students opinion on gender bias in education system 35.4 per cent reported that, there is gender

bias in education system. 64.6 per cent felt that there is no gender bias.

- Respondent women students awareness on globalization. 29.1 per cent felt that globalization is networking with markets/institutions. 20.1 per cent felt that, it's a trade without barriers. 25.7 per cent felt that, it is an open economy.
- Awareness on globalization and its impact on expenses on Higher Education 78.6 per cent of respondent women felt that, the globalization process has increased expenses on Higher Education. 21.4 per cent felt that, the process of globalization has not increased the Higher Education expenses.

Conclusion

Globalization process has both positive and native impact on women higher education in general and weaker section women in particular.

Higher education has to undergo some modifications and the admission approaches need to be modified in order to get admission for more number of weaker section women in higher education arena.

The impact of globalization has also given boost for weaker sections women students. However higher education has positive as well as negative impact on women empowerment processes.

I have attempted to traverse the entire spectrum of globalization with a focus on studying its impact on and implications for the educational system. Even at the cost of repetition, it may be stated that globalization is a recent phenomenon in the world's socio-economic system. Although it is too early to assess the impact of globalization on India's economy, it has so far not yielded any spectacular outcomes. It has accelerated the pace of development in some areas but has led to certain incongruities in others. It is, therefore, necessary that steps should be taken to reduce, if not remove, its baneful fall out.

Globalization, as an effective instrument of international exchange of goods and services, has to have a humane face, based on ethical considerations rather than on cut throat competition. It should play a positive role in reducing economic and social disparities within, and among, the nations. It should also be an effective tool for promoting sustainable development.

Globalization has a multi-dimensional impact on the system of education. It has underlined the need for reforms in the educational system with particular reference to the wider utilization of information technology; giving productivity dimension to the educational system and emphasis on research and development. It has also given rise to controversies relating to introducing changes in the inter-sectoral priorities in the allocation of resources leading to the misconceived policy of downsizing of secondary and higher education. It has also advocated privatization of higher education without realizing the dangerous possibility of making the system a commercial enterprise. Further, internationalization of education particularly higher education has been advocated without due regard to the needs and susceptibilities of the developing countries.

It is, therefore, necessary that each country should decide about the nature and extent of globalization that can be constructively introduced in their socio-economic and educational systems. While it is difficult to resist the temptation of falling in line with the international community, it is necessary that while doing so, the paramountcy of national interests should be kept in view. This is more so in the field of education which is intimately concerned with the development of human capital. Any thoughtless entry into the global educational market can end up in harming the vital interests of students for generations to come.

We shall conclude by quoting the prophetic statement of Mahatma Gandhi made long before globalization was ever thought of: "I do not want my house to be walled on all sides and my windows to be stuffed. I want the culture of all the lands to be blown about my house as freely as possible. But I refuse to be blown off my feet by any."

REFERENCES

Arora, Guljit, (2002). Globalization, Federalism and Decentralization, Implications for India: Bookwell.

Azad, J.L. (1971). Report of the Study of the Patterns, Procedures and Policies of Financing of Higher Education in India, Planning Commission. (mimeo).

________ (1975). Financing of Higher Education in India, Sterling.

________ (1986). Government Support for Higher Education and Research, Concept.

________ (1989). State Grants: Patterns, Procedures and Policies in Higher Education, the Institutional Context, published in Amrik Singh *et. al.* (ed.) Konark.

________ (1993). Higher Education in India: The Deepening Financial Crisis, Radiant.

________ (2003). Financing of Secondary School Education, Aravalli Publications.

Carnoy, Martin, (2000). Globalization and Educational Reforms in Globalization and Education, ed. By Nelly P. Stromquist, Rowman and Littlefield Publishers.

Douglas Albrechat and Adrian Ziderman (2000). Financing Universities in Developing Countries, The World Bank.

Five Year Plans: New Delhi, Planning Commission, Government of India. Mid-Term Reviews, Planning Commission.

Hallak, Jacques (1999). Globalization, Human Rights and Education, UNESCO, IIEP, Paris.

Higher Education in Developing Countries (2000). Peril and Praomise, Report of the Task Force; The World Bank.

Human Development in South Asia (2000). Oxford.

Human Development Reports, (1999, 2000, 2002 & 2003) UNDP, Oxford.

International Association of Universities (2001). Issues in Higher Education, the OECD, Globalization and Educational Policy, Pergamon.

Kaul J.N. (1975). (ed.): Higher Education: Social, Change National Development, Indian Institute of Advanced Study, Shimla.

Learning: The Treasure Within (1996). International Commission on Education for the Twenty-First Century, UNESCO.

National Policy on Education; Government of India, Ministry of MHRD, 1986, 1992.

Nigvekar Arun (2001). GATS and Higher Education, University Grants Commission, (mimeo).

Panchamukhi, P.R. (2002). Social Sector Development and Economic Reforms. A Focus on Education Sector in Reform and Employment, IAMR,

Parikh, Kirit S. (Ed.) 2002. India Development Report; Indira Gandhi Institute of Development Research, (Oxford).

Report of the Education Commission 1964-66, Ministry of Education, 1966.

Ryle, John, ed. (2002). Globalization, Universities and Issues of Sustainable Development; Edgar and Edgar Publishers Ltd.

Sanyal Bikas C. (1995). Innovations in University Management; UNESCO, IIEP, Paris.

Sharma, G.D. (2001). Internationalization of Higher Education; Status and Policy Suggestions, NIEPA (mimeo).

Sharma, G.D. (2001). Trade in Education Service: An Indian Response, NIEPA, New Delhi, (mimeo).

Stromquist, Nelly P. *et. al.* (ed.) (2000). Globalization and Educational Reforms, *op. cit.*

UNESCO (2000). Statistical Year Book, various years.

Wells Amy Stuart, *et. al.* (1998). Globalization and Educational Changes in Andy Hergreaves (ed.) International Hand Book of Educational Change, Vol. 5, Kluwer Academic Publishers, London.

World Bank (2002). Higher Education in Developing Countries, Peril and Promise, the Report of the Task Force on Education and Society, Washington.

World Bank Country Study (1999). India, Reducing Poverty, Accelerating Development, Oxford.

12

Financial Inclusion for Women Empowerment in South Asia Context

DR. B. RATNA KUMARI, INDIA

Prologue

For the first time in the history of Indian planning there is an attempt to move beyond empowerment and recognize women as agents of sustained socio-economic growth and change. The Eleventh Five Year Plan acknowledges women's agencies and tries to ensure that their needs, rights and contribution are reflected in every section of the Plan document. Gender is, therefore, a cross-cutting theme; it is not confined to a single issue on Women. The vision is to develop an integrated approach which would eventually dispense the need of Financial Inclusion for women empowerment.

While endeavouring to guarantee the rights and entitlements of all women, the Eleventh Plan recognized that women are not a homogenous category. Their situations, and consequently requirements, differ based on their locations within various castes, communities, religions, geographic and development zones and the effort during the Eleventh Plan is to cater to all these differential and specific requirements. Further, the central vision of the Eleventh Plan is to build on our strengths to trigger a development process which ensures broad-based improvement in the quality of life of the people, especially the poor, SCs/STs, Other Backward Castes (OBCs), minorities and women (GoI, 2008 p. 2).

Therefore, the broad vision of the Eleventh Plan included several inter-related components: rapid growth that reduces poverty and creates employment opportunities, access to essential services in health and education especially for the poor, equality of opportunity, empowerment of women through Financial Inclusion.

Let me start by giving a general definition for access to finance and Financial Inclusion and challenges for Women empowerment through Financial Inclusion in India in general and Andhra Pradesh in particular.

Human Development and Gender Situation

As per the UNDPs Global Human Development Report (HDR) 2007, in spite of the absolute value of the Human Development Index (HDI) for India improving from 0.577 in 2000 to 0.611 in 2004 and further to 0.619 in 2005, the relative ranking of India has not changed much. India ranks at 128 among the countries with medium human development out of 177 countries of the world as against 126 in the previous year. In terms of Gender Development Index (GDI), India ranks 113 out of 157 countries ranked on the basis of their GDI value. A zero count for HDI rank minus for India is indicative of almost similar status of ranking in terms of gender development and human development. At the same time, while India's HDI rank reflects low relative achievement in the level of human development, a negative count of (-11) for GDP per capita (PPP US$) rank minus HDI rank is also indicative that the country has done better in terms of per capita income than in other components of human development (See Table 1). The other indicators related to Health and Education also indicate the same. The situation reinforces the need for greater focus on this area in our development planning. It is this concern that is reflected in the *Eleventh Plan which seeks to reduce not only poverty but also the various kinds of disparities across regions and communities by ensuring better access to not only basic physical infrastructure but also health and education services to one and all*. In order to empower women the Eleventh Plan has initiated Financial Inclusion.

Research Questions

1. What is access to Finance?
2. What is Financial Inclusion?
3. What do you mean by Women Empowerment?
4. Is it sufficient for women to empower economically?
5. How these processes help the women to strengthen their *'Self'* concept?
6. What are the key entry points for Financial Inclusion?
7. What are the new initiatives for Financial Inclusion of women?

Table-1
India's Global Position on Human and Gender Development

Country	HDI Bank		GDP Per Capita (PPP US$) Minus HDI Rank	GDI Rank		HDI Rank Minus GDI Rank	Life Expectancy at Birth (Years)	Combined GER (Primary, Secondary and Tertiary Education)	Physians per one Lakh People	Infants with Low Birth Weight (%)
	2000	2005	2005	2000	2005	2005	2005	2005	2000-04	1998-05
Norway	1	2	1	3	3	-1	79.8	99.2	313	5
Australia	5	3	13	1	2	1	80.9	113	247	7
Sri Lanka	89	99	07	70	89	-1	71.6	62.7	55	22
China	96	81	05	77	73	1	72.5	69.1	106	4
Indonesia	110	107	06	91	94	1	69.7	68.2	13	9
India	124	128	-11	105	113	0	63.7	63.8	60	30
Pakistan	138	136	-8	120	125	-7	64.6	40	74	19
Bangladesh	145	140	0	121	121	1	63.1	56	26	36
Nepal	142	142	08	119	128	-4	62.6	58.1	21	21
Mozambique	170	172	-16	144	150	2	42.8	52.9	3	15
Nigeria	172	174	-1	146	155	-1	55.8	22.7	2	13

Source: UNDP Human Development Reports, 2002 and 2007.

8. What are the drawbacks in Financial Inclusion and uneven ground situation?
9. How can women empowered through financial inclusion? some case studies

In view of the above questions, there is a strong need to analyze the Financial Inclusion for women and it needs a Comprehensive Programme to sustain women empowerment. The emergence of Women entrepreneurs and their contribution to the national economy is quite visible in India. From the early 1970s, women's movements in a number of countries identified credit as a major constraint on women's ability to earn an income and became increasingly interested in the degree to which poverty-focused credit programmes and credit cooperatives were actually being used by women. SEWA in India, for example, set up credit programmes as part of a multi-pronged strategy for an organization of informal sector women workers.

Since the 1970s, many women's organizations worldwide have included credit and savings, both as a way of increasing women's incomes and to bring women together to address wider gender issues. The 1980s saw the emergence of poverty-targeted micro-finance institutions like Grameen Bank. Many of these programmes see themselves as empowerment-oriented. In the 1990s, a combination of evidence of high female repayment rates and the rising influence of gender lobbies within donor agencies and NGOs led to increasing emphasis on targeting women in micro-finance programmes.

Throughout the developing countries, innovative lending programmes have emerged that specializes in supplying small capital loans to low-income entrepreneurs. In many of these programmes it is common to find that a large percentage of borrowers are women. For example, based on a 1996 survey of micro-finance institution around the world, the World Bank estimated that 61 per cent of all clients were women (World Bank, 1997). In two rather well documented lending programmes, the Grameen Bank in Bangladesh and Bancosol in Bolivia, the percentages are 95 per cent and 72 per cent respectively. These high female participation rates have raised a number of research questions and have in turn, inspired a growing number of empirical investigations. One question that is commonly raised is how a woman's borrowing impacts household consumption. For example, using data from Bangladesh, Pitt and Khandke (1999) estimate how participation in a credit programme impacts household consumption, depending on the participant's gender. They conclude that household consumption increases more if a woman takes out a loan than a man. On the other hand, Morduch (1999) finds that participation in a credit programme in Bangladesh, everything else equal, tends to imply lower household consumption. It turns out that disagreement such as this is rather common in the literature.

Another area of debate surrounds the question of whether a woman's participation in a credit programme raises her "bargaining power" or "empowerment" in the household. Hashemi *et. al.* (1996) for example, attempt to measure a woman's empowerment using indicators such as level of mobility, ability to make large purchases, and political and legal awareness. However, in other studies, such as Goetz and Sen Gupta (1996) and Rahaman (1999), evidence is offered that a woman's participation in a credit programme reinforces her dominated role in the household, and in some cases, the loan ends up under the control of her husband.

Given this backdrop the objective of the paper is to examine the two basic research questions. First, the study attempts define the Financial Inclusion and how can be it helps the woman's tendency to invest in safer investment projects and linked to her desire to raise her bargaining position in the households. Second, in addition to the project choice, women empowerment is examined with respect to control of savings, control of income, control over loans, control over purchasing capacity and family planning in some sample households through Chaitanya Sravanthi (MACTS Society) and Visakhapatnam.

What is Access to Finance?

In simple terms, this means to provide an environment in which people, in general, have accesses to the formal financial system, through the use of different financial products at affordable prices. The access could be to any formal financial institution, market, and payment system or to a financial instrument, including savings, loans, remittances and insurance services.

What is Financial Inclusion?

This means the process of facilitating those sectors and segments of the population that are outside, to become a part of the formal financial system and enrolling individuals or groups into the formal financial sector.

Key Entry Points for Financial Inclusion

These could be through:

- *(a)* Direct loans or banking facilities to the targeted vulnerable communities or groups;
- *(b)* Facilitation of economic activity in a particular geographical area of operations or location;
- *(c)* Development of local or national infrastructure to enable a particular type of business activity, which could then be

practiced or performed by a group or groups which can include women; and

(d) Providing an enabling environment and/or enhancements for such economic activity to take place. The enabling environment includes laws, regulations, taxation, skills development, duty waivers, subsidies, etc. In this context, tax concessions and duty waivers given to make enterprises be "financially inclusive" are often forgotten. In fact, due to lack of awareness, enhancement of access to finance or financial inclusion that has already taken place in various sectors, and the enabling environment that has been created, are taken for granted with no value attached to them.

Women's Contribution to Economic Development

Let me now deal with the importance of women's contribution to the economic development in India in general and Andhra Pradesh in particular and assess whether financial inclusion of, and access to finance by women are on per with the contribution they make.

Women in India have been engaged in economic activities over centuries of history primarily through employment. Due to low productivity and inadequate incomes in the agricultural sector, women in small farm families have moved from unpaid family labour to other occupations, in particular, small scale enterprises through SHG movement. According to 2001 census of the total work participation rate, women accounted for 25.7 per cent, however this is still low compared to male work participation rate. And women occupied 85 per cent in agriculture as farmers, who are small and marginal finds difficult to access inputs, credit, and extension or to market their output (GoI, 2008, p. 8).

Drawbacks in Financial Inclusion and Uneven Ground Situation

The banking and financial sector in the country must be strong for financial inclusion to take place. Our banking sector has been showing advancement and growth. The financial system is stable and resilient. The financial institutions are committed to engage in social responsibility related work as well, or to reach out to vulnerable and disadvantaged groups, of which women occupy an important place. Despite the advancement of the financial sector and the resilience of the system as a whole, we are still unable to appreciate or criticize its commitment towards financial inclusion of and access to finance by women, *due to lack of disaggregated data from banks and financial institutions*. This, I believe, is the biggest drawback in initiating policy responses to remedy the deficiencies in financial inclusion of women.

What action is needed and how quickly it can be implemented are challenging tasks, but financial inclusion, in general, and for women, in particular, is an area that should be given priority.

The main credit needs among people in low growth areas with low incomes, in particular, women are in need of

- Access to small, unsecured, fixed term loans in cash;
- Quick access to credit without lengthy or intrusive application procedures;
- Affordable weekly payments with no hidden or extra charges;
- Automatic repayment arrangements, such as deduction from benefit or home visits by a collector; and
- Opportunities for making late payments or rescheduling loans without incurring charges when temporary financial problems occur.

If anyone of these or a combination of these factors tend to deny access to financial institutions or to products, that is known as financial exclusion, which is often reflected as a symptom of poverty as well as a cause. As much as we are interested in financial inclusion, it is also necessary to reduce financial exclusion to a minimum, which is also a policy challenge. These are two sides of the same coin.

Visible Areas of Financial Exclusion

Financial exclusion and denial of access to credit exists in two clear areas, in particular, in *formal credit markets and the payment system.* According to available data, in India, at least 40 per cent of the farm households do not have access to formal sources of credit or bank accounts. The reliability of this number depends on the type of survey done and the source of information. Nevertheless, it is a significant number to work with. Comparatively, however, we are ahead in the region as 51 per cent of about 89 million farm households in India have no access to formal or informal sources of credit while 73 per cent have no access to formal sources of credit. Although both in India and Sri Lanka, the shares of non-institutional sources of credit have decreased compared to the 1970's and 1980's, there still remains a significant gap in accessing the formal financial sector by men and women in rural areas and the unemployed in the urban areas. Among many reasons for financial exclusion of women from the formal system, however, literacy barriers and language barriers are becoming less important factors. It is primarily *the approach of banks and financial institutions and the strenuous processes and procedures adopted by them, which matters more in financial exclusion.*

The second important area of financial *exclusion is the denial of access to efficient and safe payment systems.* This area of activity is unknown to many and it has been taken for granted. Among the main payment instruments, cash is straightforward. However, the other payment instruments, such as cheques, bank drafts, electronic payments, card payments etc., can have delays in both clearing and settlement, which can cause problems to those who receive money through these payment modes. This is common to both men and women.

Initiatives for Financial Inclusion of Women

In order to fulfill MDGs, some initiatives were taken, not only by India and Andhra Pradesh in particular through SHG movement, but also in the South Asian Region towards financial inclusion. By 2005, micro-finance institutions covered at least 35 mn of some 270 mn people in the South Asian region and met around 15 per cent of the overall credit requirements of low-income families. In Sri Lanka, the coverage is particularly high at 60 per cent. The high outreach in Sri Lanka is based on an extensive network of community-based organizations that receive considerable government subsidies. Almost all rural financial institutions in Sri Lanka and India have provided easy access to women, particularly in the villages, slums and among fishing communities. Financial institutions that are directly involved in this area, are the licensed commercial banks, licensed specialized banks, micro-finance institutions, cooperative rural banks. Let us examine the extent to which financial inclusion for women has taken place through the existing institutional network and assess the deficiencies and gaps, although we may not be able to do a comprehensive analysis. The participation of women in credit programs as at end.

Extent of Microfinance Outreach in South Asia

An important factor, *i.e.*, due to lack of statistics and information, it is difficult to assess the ratio of loans granted exclusively for women by Commercial Banks.

As shown in Table: 2 exclusivity conditions are not necessarily applicable to India and Sri Lanka given the large-scale membership of women in the widespread banking arm of the Cooperative Societies, *i.e.* about 1,500 cooperative rural banks and 7,400 Sanasa Societies and SHGs in Sri Lanka and Commercial Banks and Regional Rural Banks in India. In effect, in the micro-finance delivery chain, NABARD in India with CBs and RRBs while Sri Lanka with Cooperative Societies and Sanasa Societies appear to be very significant.

Table-2
Extent of Micro-finance Outreach in South Asia

Country	*Population (Million)*	*Poverty Ratio (%)*	*Poor Families (Millions)*	*Poor Clients (Millions)*	*MF Poverty Outreach %*	*MF Coverage of Poor Families %*	*Borrowing Clients, % of Population*
Afghanistan	22	55	2	0.12	50	3	-
Bangladesh	143	50	13	16	50	62	13.1
India	1100	30	60	15	35	9	1.1
Nepal	26	35	1.6	0.5	45	14	1.5
Pakistan	155	33	8.5	0.58	35	2	-
Sri Lanka	20	25	1	2.5	25	63	4.3

Source: Getting Finance in South Asia, Phase IV, 2008, World Bank Publication.

Women still feature significantly in the vulnerable groups and it is imperative to include them in the facilities offered by the formal financial sector. However, in terms of micro-finance coverage of poor families, India coverage's 9 per cent families while Sri Lanka covers 63 per cent families, which is the highest in South Asia. Similarly, women account for 1.1 per cent in India and 4.3 per cent of the borrowing clients in Sri Lanka. India at 1.1 per cent is the lowest than Bangladesh, which is at 13 per cent and Sri Lanka at 4.3 per cent but way above others. Even than in India in general and Andhra Pradesh in particular we had high hopes of enhancing financial inclusion of women through the Millennium Development Goals, which would have provided a smooth path for financial inclusion for women. However, even after several rounds of discussions, the programme has not got off the ground as yet.

Recent Initiatives taken by the Reserve Bank of India and the Banking and Financial Sector

As in India, banks and financial institutions in India, at the grass-root levels, have been advised to engage in basic banking with 'no frills', or to entertain minimum balances and reduce charges where possible to enhance access to finance and financial inclusion. The recent efforts taken by the Reserve Bank of India as well as some banking institutions have enhanced access to finance and financial inclusion.

RBI feels that banks have been bestowed with several privileges, especially in mobilizing public deposits on a highly leveraged basis and therefore, they should be obliged to provide banking services to all the segment of the population on equitable basis. RBI, through its Annual Policy/Quarterly Policy Review Statements has been urging the banks to empower the depositors by providing wider access and better quality services. With this in view, RBI has initiated a number of measures in which banks have to play an active role in the years to come in the direction of financial inclusion.

Coming to the initiatives taken by Banks in the direction of Financial Inclusion in the State of Andhra Pradesh, the progress is judged in terms of the following components

1. Opening of Savings bank A/Cs (no-frills A/Cs).
2. Strengthening SHG lending.
3. Mapping indebtedness of the farmers and to identify the un-indebted farmers.
4. Coverage of Tenant farmers/share croppers.
5. Defaulters cleansing mechanism.
6. Appointment of Business Facilitators/Business Correspondents.
7. IT connectivity.
8. Insurance Products.
9. Issue of General Purpose Credit Cards (GCC).
10. Financial Literacy cum Credit Counseling Centres.
11. Rural Training Institutes.
12. A.P. Smart Card Project.

SHGs-Bank Linkage Programme in India and Andhra Pradesh

The SHGs emerged as a component of the Indian financial system after 1996. In India, the SHG-Bank Linkage model is one of the world's largest microfinance initiatives in terms of outreach (Kropp & Suran, 2002). NABARD is the processing agency of the SHG – Bank Linkage Model. It provides financial as well as Capacity Building support to the bank officials, NGO staff, Government socials and SHG members (See for more details Table 3).

Table-3
SHGs–Bank Linkage Programme, India

Year (end March)	*No. of SHGs Linked*	*No. of SHGs (Cumulative)*	*Bank Loan (in Rs. Crore)*	*Cumulative Bank Loan*
1992-93	255	255	0.29	0.29
1993-94	365	620	0.36	0.65
1994-95	1502	2122	1.79	2.44
1995-96	2635	4757	3.62	6.06
1996-97	3841	8598	5.78	11.84
1997-98	5719	14317	11.92	23.76
1998-99	18678	32995	33.31	57.07
1999-2000	81780	114775	135.91	192.98
2000-01	149050	263825	287.89	480.87
2001-02	197653	461478	545.47	1026.34
2002-03	255882	717360	1022.33	2048.67
2003-04	361731	1079091	1855.53	3904.2
2004-05	539365	1618456	2994.26	6898.46
2005-06	620109	2238565	4499.09	11397.55

Source: NABARD, 2006.

In addition to NABARD, several other apex bodies or wholesalers provide loans to financial intermediaries for on lending to SHGs. These include the Small Industries Development Bank of India (SIDBI), Rashtriya Mahila Kosh (RMK), Housing and Urban Development Corporation (HUDCO), Housing Development Finance Corporation (HDFC) and Friends of Women's World Banking (FWWB). Some donors and banks (*e.g.* Rabobank) also provide grants and loans to micro-finance institutions for on lending to SHGs and SHG federations (Tankha, 2002).

It is revealed from Table 4 that three-micro-finance finance agencies, namely, Commercial Banks (CBs), Regional Rural Banks (RRB) and Cooperative Banks played an important role in the

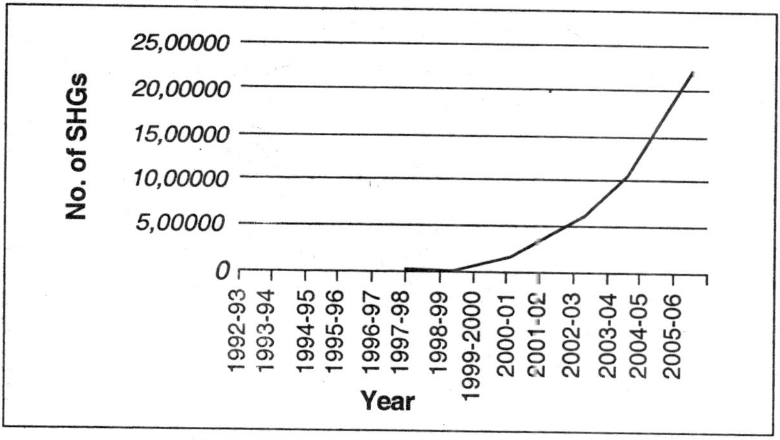

Fig. 1. SHGs–Bank Linkage Programme

Table–4

Agency-wise Cumulative Position of SHGs up to March 2006

S. No. State/Region	*CBs No. of SHGs*	*RRBs No. of SHGs*	*Co-oper. Bank No. of SHGs*	*Total No. of SHGs*
Southern Region				
Andhra Pradesh	3,82,422	1,90,120	14,696	5,87,238
Karnataka	81,213	81,839	61,876	2,24,928
Kerala	54,966	9,055	22,967	8,12,166
Tamil Nadu and UT of Pondicherry	2,17,378	55,664	42,235	3,15,277
Total	**7,35,979**	**3,36,678**	**1,41,774**	**12,14,431**

Source: NABARD, 2006.

formation of SHGs-bank linkage programme in different states of India. The Commercial Banks and Regional Rural Banks formed the maximum number of SHGs in Andhra Pradesh (See Figs. 3 and 4). The distribution of the number of SHGs is concentrated in the southern states. Andhra Pradesh ranks first, Tamil Nadu ranks second and Karnataka the third position in the number of SHGs formation.

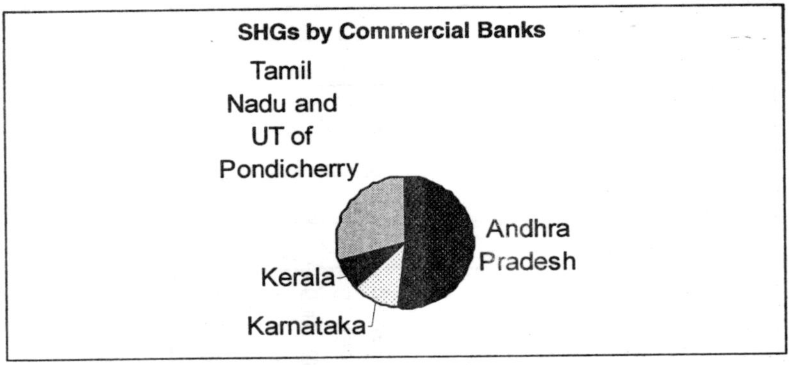

Fig. 2. SHGs by Commercial Banks

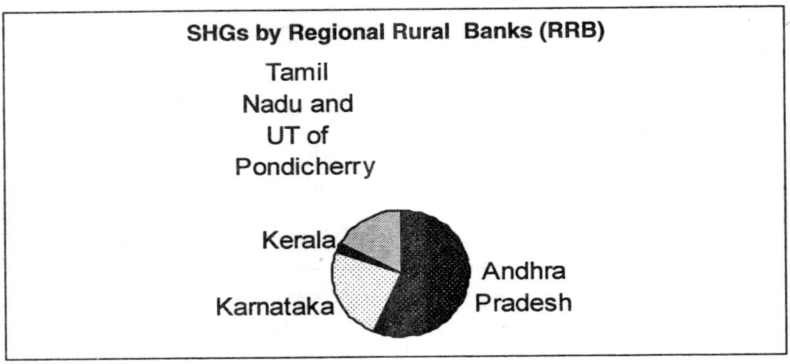

Fig. 3. SHGs by Regional Rural Banks (RRB)

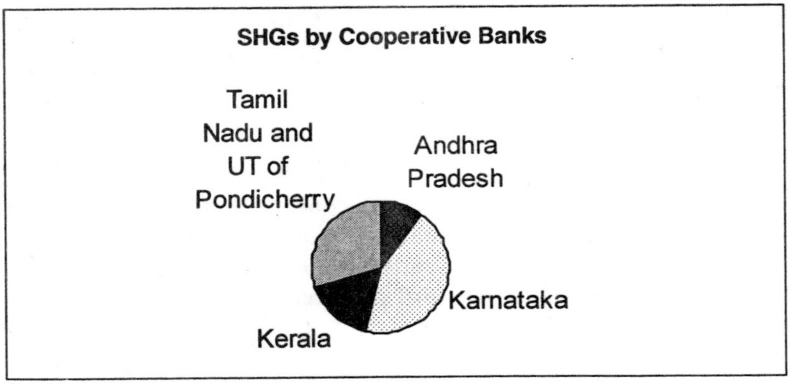

Fig. 4. SHGs by Cooperative Banks

Table-5
SHG-Bank Linkage–Region-wise Physical and Financial Progress (March 2005)

S. No.	*State/ Region*	*No. of SHGs*	*Bank Loan (Rs. Milllion)*
Southern Region			
1.	Andhra Pradesh	5,87,238 (1)	43,455.18
2.	Karnataka	2,24,928 (3)	9,927.53
3.	Kerala	86,988	4,821.48
4.	Tamil Nadu and UT of Pondicherry	3,15,277 (2)	27,472.73
	Total	**12,14,431**	**85,676.92**

Source: NABARD, 2006.

While a gender-disaggregated, comprehensive database on the sector is not available, there is ample evidence to prove that a majority of women are engaged in the Micro Small Enterprises (MSEs). In sectors such as handloom, over 60 per cent of the workforce comprises women. Chemical and plastics, food processing and village industries also employ a large number of women. The proportion of women entrepreneurs is, however, quite low. As per the Third All-India Census (2001-02), only 9,95,141 (9.46%) MSEs are actually manages by women. As against this, in the US, women own 38 per cent of the small enterprises, which employ more than 50 per cent of the private sector workforce. In countries such as Brazil, Ireland, Spain and the US, women are creating new enterprises at a faster rate than men (OECD, 2001).

The absence of property rights and the concomitant difficulty in accessing credit may be responsible for the low proportion of women entrepreneurs in India. Most women either do job work, assist their family members, or employed as workers in small-scale units. They face widespread discrimination and exploitation. *Zari* workers, *agarbatti* and *bidi* rollers, embroidery workers make as little as Rs. 10 for an eight-hour day. During the Eleventh Plan period, it is essential to provide a social security cover that is sensitive to women's special needs. Hence, there is a strong need to pay attention so that women entrepreneurs has to be provided easy access to credit and appropriate advisory and mentoring services.

Gender inequality also remains a pervasive problem and some of the structural changes taking place have an adverse effect on women. The lack of inclusiveness is borne out by data on several dimensions of performance.

Need for a Comprehensive Programme to Increase Financial Inclusion of Women

It is important to note that initiatives cannot be taken and implemented by the Government alone. Government could perhaps be the main motivator and driver. The promotion of women entrepreneurial activities and financial inclusion has to be elevated to a policy debate. There should be a serious commitment by banks and financial institutions, and their business development sections should be proactive and ensure that credit delivery to women engaged in relevant sectors is given priority.

In addition to the major infrastructure development projects, many village level enterprises and projects are coming up within a short period of time. Crop agriculture, the dairy industry, fishing industry and livestock are three key areas, which can make a significant contribution to growth. Women's participation in each of these activities is estimated to be high and there are clear opportunities for women, seeking banking and financial services.

It is time to prepare a *comprehensive plan* and that should have new entry points to accommodate *women's financial requirements.* Some of the new entry points include the following:

- Information technology application and usage
- Introduce products/supply chain focused credit facilities and payment instruments.

Over half a million SHGs have been linked to banks over the years but a handful of states, mostly in South India, account for over three-fourth of this figure with Andhra Pradesh being an undisputed leader. In spite of the impressive figures, micro-finance in India is still presently too small to create a massive impact in poverty alleviation, but if pursued with skill and opportunity development of the poor, it holds the promise to alter the socio-economic. This paper reviews the current level and pattern of access to finance for India's rural poor and examines some of the key micro-finance approaches in India, taking a close look at the most dominant among these, the Self-Help Group (SHG) Bank Linkage initiative. It empirically analyzes the success with which SHG Bank Linkage has been able to reach the poor, examines the reasons behind this, and the lessons learned. The analysis in the paper draws heavily on a recent rural access to finance survey of 6,000 households in India, undertaken by the authors. The main findings and implications of the paper are as follows: India's rural poor currently have very little access to finance from formal sources. Micro-finance approaches have tried to fill the gap. Among these, the growth of SHG Bank Linkage has been particularly remarkable, but outreach remains modest in terms of the proportion of poor households served.

Women Empowerment Practices

Women constitute one-half of the world's population and a visible majority of the poor. Women either solely or largely support an increasing number of families. Projects aiming to improve the living conditions of the poor cannot, therefore, be effective unless women participate in their formulation and implementation, as contributors as well as beneficiaries.

The following important conclusions are drawn from the briefs:

- To empower women is to increase their control over the decisions that affect their lives both within and outside the household;
- Women should be encouraged to bring their vision and leadership, knowledge and skills, views and aspirations into the development agenda from the grassroots to international levels;
- Women should be assisted in conflict situations and their participation in peace processes supported; and
- Emphasis should be given to advocacy of gender responsive legislation and constitutional revisions to increase women's opportunities to influence the direction of society and to remove obstacles to women's access to power;

The progress made in implementing the Beijing Declaration and Platform for Action, adopted at the Fourth World Conference on Women, 1995; the Tokyo Declaration on African Development, 1993; the recommendations of the first and second Asia/Africa Forums in Bandung, 1994, and Bangkok, 1997; and, the work of the First Global Women Entrepreneurs' Trade Fair and Investment Forum in Ghana, 1996.

That significant further actions, including affirmative action, were needed from all key actors in the economic empowerment of women—government agencies, non-governmental organizations, regional and international organizations, donor countries, female entrepreneurs and women in the labour force—to develop policies, programmes and projects, including strengthening of legal mechanisms and institutional frameworks, to address key constraints on the economic empowerment of women in Asia and Africa:

- The Forum identified the need for an enabling legal and policy framework and action to address five priority areas to promote women's economic empowerment.
- Increased access to educational and training opportunities, and encouragement of positive socialization to promote self-development and enable full utilization of opportunities.
- Improved access to credit and finance.
- Improving access to management and marketing skills and appropriate technology.
- Building and strengthening networks among female entrepreneurs, non-governmental organizations, relevant governmental organizations, regional and international organizations; and
- Increased Asia-Africa cooperation.

Let me sum up the substance in a few sentences. More than anything, there is an urgency on the part or any other institution to conduct research, surveys and statistical analyses to assess the status of enhancement of access to credit and financial inclusion among women in India. It is hard to come to conclusions without adequate and reliable statistics or even to initiate policy action to fill in gaps that exist in this area. It is equally important for the relevant Ministry or Ministries and other public and private organizations to coordinate and prepare a strategic plan to spearhead the campaign of financial inclusion for women and suggest policy and operational measures as they deem fit. This initiative too should be supported by well-recognized research institutions like NABARD. I hope the deliberations during the next few days would lead the way to prepare an action plan or road map to take forward the financial inclusion for women initiative.

Table-6
Commonly used Dimensions of Empowerment and Potential Operationalization in the Household, Community and Broader Arenas

Dimension	*Household*	*Community*	*Broader Arenas*
Economic	Women's control income; relative contribution to family support; access to and control of family resources	Women's access to employment; ownership assets and land; access credit; involvement representation in local associations; access to markets	Women's in high paying jobs; women CEO's; representation of economic interests in macro-conomic state and federal
Socio-Cultural	Women's freedom of movement; lack of discrimination against daughters; to educating daughters	Women's visibility in access to social spaces; access to modern transportation; in extra-familial groups social networks; sift in patriarchal norms (such son preference); representation of the female in myth and	Women's literacy and access to a broad range educational options; Positive media images women, their roles and contributions.
Familial/ Interpersonal	Participation in decision-making; over sexual relations; ability to make child-bearing use contraception, abortion; control over spouse selection and marriage timing; freedom from violence	Shifts in marriage and kinship systems greater vale and for women (*e.g.* later marriages, self-selection spouses, reduction in the practice of dowry; acceptability of dowry; acceptability of divorce); local campaigns against domestic violence.	Regional/National in timing of marriage, options for divorce; political, legal, support for (or lack of active opposition to shifts; systems easy access to contraception, safe abortion, reproductive health services.
Legal	Knowledge of legal rights; domestic for exercising rights	Community for rights; campaigns for rights awareness;	Laws supporting rights, access to and options;

Contd...

Dimension	*Household*	*Community*	*Broader Arenas*
		local enforcement of rights	Advocacy rights and legislation; of judicial system to redress rights violations.
Political	Knowledge of system and means of access to it; domestic support for political engagement; the right to vote	Women's involvement mobilization in the local political support for specific candidates or legislation; representation in local bodies of government	Women's in regional and national bodies of government; strength as a voting representation of interests in effective lobbies and interest
Psychological	Self-esteem; self-efficacy; well-being	Collective awareness of injustice, potential of mobilization	Women's sense of inclusion and systemic acceptance of women's entitlement inclusion.

Three Types of Empowerment

- Economic empowerment.
- Increased well-being.
- Social and political empowerment.

Level of Empowerment

Empowerment is measured by the degree of economic independence, decision-making at household level, decision-making within the group and self-perception. These individual factors influence the overall level of empowerment.

Overall, group members in Andhra Pradesh (68%), Assam (73%), Kerala (78%), Mizoram (68%), Tamil Nadu (77%), and West Bengal (72%) are relatively more empowered than others.

In all these states, their role in decision-making at household-level is much lower when compared to decision-making at the collective group level. This is quite understandable as the women are in a better position to take decisions as a collective than at the household level, where the individual woman is confronted with other family members and might not always have the decision-making power (due to patriarchy and hierarchy).

The dispersed, unorganized and often household-based micro and small enterprises are capital-saving labour-intensive, and environment-friendly tools of inclusion. In India, they are the largest source of employment after agriculture and are found in both rural as well as urban areas.

In developing countries across Asia, Small and Medium Enterprises (SMEs)

(i) Make up 80-90 per cent of all enterprises,
(ii) Provide over 60 per cent of the private sector jobs,
(iii) Generate over 30-40 per cent of total employment, and
(iv) Contribute about 50 per cent of sales or value added.

In India, they constitute 95 per cent of all enterprises. Labour productivity of Small-Scale Industries (SSIs) in India during 1990-98 at the compound growth rate was 8.5 per cent whereas labour productivity of Large-Scale Industries (LSIs) was 7.54 per cent. however, recently in a study of 53 countries done by Fortune Small Business Survey, June 2007 on 'Most and Least Friendly Countries to Small Businesses', India ranked 46th, well behind the other neighbouring Asian countries such as Singapore (5th), Hong Kong (6th), Thailand (15th), Malaysia (28th) etc.

Inadequate working capital, lack of information to access markets and foreign business opportunities, lack of trained personnel, and obsolete technology are the major barriers to the growth of MSEs across the world in general and in India in particular.

Shortage of working capital is widely recognized as the biggest hurdle in the growth of unorganized and organized MSEs. Securing bank credits, difficulties in documentation for bank loans, and lack of collateral security are bigger problems in India than in majority of the other developing countries in Asia. It is estimated that less than 8 per cent of the total bank credit finds its way to the MSE sector.

The vision of inclusiveness must go beyond the traditional objective of poverty alleviation to encompass equality of opportunity, as well as economic and social mobility for all sections of society, with affirmative action for SCs, STs, OBCs, minorities and women. There must be equality of opportunity to all with freedom and dignity, and without social or political obstacles. This must be accompanied by an improvement in the opportunities for economic and social advancement. In particular, individuals belonging to isadvantaged groups should be provided special opportunities to develop their skills and participate in the growth process.

An Empirical Study on Journey Towards Empowerment of Women

The report of an evaluation study on empowerment of women at urban slums of Visakhapatnam through SHGs by Chaitanya Sravanthi emphasizes the compelling need to focus on Women Socio-economic and empowerment through *Indira Kranti Padhakam.*

Objectives

- To analyze the growth and performance of the SHGs of Chaitanya Sravanti;
- To examine the empowerment process of the members as a result of participation in the SHGs programme; and
- To suggest a strategy for sustainable development of SHGs of Chaitanya Sravanthi.

Methodology

The study was confined on purposive basis, only to I town area of Visakhapatnam city where SHGs of Chaitanya Sravanthi are located. The progress of our analysis bears on the progress of SHGs and their member's empowerment status. Secondary data were collected to analyze the performance of the SHGs in Visakhapatnam through DRDA, SC Corporation and BC corporation officials. As a preliminary step means and Standard Deviation (SD) were computed for SHGs and members of SHGs of Chaitanya Sravanthi.

Sample

400 members (women) of SHGs of Chaitanya Sravanthi were administered with well structured schedule during 7th November 2007–12th November 2007 on random basis. The collected data has been classified and computed and analyzed by using appropriate statistical tools.

Findings:

Following are the major findings of the present study:

- 41.0 per cent of respondent women are in 20-30 years age group 41.3 per cent of the respondent women are in 31-40 years age group. 14.3 per cent of the respondent women are in 41-50 years age group. A small percentage (4) women are in 51 years and above age group.

- 85.3 per cent of women (respondent) were married. 4.5 per cent of women remained has spinster (unmarried). 9.5 per cent of respondent women are widows. 0.5 per cent of respondent women are separated. 0.3 per cent was divorced.
- 23.3 per cent of respondent women are illiterates and 23.5 per cent of respondent women had primary level of education. 43.8 per cent of respondent women had secondary level of education. 4.3 per cent of respondent women had intermediate level of education. 5.3 per cent of respondent women have graduation and above level of education.
- 62.0 per cent of respondent women family size is small *i.e.,* 1-4 members. 38.0 per cent of respondent women family size is large i.e., 5-10 members.
- Monthly income of family has been raised drastically after joining SHGs. Before joining SHGs 85.0 per cent of respondent women family income was 500-1500 p.m. It has comedown (after joining the SHGs) to 22.5 per cent. In the same manner 12.3 per cent of respondent women family income was 1600-2500 p.m. It has raised to 69.3 per cent (after joining the SHGs). 2.8 per cent of respondent women family income was 2600-above p.m. before joining the SHGs and it has raised to 8.3 per cent.
- Majority of respondent women had not aware of vocational training programmes, employment opportunities, income generating activities and knowledge on banks and loans before joining the SHGs. After their admission in SHGs the awareness on these issues has increased tremendously.
- Majority of respondent women earning capacity, participation in social development activities, participation in economic decision, economic independence self-sufficiency, self-confidence, self-esteem and personality development has changed remarkable and a positive result is noticed in this direction.
- Majority of respondent women's children education level, health and nutritional levels has increased. Awareness of Government health schemes and programmes and availing medical services has increased remarkably after joining SHGs.

Conclusions

The Chaitanya Sravanthi aiming to improve the capacities of urban slum women by strengthening the micro level credit system and also to empower women in urban slums.

This study examining the performance and sustainability of SHGs in Chaitanya Sravanthi. The data analysis revealed that, the growth of SHGs is so rapid and dynamic in Chaitanya Sravanthi. Majority household income level (respondent women) has increased considerably. There is perceptible change in the living styles of women.

The movement of SHGs in Chaitanya Sravanthi appears to be creating a lot of hope enthusiasm among women belonging to weaker sections.

Suggestions

Following are few suggestions made after examining the major findings of the study for sustainable development of Chaitanya Sravanthi SHGs.

- Ensure equal access to the illiterate poor women to get the benefits from PMRY programme.
- Bank transactions must be user friendly.
- The loan amount should be enhanced from the present level of 4-10 times of savings.
- Production cum-training centers should be opened at community level according to the market driven forces.
- Individual awareness programmes on health and nutritional issues should be strengthened and to improve the health status of members as well as family.
- Promote lifelong education and vocational training for girls and women.
- Develop non-discriminatory education and training.
- Provide business services, training and access to markets, information and technology particularly to low income women.

REFERENCES

Chaurasia Alok Ranjan, S.C. Gulati (2007) *India: The State of Population*, Oxford University Press, New Delhi.

Government of India (2008): *Economic Survey 2007-08*, Oxford University Press, New Delhi.

GoI (2008): Planning Commission Government of India, 2008 *Eleventh Five Year Plan* (2007-2012), Vol-III, Oxford University Press, New Delhi.

GoI (2008): Planning Commission Government of India, 2008 *Eleventh Five Year Plan* (2007-2012), Vol-I, Oxford University Press, New Delhi.

Hashemi, S.M., Schuler, S.R., Riley, A.P. (1996): *Rural Credit Programmes and Women's Empowerment in Bangladesh, World Development* 24 (4), 635-653.

Jayamaya Dr. Ranee (2008), Deputy Governor, Central Bank of Sri Lanka *Access to Finance and Financial Inclusion for Women.*

Lalitha, N. and B.S. Nagarajan, (2002) : *Self-help Groups in Rural Development* New Delhi, Dominant Publishers and Distributors.

Morduch, J. (1999): Thes Micro-finance Promise. *Journal of Economic Literature* 37 (4), 1569-1614.

NIPCCD (2005): *Factsheet on Women in India 2005,* New Delhi.

Pitt, M.M., Khandker, S.R., (1998): *The Impact of Group-based Credit Programmes on Poor Households in Bangladesh:* does the gender of participants matter? *Journal of Political Economy* 106 (5), 995-96.

Rahman, A., (1999): *Micro-credit Initiatives for Equitable and Sustainable Development: Who Pays? World Development* 27 (1), 67-82.

World Bank, (1997): *Sustainable Banking with the Poor: An Inventory of Microfinance Institutions in Latin America and the Caribbean.* World Bank Publication, Washington, DC.

Index

Abolishment, 81, 82, 180
Advancement of women, 232
Affirmative action, 62, 75, 107, 124, 196, 198, 274, 277
Agrarian capitalism, 33, 34, 41
Ailments, 219, 222-23
Analytical tools, 89
Andhra University, 195, 225, 244
Andocentric claims, 9
Anxiety, 218
Assessment, 5, 6, 21, 23, 71, 139, 239

Benhabib, Seyla, 72, 83, 86
Blatter, Fliegende, 176
Blue-collar women, 126-27
Breadwinner Models, 41, 42, 61, 64, 66, 68
Businesswomen, 124

Capitalism, 8, 31, 33-35, 40, 43
Caregiver parity models, 64
Care-work, 61, 64-66, 68, 79
Central America, 37
Central European Countries, 96
Children education, 216, 226
Civil codes, 10
Civil society, 64, 65, 68, 223
Clothing industries, 38, 142
Clustering, 62, 63
Commercialization of education, 243
Communist era, 100-1
Competition prohibition, 168
Cooperative rural banks, 265-66
Crèches, 132, 223
Credit Counseling Centres, 267
Credit programme, 261-62

Day-care centers, 132, 231
Decision-making processes, 109, 177
Decommodification, 62
Democratic theory, 77, 83, 85, 86
Democratization, 86, 97, 182
Developed market economy, 105, 107-8
Developing countries, 107, 186, 234-35, 238, 255, 261, 277
Development and Women Empowerment, 225-26
Discrimination, 3, 4, 11, 18, 66, 75, 78, 97, 109, 118, 124, 128, 148, 173, 180, 271
Domestic
  chores, 215, 222
  firms, 198
  work, 24, 131, 173, 176, 181, 183-84, 201
Dual-income family models, 130
Durgabhai Deshmukh Centre, 195

East and Central European countries, 96, 109-10
East Germany, 61, 68, 187
Economic development, 236, 263
Economic empowerment, 274, 276
Economic inequalities, 81, 82
Elderly women, 67, 69
Employment
alternative forms of, 111, 115
hierarchy, 120
informal, 145
motivation, 115, 137
patterns, 53, 63
policies, 62, 133, 140-41, 192
preferred, 250, 253
structure, 114, 129
Empowerment, 25, 80, 225, 228, 244, 252, 258, 262, 276, 278
Engendering processes, 18, 24
Entrepreneurial interests, 124
Ethnicity, 48, 78, 80-82
European Commission, 113-15, 187
European Union, 53, 98, 102, 112, 114-15, 117, 186-87, 189-90, 192-93
Exclusion, 6, 15, 82, 87, 89, 153, 162
Export Processing Zones, 194

False dichotomy, 78
Family
double wage-earner, 44
duties, 18, 148
farm, 263
law, 66
nuclear, 76, 130
obligations, 147
respondent women workers, 207
Female
employment, 16, 61, 110-11, 114, 118-19, 128-31, 133
entrepreneurs, 120-23, 274
pensioners, 112
Feminism, 51, 71, 72, 74, 82
Feminist movement, 51, 82, 85
Feminist theory, 2, 71, 74, 88
Feminist theory of democracy, 71, 72, 87, 89
Feminization, 44, 128-30, 147
Feminized jobs, 128
Financial
exclusion, 264-65
inclusion, 258-60, 262-67, 272, 274
institutions, 263-65, 267, 272
Fiscal policies, 31
Fordist Family Breadwinner Model, 44
Fordist period, 40, 42, 43, 46
Fordist production techniques, 38
Formal economy, 38, 44, 45, 47
Fraser, Nancy, 49, 52, 61, 63-68, 72, 74, 81-83, 86-89
Full-time employment, 114, 179, 184, 191

Gainful employment, 8, 17, 18, 21, 65, 74, 120, 156, 174-76, 181
Gender
analysis, 40
arrangements, 1, 9, 10, 13, 23
assignment, 162
asymmetry, 148
barriers, 164
-based contract, 191
-based division, 11, 17, 23, 153
bias, 9, 19, 187, 251, 253-54
classification, 12, 15
-coded work, 158, 166
component, 61
composition, 158
contract, 152, 166, 168-69
democracy, 13
designation, 162
development index, 259
development, 259
differences, 73, 77, 78, 80, 85, 86, 160, 162, 166, 168
differentiation, 166
discrimination, 4, 87, 186
equity, 63, 64
gaps, 2, 117, 127, 187, 192, 232

groups, 4-7, 9, 11, 12, 14, 15, 19, 20
hierarchy, 9, 12, 39, 66, 75, 152, 157, 161, 166-68, 183
history, 5
imbalance, 226
inequality, 3, 4, 13, 272
inequities, 186
interrelatedness, 5
lobbies, 261
membership, 4, 9, 11, 14, 118, 156, 162-63
norms, 153, 159, 169
perspective, 86
policy, 13
positions, 20
practices, 40
prejudice, 165
quality, 11
regimes, 2, 33, 39-41
relations, 2, 5, 39, 42, 53, 62
relationships, 2, 3, 7, 12, 13, 18, 24
segregation, 152-53, 155, 157-59, 161-62, 164, 166-68
separation, 76, 153, 160, 166
situation, 259
stereotypes, 137, 159, 164-65, 168
stereotyping, 157, 163
structuring, 161
studies, 2-4, 13, 152
Genderization, 15, 24
Genderized clichés, 24
German Civil Code, 7, 9
Germany, 23, 47, 60, 61, 66, 69, 71, 72, 74, 159, 174, 188, 190
Global economy, 32, 34, 37, 43, 46, 48-50, 54
Global factories, 36, 37, 39, 53
Globalization, 1, 25, 31-33, 35, 36, 38, 39, 44, 48, 49, 53, 55, 194-99, 225-26, 233-37, 239-40, 251-52, 254-55
Globalization literature, 33, 50, 53
Governing bodies, 107-9

Hakim, Catherine, 154-56, 158
Hegemony, 13, 14, 20, 22, 234
Hensman, Rohini, 196-97
Hetero-patriarchal family, 49
Hetero-sexual nuclear family, 65
Higher education, 138, 177, 198, 225-28, 232, 235-36, 239-44, 250, 252-55
Hill, Anita, 87, 88
Human development, 259
Human rights, 54, 104, 235
Hungarian women, 101, 126
Hungary, 95, 96, 98, 101-2, 107-10, 113-17, 120, 124, 131

Ideal-type models, 64
Immigrants, 36, 37, 39, 176
Income differences, 117, 127
Industrial
capitalism, 3, 33, 34, 41
countries, 33, 38, 226
jobs, 42
workers, 36, 40-42
Informal economy, 37, 38, 44-46
Information processing, 34, 35
Information technology, 34, 195, 232, 237-38, 255
Integrated occupations, 155-56
Integration of women, 46, 49, 53, 54
International laws, 54
Internationalization, 32, 233, 240
IPU, 107

Job creation, 120, 190-91
Job flexibility, 187-88
Jobless women, 138

Kelly, Fernandez, 38, 39, 44, 45
Keynesian welfare state, 31, 41, 49, 50
Kruger, Helga, 17, 18

Labour Code, 147
Labour unions, 41, 53, 54, 60

Labour-market positions, 128-29
Living standards, 44, 131-32

Male breadwinner, 36, 43, 44
Male-breadwinner models, 65, 68, 69
Male-headed nuclear family, 60
Market economy, 97, 118, 130, 133-34, 144
Market-mediated work, 9, 16
Marriage contract, 66, 75
Marxism, 74
Masculinity, 2, 11, 15, 39, 40, 75, 167
Mass production, 31, 41, 43
Maternity, 111, 131, 143, 147-48, 179
Medical
 aid, 218, 223
 dispensary, 219-20
 facilities, 202, 218
Micro-finance institutions, 261, 265, 268
Money society, 44, 48
Moral orientation, 77
Moral psychology, 73
Municipal elections, 104

NABARD, 266, 268, 274
National anti-cyclical monetary, 31
National identity, 48, 234, 236
National Policy on Education, 227, 232
National territory, 36, 37, 48
Network society, 33, 35, 50, 53
Non-governmental organization, 54, 274
Norway, 101, 106-7

Occupational segregation, 130, 145, 148, 152, 156
Occupational society, 175

Parliamentary parties, 102, 104
Parliamentary ratio of women, 105, 107
Part-time
 employment, 64, 116, 163, 178
 jobs, 115-16, 133
 women research associates, 231
 work, 63, 178, 188
 workers, 115, 187
Pateman, Carole, 48, 75, 76
Patriarchal family law, 9
Polish women, 108
Political decision-making processes, 97, 109
Political participation, 2, 3, 107-9
Political theory, 75, 78, 82
Post-modern critique, 71, 72
Primary health centers, 201
Production process, 34, 38, 143
Professional activities, 155
Public services, 42, 47, 49, 50, 52

Quota system, 107

Ranking family, 19
Reciprocity, 12, 241
Redistribution of labour, 133
Reorganization, 13, 50, 53, 186
Reserve Bank of India, 267

Sanders, Helke, 173
Sassen, Saskia, 36, 37, 47
Sectoral differences, 143, 191
Self-employment, 124, 246, 253
Self-motivation, 248, 250, 253
Sexual division of labour, 42
Sexual harassment, 87, 88, 230
Sexual orientation, 78-82
SEZs, 194, 222-23
SHGs, 267-69, 272, 278-80
Single mothers, 44, 67, 69, 76, 89
Social activities, 24, 189
Social compromise, 49
Social conflicts, 7, 10, 196
Social democratic, 62, 63
Social differences, 4, 14
Social division, 20, 44, 48, 49, 131
Social inequalities, 3, 4, 71, 80, 160, 184
Social services, 42, 46, 187, 241

Social spheres, 3-5, 11, 12, 14, 20-22, 24
Socialization processes, 95, 130-31
Societal reproduction processes, 12, 20, 24
Socio-economic development, 226, 236
Solo-mother family, 61
Sravanthi, Chaitanya, 262, 280
SSA, 231
State-market relations, 62
Supreme Court, 87, 88, 195, 199, 226
Sustainable development, 254, 278, 280
Sweatshops, 37, 39

Textile industries, 38, 39, 127
Trade unions, 98, 107-8, 189, 223
Transitional period, 96, 114, 119
Two-income family models, 110

UGC, 225-26, 228, 230, 232
Unemployment rates, 117, 187
Unemployment, 60, 110-11, 116, 118, 122, 134, 137, 141, 145, 149, 174-77, 181, 188
Unification, 60, 61, 69
Universalism, 83
University education, 241-42
Unpaid family labour, 263

Value education, 238
Violence, 10, 74, 78, 79, 230
Voluntary organizations, 221-22
VSEZ company, 201-2

Welfare recipients, 69, 180
Welfare regimes, 62, 63
Welfare rights, 62, 65, 67
Welfare state analysis, 61, 62
Welfare state, 3, 5, 11, 42, 48-50, 52, 60-63, 67, 69, 76
West Germany, 66-69, 173
Women
  employment, 118-19, 133
  empowerment, 225-27, 232, 258-59, 262, 278
  entrepreneurs, 124, 260, 271
Work society, 48, 49
Workforce, 125, 128-29, 152-53, 157, 165, 271
World Bank, 52, 197, 235, 241-42, 261
World War, 32, 108, 225-26